The Lonely Londoners

Novel by Sam Selvon
Adapted by Roy Williams

methuen | drama

LONDON • NEW YORK • OXFORD • NEW DELHI • SYDNEY

METHUEN DRAMA
Bloomsbury Publishing Plc
50 Bedford Square, London, WC1B 3DP, UK
1385 Broadway, New York, NY 10018, USA
29 Earlsfort Terrace, Dublin 2, Ireland

BLOOMSBURY, METHUEN DRAMA and the Methuen
Drama logo are trademarks of Bloomsbury Publishing Plc

The Lonely Londoners first published in Great Britain by Allan Wingate in 1956

Play adaptation first published in Great Britain by Methuen Drama in 2024

Novel copyright © Sam Selvon, 1956

Adaptation copyright © Roy Williams, 2024

Roy Williams has asserted his right under the Copyright, Designs
and Patents Act, 1988, to be identified as author of this work.

Cover design: Ciaran Walsh (CIWA Design)

A catalogue record for this book is available from the British Library.

A catalog record for this book is available from the Library of Congress.

ISBN: PB: 978-1-3504-9657-6
ePDF: 978-1-3504-9658-3
eBook: 978-1-3504-9659-0

Series: Modern Plays

Typeset by Mark Heslington Ltd, Scarborough, North Yorkshire

To find out more about our authors and books visit
www.bloomsbury.com and sign up for our newsletters.

The Lonely Londoners

Performed at the Jermyn Street Theatre, London from 29 February–6 April 2024 with the following cast:

Cast

Lewis	TOBI BAKARE
Moses	GAMBA COLE
Agnes	SHANNON HAYES
Big City	GILBERT KYEM JNR
Tanty	CAROL MOSES
Christina	AIMEE POWELL
Galahad	ROMARIO SIMPSON

Production Team

Author	SAM SELVON
Adaptor	ROY WILLIAMS
Director	EBENEZER BAMGBOYE
Designer	LAURA ANN PRICE
Costume Designer	ANETT BLACK
Lighting Designer	ELLIOT GRIGGS
Sound Designer	TONY GAYLE
Casting Director	ABBY GALVIN
Assistant Director	PALOMA SIERRA
Movement Director	NEVENA STOJKOV
Voice and Dialect Coach	AUNDREA FUDGE
Production Manager	LUCY MEWIS-McKERROW
Stage Manager	SUMMER KEELING
Set Builder	TOM BAUM
Set Electrics	EDWARD CALLOW
Production Technician	HEATHER SMITH
Executive Producer	DAVID DOYLE
Producer	GABRIELE UBOLDI

Special thanks to Michael Buffong at Talawa Theatre, Kara Fitzpatrick, Doreene Blackstock, Tia Bannon, Rebecca Hesketh-Smith, Tyrone Huntley, CJ Beckford, Elliot Barnes-Worrell, Stephen Pemble, Amelia Carr, the Estate of Sam Selvon, and Susheila Nasta, Consultant and Literary Representative.

Cast

Tobi Bakare
Lewis

Theatre includes: *Gone Too Far* (Royal Court Theatre); *Greenland* (National Theatre); *Crawling in the Dark* (Almeida Theatre); *Iya Ile*, *Utopia* (Soho Theatre).

Television includes: *Death in Paradise*, *Shadowline*, *One Child* (BBC); *The Tunnel* (Sky Atlantic); *Outlander* (Lionsgate); *The Smoke* (Sky One).

Gamba Cole
Moses

Theatre includes: *Chicken Burger n Chips* (Brixton House/Oisel Productions); *POT* (Oval House Theatre/UK tour); *Antigone* (Pilot Theatre/UK tour); *Kingston 14* (Theatre Royal Stratford East).

Television includes: *The Outlaws* (BBC/Amazon Studios); *Three Little Birds* (Tiger Aspect/Douglas Road); *A Death in Paradise* (Red Planet Pictures); *A Discovery of Witches* (Bad Wolf); *Hanna* (Amazon Studios/NBC); *The Windrush Monologues* (BBC Arts/Endemol); *Guerrilla* 9 (Showtime/Sky Atlantic); *Our Loved Boy* (BBC).

Film includes: *His House* (New Regency); *Gone Too Far* (Poisson Rouge).

Shannon Hayes
Agnes

Theatre includes: *Bitter Lemons* (Bristol Old Vic); *The Seven Pomegranate Seeds* (Rose Theatre); *Raya* (Hampstead Theatre).

Television includes: *Vigil S2*, *Years and Years* (BBC); *Ted Lasso* (Apple TV); *I Hate Suzie* (Sky); *Cold Feet* (ITV).

Gilbert Kyem Jnr
Big City

Theatre includes: *Hamlet*, *Oresteia* (Broadway/Almeida Theatre); *Never Not Once* (Park Theatre).

Television includes: *Rivals* (Disney/Happy Prince).

Film includes: *Prizefighter* (Amazon).

Carol Moses
Tanty

Theatre includes: *Unseen Unheard* (Theatre Peckham); *Hoxton St* (Hoxton Hall); *Forty* (Hackney Empire); *Clockwork* (National Theatre).

Television includes: *The Ballad of Renegade Nell* (Disney+); *Holby City*, *A Class Apart*, *Call the Midwife* (BBC); *The Bill*, *Perrin* (ITV).

Film includes: *Mama*, *The Change*, *In Da Mix*, *Side Hustle*.

Carol Moses trained at Rose Bruford College.

Aimee Powell
Christina

Theatre includes: *Family Tree*, *Crongton Knights* (UK tour); *Nothello* (Belgrade Theatre); *Freeman* (international tour); *Feed The Beast* (Birmingham REP).

Television includes: *Doctors* (BBC), *SeaView* (Prime Video).

Film includes: *Sent to Cov* (Sky Arts).

Romario Simpson
Galahad

Theatre includes: *Syndrome* (Tristan Bates Theatre); *Coming Home* (ALRA); *Sket* (Park Theatre); *Think* (Edinburgh Fringe); *And Then There Was War* (Stratford Circus Theatre);

Reflection, Scratch Me If You Can (Southbank Vaults); *Love Clc* (Mountview); *Our Country's Good* (WKC Theatre).

Television includes: *Granite Harbour S1/S2* (BBC Scotland) *Riches* (ITV); *Django* (Sky Atlantic); *Andor* (Disney+); *Sm(Axe: Lover's Rock* (BBC); *Noughts + Crosses* (BBC); *Timew, S2* (ITV); *Dixi* (CBBC).

hild

ST TEN the following morning Troy, hung
nd carrying a roll of canvas and stretchers,
he little theatre. Guided by Paul and Cedric,
tudio easel between them, she went down a
l led out of the hall, turned right at a green
bond which,' Cedric panted, 'the Difficult
Cat will,' and continued towards the rear of that
to Their journey was not without incident, for as
the door of what, as Troy later discovered, was
a room, it was flung open and a short plumpish
m his back towards them, shouting angrily: 'If
voin my treatment, Sir Henry, you have an obvious
erll be glad to be relieved of the thankless task
of for a damned obstinate patient and his grand-
lauy made a valiant effort to forge ahead, but was
locedric, who stopped short, holding the easel diago-
all he passage and listening with an air of the liveliest

This time she

edly bade her goo

and left them barel

before they fell to ag

Only a solitary

completely silent, and

While Troy climbed the

in this enormous house

stretched out on all side

It housed, as well as the

deeper thoughts and the t

she reached the gallery, wh

drawing-room was now pr

island. The rows of mediocr

that she now passed had a li

and seemed to be indifferentl

last, was her own passage with

halted for a moment before clim

or had the door, out of sight or

been softly closed? 'Perhaps,' she

the room below me,' and for some

her unpleasantly. 'Ridiculous!' thou

switch at the foot of the stairs. A lan

first spiral, brought the curved wall

Troy mounted briskly, hoping th

in her white room. As she turned the

her long dress with her right hand an

out for the narrow rail.

The rail was sticky.

She snatched her hand away wit

looked at it. The palm and the under-su

stood in the shadow of the inner wall, b

into light. By the single lamps she saw

hand was red.

Five seconds must have gone by befo

the stuff on her hand was paint.

interest. 'Now, now, keep your temper,' rumbled the invisible Sir Henry. 'I wash my hands of you,' the other proclaimed. 'No, you don't. You keep a civil tongue in your head, Withers. You'd much better look after me and take a bit of honest criticism in the way it's intended.' 'This is outrageous,' the visitor said, but with a note of something like despair in his voice. 'I formally relinquish the case. You will take this as final.' There was a pause, during which Paul attempted, without success, to drag Cedric away. 'I won't accept it,' Sir Henry said at last. 'Come, now, Withers, keep your temper. You ought to understand. I've a great deal to try me. A great deal. Bear with an old fellow's tantrums, won't you? You shan't regret it. See here, now. Shut that door and listen to me.' Without turning, the visitor slowly shut the door.

'And *now*,' Cedric whispered, 'he'll tell poor Dr Withers he's going to be remembered in the Will.'

'Come on, for God's sake,' said Paul, and they made their way to the little theatre.

Half an hour later Troy had set up her easel, stretched her canvas, and prepared paper and boards for preliminary studies. The theatre was a complete little affair with a deepish stage. The *Macbeth* backcloth was simple and brilliantly conceived. The scenic painter had carried out Troy's original sketch very well indeed. Before it stood three-dimensional monolithic forms that composed well and broke across the cloth in the right places. She saw where she would place her figure. There would be no attempt to present the background in terms of actuality. It would be frankly a stage set. 'A dangling rope would come rather nicely,' she thought, 'but I suppose they wouldn't like that. If only he'll stand!'

Cedric and Paul now began to show her what could be done with the lights. Troy was enjoying herself. She liked the smell of canvas and glue and the feeling that this was a place where people worked. In the little theatre even Cedric improved. He was knowledgeable and quickly responsive to her suggestions, checking Paul's desire to flood the set with a startling display of lighting and getting him to stand in position while he himself focussed a single spot. 'We must find the backcloth discreetly,' he cried. 'Try the ground row.' And presently a luminous glow appeared, delighting Troy.

'But how are you going to *see*?' cried Cedric distractedly. 'Oh, lawks! How *are* you going to see?'

'I can bring down a standard spot on an extension,' Paul offered. 'Or we could uncover a window.'

Cedric gazed in an agony of inquiry at Troy. 'But the window light would infiltrate,' he said. 'Or wouldn't it?'

'We could try.'

At last by an ingenious arrangement of screens Troy was able to get daylight on her canvas and a fair view of the stage.

The clock—it was, of course, known as the Great Clock—in the central tower struck eleven. A door somewhere backstage opened and shut, and dead on his cue Sir Henry, in the character of Macbeth, walked onto the lighted set.

'Golly!' Troy whispered. 'Oh, Golly!'

'Devastatingly fancy dress,' said Cedric in her ear, 'but in its ridiculous way rather exciting. Or not? Too fancy?'

'It's not too fancy for me,' Troy said roundly, and walked down the aisle to greet her sitter.

At midday Troy drove her fingers through her hair, propped a large charcoal drawing against the front of the stage and backed away from it down the aisle. Sir Henry took off his helmet, groaned a little, and moved cautiously to a chair in the wings.

'I suppose you want to stop,' said Troy absently, biting her thumb and peering at her drawing.

'One grows a trifle stiff,' he replied. She then noticed that he was looking more than a trifle tired. He had made up for her sitting, painting heavy shadows round his eyes and staining his moustache and the tuft on his chin with water-dye. To this he had added long strands of crêpe hair. But beneath the greasepaint and hair his face sagged a little and his head drooped.

'I must let you go,' said Troy. 'I hope I haven't been too exacting. One forgets.'

'One also remembers,' said Sir Henry. 'I have been remembering my lines. I played the part first in 1904.'

Troy looked up quickly, suddenly liking him.

'It's a wonderful role,' he said. 'Wonderful.'

'I was very much moved by it when I saw you five years ago.'

'I've played it six times and always to enormous business. It hasn't been an unlucky piece for me.'

'I've heard about the Macbeth superstition. One mustn't quote from the play, must one?' Troy made a sudden pounce at her drawing and wiped her thumb down a too dominant line. 'Do you believe it's unlucky?' she asked vaguely.

'It has been for other actors,' he said, quite seriously. 'There's always a heavy feeling offstage during performance. People are nervy.'

'Isn't that perhaps because they remember the superstition?'

'It's there,' he said. 'You can't escape the feeling. But the piece has never been unlucky for me.' His voice, which had sounded tired, lifted again. 'If it were otherwise, should I have chosen this role for my portrait? Assuredly not. And now,' he said with a return of his arch and over-gallant manner, 'am I to be allowed a peep before I go?'

Troy was not very keen for him to have his peep, but she took the drawing a little way down the aisle and turned it towards him. 'I'm afraid it won't explain itself,' she said. 'It's merely a sort of plot of what I hope to do.'

'Ah, yes!' He put his hand in his tunic and drew out a pair of gold-rimmed pince-nez and there, in a moment, was Macbeth, with glasses perched on his nose, staring solemnly at his own portrait. 'Such a clever lady,' he said. 'Very clever!'

Troy put the drawing away and he got up slowly. 'Off, ye lend-
ings!' he said. 'I must change.' He adjusted his cloak with a
practised hand, drew himself up, and, moving into the spot-
light, pointed his dirk at the great naked canvas. His voice, as
though husbanded for this one flourish, boomed through the
empty theatre.

> Well, may you see things well done there: adieu!
> Lest our old robes sit easier than our new!

' "God's benison go with you!" ' said Troy, luckily remembering the line. He crossed himself, chuckled and strode
off between the monoliths to the door behind the stage. It
slammed and Troy was alone.

She had made up her mind to start at once with the
laying out of her subject on the big canvas. There would be
no more preliminary studies. Time pressed and she knew now
what she wanted. There is no other moment, she thought, to
compare with this, when you face the tautly stretched surface
and raise your hand to make the first touch upon it. And,
drawing in her breath, she swept her charcoal across the
canvas. It gave a faint drumlike note of response. 'We're off,'
thought Troy.

Fifty minutes went by and a rhythm of line and mass
grew under her hand. Back and forward she walked, making
sharp accents with the end of her charcoal or sweeping it
flat across the grain of the canvas. All that was Troy was
now poured into her thin blackened hand. At last she stood
motionless, ten paces back from her work, and, after an
interval, lit a cigarette, took up her duster and began to flick
her drawing. Showers of charcoal fell down the surface.

'Don't you like it?' asked a sharp voice.

Troy jumped galvanically and turned. The little girl she
had seen fighting on the terrace stood in the aisle, her hands
jammed in the pockets of her pinafore and her feet planted
apart.

'Where did you come from?' Troy demanded.

'Through the end door. I came quietly because I'm not allowed. Why are you rubbing it out? Don't you like it?'

'I'm not rubbing it out. It's still there.' And indeed the ghost of her drawing remained. 'You take the surplus charcoal off,' she said curtly. 'Otherwise it messes the paints.'

'Is it going to be Noddy dressed up funny?'

Troy started at this use of a name she had imagined to be Miss Orrincourt's prerogative and invention.

'I call him Noddy,' said the child, as if guessing at her thought, 'and so does Sonia. She got it from me. I'm going to be like Sonia when I'm grown up.'

'Oh,' said Troy, opening her paint box and rummaging in it.

'Are those your paints?'

'Yes,' said Troy, looking fixedly at her. 'They are. Mine.'

'I'm Patricia Claudia Ellen Ancred Kentish.'

'So I'd gathered.'

'You couldn't have gathered all of that, because nobody except Miss Able ever calls me anything but Panty. Not that I care,' added Panty, suddenly climbing onto the back of one of the stools and locking her feet in the arms, 'I'm double jointed,' she said, throwing herself back and hanging head downwards.

'That won't help you if you break your neck,' said Troy.

Panty made an offensive gargling noise.

'As you're not allowed here,' Troy continued, 'hadn't you better run off?'

'No,' said Panty.

Troy squeezed a fat serpent of Flake White out on her palette. 'If I ignore this child,' she thought, 'perhaps she will get bored and go.'

Now the yellows, next the reds. How beautiful was her palette!

'I'm going to paint with those paints,' said Panty at her elbow.

'You haven't a hope,' said Troy.

'I'm going to.' She made a sudden grab at the tray of long brushes. Troy anticipated this move by a split second.

'Now, see here, Panty,' she said, shutting the box and facing the child, 'if you don't pipe down I shall pick you up by the slack of your breeches and carry you straight back to where you belong. You don't like people butting in on your games, do you? Well, this is my game, and I can't get on with it if you butt in.'

'I'll kill you,' said Panty.

'Don't be an ass,' said Troy mildly.

Panty scooped up a dollop of vermilion on three of her fingers and flung it wildly at Troy's face. She then burst into peals of shrill laughter.

'You can't whack me,' she shrieked. 'I'm being brought up on a system.'

'Can't I!' Troy rejoined. 'System or no system—' And indeed there was nothing she desired more at the moment than to beat Panty. The child confronted her with an expression of concentrated malevolence. Her cheeks were blown out with such determination that her nose wrinkled and turned up. Her mouth was so tightly shut that lines resembling a cat's whiskers radiated from it. She scowled hideously. Her pigtails stuck out at right angles to her head. Altogether she looked like an infuriated infant Boreas.

Troy sat down and reached for a piece of rag to clean her face. 'Oh, Panty,' she said, 'you do look so exactly like your Uncle Thomas.'

Panty drew back her arm again. 'No, don't,' said Troy. 'Don't do any more damage with red paint, I implore you. Look here, I'll strike a bargain with you. If you'll promise not to take any more paint without asking, I'll give you a board and some brushes and let you make a proper picture.'

Panty glared at her. 'When?' she said warily.

'When we've asked your mother or Miss Able. I'll ask. But no more nonsense. And especially,' Troy added, taking a shot in the dark, 'no more going to my room and squeezing paint on the stair rail.'

Panty stared blankly at her. 'I don't know what you're talking about,' she said flatly. 'When can I paint? I want to. Now.'

'Yes, but let's get this cleared up. What did you do before dinner last night?'

'I don't know. Yes, I do. Dr Withers came. He weighed us all. He's going to make me bald because I've got ringworm. That's why I've got this cap on. Would you like to see my ringworm?'

'No.'

'I got it first. I've given it to sixteen of the others.'

'Did you go up to my room and mess about with my paints?'

'No.'

'Honestly, Panty?'

'Honestly what? I don't know where your room is. When can I paint?'

'Do you promise you didn't put paint…'

'You are *silly*!' said Panty furiously. 'Can't you see a person's telling the truth.'

And Troy, greatly bewildered, thought that she could.

While she was still digesting this queer little scene, the door at the back of the stalls opened and Cedric peered round it.

'*So* humble and timid,' he lisped. 'Just a mouse-like squeak to tell you luncheon is almost on the table. *Panty!*' he cried shrilly, catching sight of his cousin. 'You gross child! Back to the West Wing, miss! How dare you muscle your hideous way in here?'

Panty grinned savagely at him. 'Hallo, Sissy,' she said.

'Wait,' said Cedric, 'just wait till the Old Person catches you. What he won't do to you!'

'Why?' Panty demanded.

'Why! You ask me why. Infamy! With the grease-paint fresh on your fingers.'

Both Panty and Troy gaped at this. Panty glanced at her hand. 'That's her paint,' she said, jerking her head at Troy. 'That's not grease-paint.'

'Do you deny,' Cedric pursued, shaking his finger at her, 'do you deny, you toxic child, that you went into your grandfather's dressing-room while he was sitting for Mrs Alleyn, and scrawled some pothouse insult in lake-liner on his looking-glass? Do you deny, moreover, that you painted a red moustache on the cat, Carabbas?'

With an air of bewilderment that Troy could have sworn was genuine, Panty repeated her former statement. 'I don't know what you're talking about. I didn't.'

'Tell that,' said Cedric with relish, 'to your grandpapa and see if he believes you.'

'Noddy likes me,' said Panty, rallying. 'He likes me best in the family. He thinks you're awful. He said you're a simpering popinjay.'

'See here,' said Troy hastily. 'Let's get this straight. You say Panty's written something in grease-paint on Sir Henry's looking-glass. What's she supposed to have written?'

Cedric coughed. 'Dearest Mrs Alleyn, we mustn't allow you for a second to be disturbed...'

'I'm not disturbed,' said Troy. 'What was written on the glass?'

'My mama would have wiped it off. She was in his room tidying, and saw it. She hunted madly for a rag but the Old Person, at that moment, walked in and saw it. He's roaring about the house like a major prophet.'

'But what was it, for pity's sake?'

'"Grandfather's a bloody old fool,"' said Cedric. Panty giggled. 'There!' said Cedric. 'You see? Obviously she wrote it. Obviously she made up the cat.'

'I didn't. I *didn't*.' And with one of those emotional *volte-faces* by which children bewilder us, Panty wrinkled up her face, kicked Cedric suddenly but half-heartedly on the shin, and burst into a storm of tears.

'You odious child!' he ejaculated, skipping out of her way.

Panty flung herself on her face, screamed industriously and beat the floor with her fists. 'You all hate me,' she sobbed. 'Wicked beasts! I wish I was dead.'

'Oh, la,' said Cedric, 'how tedious! Now, she'll have a fit or something.'

Upon this scene came Paul Kentish. He limped rapidly down the aisle, seized his sister by the slack of her garments and, picking her up very much as if she was a kitten, attempted to stand her on her feet. Panty drew up her legs and hung from his grasp, in some danger, Troy felt, of suffocation. 'Stop it at once, Panty,' he said. 'You've been a very naughty girl.'

'Wait a minute,' said Troy. 'I don't think she has, honestly. I mean, not in the way you think. There's a muddle, I'm certain of it.'

Paul relinquished his hold. Panty sat on the floor, sobbing harshly, a most desolate child.

'It's all right,' said Troy, 'I'll explain. You didn't do it, Panty, and you shall paint if you still want to.'

'She's not allowed to come out of school,' said Paul. 'Caroline Able will be here in a minute.'

'Thank God for that,' said Cedric.

Miss Able arrived almost immediately, cast a professionally breezy glance at her charge and said it was dinner-time. Panty, with a look at Troy which she was unable to interpret, got to her feet.

'Look here...' said Troy.

'Yes?' said Miss Able cheerfully.

'About this looking-glass business. I don't think that Panty...'

'Next time she feels like that we'll think of something much more sensible to do, won't we, Patricia?'

'Yes, but I don't think she did it.'

'We're getting very good at just facing up to these funny old things we do when we're silly, aren't we, Patricia? It's best just to find out why and then forget about them.'

'But…'

'Dinner!' cried Miss Able brightly and firmly. She removed the child without any great ado.

'Dearest Mrs Alleyn,' said Cedric, waving his hands. 'Why are you so sure Panty is not the author of the insult on the Old Person's mirror?'

'Has she ever called him "Grandfather"?'

'Well, no,' said Paul. 'No, actually she hasn't.'

'And what's more…' Troy stopped short. Cedric had moved to her painting table. He had taken up a piece of rag and was using it to clean a finger-nail. Only then did Troy realize that the first finger of the right hand he had waved at her had been stained dark crimson under the nail.

He caught her eye and dropped the rag.

'Such a Paul Pry!' he said. 'Dipping my fingers in your paint.'

But there had been no dark crimson laid out on her palette.

'Well,' said Cedric shrilly, 'shall we lunch?'

By the light of her flash-lamp Troy was examining the stair rail in her tower. The paint had not been cleaned away and was now in the condition known as tacky. She could see clearly the mark left by her own hand. Above this, the paint was untouched. It had not been squeezed out and left, but brushed over the surface. At one point only, on the stone wall above the rail, someone had left the faint red print of two fingers. 'How Rory would laugh at me,' she thought, peering at them. They were small, but not small enough, she thought, to have been made by a child. Could one of the maids have touched the rail and then the wall? But beyond the mark left by her own grip there were no other prints on the rail. 'Rory,' she thought, 'would take photographs, but how could one ever get anything from these things? They're all broken up by the rough surface. I couldn't even make a drawing of them.' She was about to move away when the light from her torch fell on an object that seemed to be wedged in the gap between a step and the stone wall. Looking more closely she discovered it to be one of her own brushes. She worked it out, and found that the bristles were thick with half-dry Rose Madder.

She went down to the half-landing. There was the door that she had fancied she heard closing last night when she went to bed. It was not quite shut now and she gave it a tentative shove. It swung inwards, and Troy was confronted with a Victorian bathroom.

'Well,' she thought crossly, remembering her long tramp that morning in search of a bath, 'Fenella might have told me I'd got one of my own.'

She had dirtied her fingers on the brush and went in to wash them. The soap in the marble hand-basin was already stained with Rose Madder. 'This is a mad-house,' thought Troy.

Sir Henry posed for an hour that afternoon. The next morning, Sunday, was marked by a massive attendance of the entire family (with Troy) at Ancreton church. In the afternoon, however, he gave her an hour. Troy had decided to go straight for the head. She had laid in a general scheme for her work, an exciting affair of wet shadows and sharp accents. This could be completed without him. She was painting well. The touch of flamboyancy that she had dreaded was absent. She had returned often to the play. Its threat of horror was now a factor in her approach to her work. She was strongly aware of that sense of a directive power which comes only when all is well with painters. With any luck, she thought, I'll be able to say: 'Did the fool that is me, make this?'

At the fourth sitting, Sir Henry returning perhaps to some bygone performance, broke the silence by speaking without warning the lines she had many times read:

Light thickens, and the crow
Makes wing to the rooky wood...

He startled Troy so much that her hand jerked and she
waited motionless until he had finished the speech, resenting
the genuine twist of apprehension that had shaken her. She
could find nothing to say in response to this unexpected and
oddly impersonal performance, but she had the feeling that
the old man knew very well how much it had moved her.

After a moment she returned to her work and still it
went well. Troy was a deliberate painter, but the head grew
with almost frightening rapidity. In an hour she knew that she
must not touch it again. She was suddenly exhausted. 'I think
we'll stop for today,' she said, and again felt that he was not
surprised.

Instead of going away, he came down into the front of the
theatre and looked at what she had done. She had that feeling
of gratitude to her subject that sometimes follows a sitting
that has gone well, but she did not want him to speak of the
portrait and began hurriedly to talk of Panty.

'She's doing a most spirited painting of red cows and a
green aeroplane.'

'T'uh!' said Sir Henry on a melancholy note.

'She wants to show it to you herself.'

'I have been deeply hurt,' said Sir Henry, 'by Patricia.
Deeply hurt.'

'Do you mean,' said Troy uncomfortably, 'because of
something she's supposed to have written on—on your
looking-glass?'

'Supposed! The thing was flagrant. Not only that, but she
opened the drawers of my dressing-table and pulled out my
papers. I may tell you, that if she were capable of reading the
two documents that she found there, she would perhaps feel
some misgivings. I may tell you that they closely concerned
herself, and that if there are any more of these damnable
tricks—' He paused and scowled portentously. 'Well, we shall

see. We shall see. Let her mother realize that I cannot endure for ever. And my cat!' he exclaimed. 'She has made a fool of my cat. There are still marks of grease-paint in his whiskers,' said Sir Henry angrily. 'Butter has not altogether removed them. As for the insult to me—'

'But I'm sure she didn't. I was here when they scolded her about it. Honestly, I'm sure she knew nothing whatever about it.'

'T'uh!'

'No, but really—' Should she say anything about the dark red stain under Cedric's finger-nail? No, she'd meddled enough. She went on quickly: 'Panty brags about her naughtiness. She's told me about all her practical jokes. She never calls you grandfather and I happen to know she spells it "farther," because she showed me a story she had written, and the word occurs frequently. I'm sure Panty's too fond of you,' Troy continued, wondering if she spoke the truth, 'to do anything so silly and unkind.'

'I've loved that child,' said Sir Henry with the appallingly rich display of sentiment so readily commanded by the Ancreds, 'as if she was my own. My little Best-Beloved, I've always called her. I've never made any secret of my preference. After I'm gone,' he went on to Troy's embarrassment, 'she would have known—however.' He sighed windily. Troy could think of nothing to say and cleaned her palette. The light from the single uncovered window had faded. Sir Henry had switched off the stage lamps and the little theatre was now filled with shadows. A draught somewhere in the borders caused them to move uneasily and a rope-end tapped against the canvas backcloth.

'Do you know anything about embalming?' Sir Henry asked in his deepest voice. Troy jumped.

'No, indeed,' she said.

'I have studied the subject,' said Sir Henry, 'deeply.'

'Oddly enough,' said Troy after a pause, 'I did look at that queer little book in the drawing-room. The one in the glass case.'

'Ah, yes. It belonged to my ancestor who rebuilt Ancreton. He himself was embalmed and his fathers before him. It has been the custom with the Ancreds. The family vault,' he rambled on depressingly, 'is remarkable for that reason. If I lie there—the Nation may have other wishes: it is not for me to speculate—but if I lie there, it will be after their fashion. I have given explicit directions.'

'I *do* wish,' Troy thought, '*how* I do wish he wouldn't go on like this.' She made a small ambiguous murmuring.

'Ah, well!' said Sir Henry heavily and began to move away. He paused before mounting the steps up to the stage. Troy thought that he was on the edge of some further confidence, and hoped that it would be of a more cheerful character.

'What,' said Sir Henry, 'is your view on the matter of marriage between first cousins?'

'I—really, I don't know,' Troy replied, furiously collecting her wits. 'I fancy I've heard that modern medical opinion doesn't condemn it. But I really haven't the smallest knowledge—'

'I am against it,' he said loudly. 'I cannot approve. Look at the Hapsburgs! The House of Spain! The Romanoffs!' His voice died away in an inarticulate rumble.

Hoping to divert his attention Troy began: 'Panty—'

'Hah!' said Sir Henry. 'These doctors don't know anything. Patricia's scalp! A common childish ailment, and Withers, having pottered about with it for weeks without doing any good, is now going to dose the child with a depilatory. Disgusting! I have spoken to the child's mother, but I'd have done better to hold my tongue. Who,' Sir Henry demanded, 'pays any attention to the old man? Nobody. Ours is an Ancient House, Mrs Alleyn. We have borne arms since my ancestor, the Sieur d'Ancred, fought beside the Conqueror. And before that. Before that. A proud house. Perhaps in my own humble way I have not disgraced it. But what will happen when I am Gone? I look for my Heir and what do I find? A Thing! An emasculated Popinjay!'

He evidently expected some reply to this pronouncement on Cedric, but Troy was quite unable to think of one.

'The last of the Ancreds!' he said, glaring at her. 'A family that came in with the Conqueror to go out with a—'

'But,' said Troy, 'he may marry and...'

'And have kittens! P'shaw!'

'Perhaps Mr Thomas Ancred...'

'Old Tommy! No! I've talked to old Tommy. He doesn't see it. He'll die a bachelor. And Claude's wife is past it. Well; it was my hope to know the line was secure before I went. I shan't.'

'But, bless my soul,' said Troy, 'you're taking far too gloomy a view of all this. There's not much wrong with a man who can pose for an hour with a helmet weighing half a hundredweight on his head. You may see all sorts of exciting things happen.'

It was astonishing, it was almost alarming, to see how promptly he squared his shoulders, how quickly gallantry made its reappearance. 'Do you think so?' he said, and Troy noticed how his hand went to his cloak, giving it an adroit hitch. 'Well, perhaps, after all, you're right. Clever lady! Yes, yes. I *may* see something exciting and what's more—' he paused and gave a very queer little giggle—'what's more, my dear, so may other people.'

Troy was never to know if Sir Henry would have elaborated on this strange prophecy, as at that moment a side door in the auditorium was flung open and Miss Orrincourt burst into the little theatre.

'Noddy!' she shouted angrily. 'You've got to come. Get out of that funny costume and protect me. I've had as much of your bloody family as I can stand. It's them or me. Now!'

She strode down the aisle and confronted him, her hands on her hips, a virago.

Sir Henry eyed her with more apprehension, Troy thought, than astonishment, and began a placatory rumbling.

'No you don't,' she said. 'Come off it and *do* something. They're in the library, sitting round a table. Plotting against me. I walked in, and there was Pauline giving an imitation of a cat-fight and telling them how I'd have to be got rid of.'

'My dear, please, I can't allow...Surely you're mistaken.'

'Am I dopey? I tell you I *heard* her. They're all against me. I warned you before and I'm warning you again and it's the last time. They're going to frame me. I know what I'm talking about. It's a frame-up. I tell you they've got me all jittery, Noddy. I can't stand it. You can either come and tell them where they get off or it's thanks for the buggy-ride and me for Town in the morning.'

He looked at her disconsolately, hesitated, and took her by the elbow. Her mouth drooped, she gazed at him dolorously. 'It's lonely here, Noddy,' she said. 'Noddy, I'm scared.'

It was strange to watch the expression of extreme tenderness that this instantly evoked; strange, and to Troy, painfully touching.

'Come,' Sir Henry said, stooping over her in his terrifying costume. 'Come along. I'll speak to these children.'

The little theatre was on the northern corner of the East Wing. When Troy had tidied up she looked out of doors and found a wintry sun still glinting feebly on Ancreton. She felt stuffed-up with her work. The carriage drive, sweeping downhill through stiffly naked trees, invited her. She fetched a coat and set out bare-headed. The frosty air stung her eyes with tears, the ground rang hard under her feet. Suddenly exhilarated she began to run. Her hair lifted, cold air ran over her scalp and her ears burned icily. 'How ridiculous to run and feel happy,' thought Troy, breathless. And slowing down, she began to make plans. She would leave the head. In two days, perhaps, it would be dry. Tomorrow, the hands and their surrounding drape, and, when he had gone, another hour or so through the background. Touch after touch and for each one the mustering of thought and muscle and the inward remembrance of the scheme.

The drive curved down between banks of dead leaves, and, overhead, frozen branches rattled in a brief visitation of wind, and she thought: 'I'm walking under the scaffolding of summer.' There, beneath her, were the gates. The sun had gone, and already fields of mist had begun to rise from the hollows. 'As far as the gates,' thought Troy, 'and then back up the terraces.' She heard the sound of hooves behind her in the woods and the faint rumbling of wheels. Out of the trees came the governess-cart and Rosinante, and there, gloved and furred and apparently recovered from her fury, sat Miss Orrincourt, flapping the reins.

Troy waited for her and she pulled up. 'I'm going to the village,' she said. 'Do you want to come? Do, like a sweet, because I've got to go to the chemist, and this brute might walk away if nobody watched it.'

Troy got in. 'Can you drive?' said Miss Orrincourt. 'Do, like a ducks. I hate it.' She handed the reins to Troy and at once groped among her magnificent furs for her cigarette case. 'I got the willies up there,' she continued. 'They've all gone out to dinner at the next-door morgue. Well, next door! It's God knows how far away. Cedric and Paul and old Pauline. What a bunch! With their tails *well* down, dear. Well, I mean to say, you saw how upset I was, didn't you? So did Noddy.' She giggled. 'Look, dear, you should have seen him. With that tin toque on his head and everything. Made the big entrance into the library and called them for everything. "This lady," he says, "is my guest and you'll be good enough to remember it." And quite a lot more. Was I tickled! Pauline and Milly looking blue murder and poor little Cedric bleating and waving his hands. He made them apologize. Oh, well,' she said, with a sigh, 'it was something happening anyway. That's the worst of life in this dump. Nothing ever happens. Nothing to do and all day to do it in. God, what a flop! If anybody'd told me a month ago I'd be that fed up I'd get round to crawling about the place in a prehistoric prop like this I'd have thought they'd gone hay-wire. Oh, well, I suppose it'd have been worse in the army.'

'Were you ever in the army?'

'I'm delicate,' said Miss Orrincourt with an air of satisfaction. 'Bronchial asthma. I was fixed up with ENSA but my
chest began a rival show. The boys in the orchestra said they
couldn't hear themselves play. So I got out. I got an under-
study at the Unicorn. It was that West End you barked your
shins on the ice. Then,' said Miss Orrincourt simply, 'Noddy
noticed me.'

'Was that an improvement?' asked Troy.

'Wouldn't you have thought so? I mean, ask yourself.
Well, you know. A man in his position. Top of the tree. Mind,
I think he's sweet. I'm crazy about him, in a way. But I've got
to look after myself, haven't I? If you don't look after yourself in this old world nobody's going to look after you. Well,
between you and I, Mrs Alleyn, things were a bit tricky. Till
yesterday. Look, a girl doesn't stick it out in an atmosphere
like this, unless there's a future in it, does she? Not if she's
still conscious, she doesn't.'

Miss Orrincourt inhaled deeply and then made a petu-
lant little sound. 'Well, I *am* fed up,' she said as if Troy had
offered some word of criticism. 'I don't say he hasn't given me
things. This coat's rather nice, don't you think? It belonged to
a lady who was in the Wrens. I saw it advertised. She'd never
worn it. Two hundred and dirt cheap, really.'

They jogged on in a silence broken only by the clop of
Rosinante's hooves. There was the little railway Halt and
there, beyond a curve in the low hills, the roofs of Ancreton
village.

'Well, I mean to say,' said Miss Orrincourt, 'when I fixed
up with Noddy to come here I didn't know what I was letting
myself in for. I'll say I didn't! Well, *you* know. On the surface
it looked like a win. It's high up, and my doctor says my chest
ought to be high up, and there wasn't much doing in the
business. My voice isn't so hot, and I haven't got the wind for
dancing like I had, and the "legitimate" gives me a pain in the
neck. So what have you?'

Stumped for an answer, as she had so often been since her arrival at Ancreton, Troy said: 'I suppose the country does feel a bit queer when you're used to bricks and mortar.'

'It feels, to be frank, like death warmed up. Not that I don't say you could do something with that Jack's-come-home up there. You know. Weekend parties, with the old bunch coming down and all the fun and games. And no Ancreds. Well, I wouldn't mind Ceddie. He's one-of-those, of course, but I always think they're good mixers in their own way. I've got it all worked out. Something to do, isn't it, making plans? It may come up in the lift one of these days; you never know. But no Ancreds when I throw a party in the Baronial Hall. You bet, no Ancreds.'

'Sir Henry?' Troy ventured.

'Well,' said Miss Orrincourt, 'I was thinking of later on, if you know what I mean.'

'Good Lord!' Troy ejaculated involuntarily.

'Mind, as I say, I'm fond of Noddy. But it's a funny old world, and there you have it. I must say it's nice having someone to talk to. Someone who isn't an Ancred. I can't exactly *confide* in Ceddie, because he's the heir, and he mightn't quite see things my way.'

'Possibly not.'

'No. Although he's quite nice to me.' The thin voice hardened. 'And, don't you worry, I know why,' Miss Orrincourt added. 'He's stuck for cash, silly kid, and he wants me to use my influence. He'd got the burns on his doorstep when the jitterbugs cleaned up his place, and then he went to the Jews and now he doesn't know where to go. He's scared to turn up at the flat. He'll have to wait till I'm fixed up myself. Then we'll see. I don't mind much,' she said, moving restlessly, 'which way it goes, so long as I'm fixed up.'

They faced each other across the bucket-cart. Troy looked at her companion's beautifully painted face. Behind it stood wraithlike trees, motionless, threaded with mist. It might have been a sharp mask, by a surrealist, hung on that darkling background, thought Troy.

A tiny rhythmic sound grew out of the freezing air. 'I can hear a cat mewing somewhere,' said Troy, pulling Rosinante up.

'That's a good one!' said Miss Orrincourt, laughing and coughing. 'A cat mewing! It's my chest, dear. This damn night air's catching me. Can you hurry that brute up?'

Troy stirred him up, and presently they clopped sedately down the one street of Ancreton village and pulled up outside a small chemist's shop, that seemed also to be a sort of general store.

'Shall I get whatever it is?' Troy offered.

'All right. I don't suppose there's anything worth looking at in the shop. No perfume. Thanks, dear. It's the stuff for the kid's ringworm. The doctor's ordered it. It's meant to be ready.'

The elderly rubicund chemist handed Troy two bottles tied together. One had an envelope attached. 'For the children up at the Manor?' he said. 'Quite so. And the small bottle is for Sir Henry.' When she had climbed back into the governess-cart, she found that he had followed her and stood blinking on the pavement. 'They're labelled,' he said fussily. 'If you'd be good enough to point out the enclosed instructions. The dosage varies, you know. It's determined by the patient's weight. Dr Withers particularly asked me to draw Miss Able's attention. Quite an unusual prescription, actually. Thallium acetate. Yes. Both labelled. Thank you. One should exercise care...So sorry we're out of wrapping paper. Good evening.' He gave a little whooping chuckle and darted back into his shop. Troy was about to turn Rosinante when Miss Orrincourt, asking her to wait, scrambled out and went into the shop, returning in a few minutes with a bulge in her pocket.

'Just something that caught my eye,' she said. 'Righty ho, dear! Home John and don't spare the horses.' On their return journey she exclaimed repeatedly on the subject of the children's ringworm. She held the collar of her fur coat across her mouth and her voice sounded unreal behind it. 'Is it tough, or is it tough? That poor kid Panty. All over her head, and her hair's her one beauty, you might say.'

'You and Panty are rather by way of being friends, aren't you?' said Troy.

'She's a terrible kiddy, really. You know. The things she does! Well! Scribbling across Noddy's mirror with a lake-liner and such a common way to put it, whatever she thought. A few more little cracks like that and she'll cook her goose if she only knew it. The mother's wild about it, naturally. Did you know the kid's favourite in the Will? She won't hold that role down much longer if she lets her sense of comedy run away with her. And then the way she put that paint on your bannister! I call it the limit.'

Troy stared at her. 'How did you know about that?'

A spasm of coughing shook her companion, 'I was crazy,' gasped the muffled voice, 'to came out in this lousy fog. Might have known. Pardon me, like a ducks, if I don't talk.'

'Did Panty tell you?' Troy persisted. '*I* haven't told anyone. Did she actually tell you she did it?'

A violent paroxysm prevented Miss Orrincourt from speaking, but with her lovely and enormous eyes fixed on Troy and still clasping her fur collar over the lower part of her face, she nodded three times.

'I'd never have believed it,' said Troy slowly. 'Never.'

Miss Orrincourt's shoulders quivered and shook. 'For all the world,' Troy thought suddenly, 'as if she was laughing.'

CHAPTER SIX

Paint

IT WAS ON THAT SAME NIGHT that there was an open flaring row between Paul and Fenella on the one hand and Sir Henry Ancred on the other. It occurred at the climax of a game of backgammon between Troy and Sir Henry. He had insisted upon teaching her this complicated and maddening game. She would have enjoyed it more if she hadn't discovered very early in the contest that her opponent disliked losing so intensely that her own run of beginner's luck had plunged him into the profoundest melancholy. He had attempted to explain to her the chances of the possible combinations of a pair of dice, adding, with some complacency, that he himself had completely mastered this problem. Troy had found his explanation utterly incomprehensible, and began by happily moving her pieces with more regard for the pattern they made on the board than for her chances of winning the game. She met with uncanny success. Sir Henry, who had entered the game with an air of gallantry, finding pretty frequent occasions to pat Troy's fingers, became thoughtful, then pained, and at last gloomy. The members of his family, aware of his mortification, watched in nervous silence. Troy moved with reckless abandon. Sir Henry savagely rattled his dice. Greatly to her relief the tide turned. She gave herself a 'blot' and looked up, to find Fenella and Paul watching her with an extraordinary expression of anxiety. Sir Henry prospered and soon began to 'bear,' Paul and Fenella exchanged a glance. Fenella nodded and turned pale.

'Aha!' cried Sir Henry in triumph. 'The winning throw, I think! The winning throw!'

He cast himself back in his chair, gazed about him and laughed delightedly. It was at this juncture that Paul, who was standing on the hearthrug with Fenella, put his arm round her and kissed her with extreme heartiness and unmistakable intention. 'Fenella and I,' he said loudly, 'are going to be married.'

There followed an electrified silence, lasting perhaps for ten seconds.

Sir Henry then picked up the backgammon board and threw it a surprising distance across the drawing-room.

'And temper,' Paul added, turning rather pale, 'never got anybody anywhere.'

Miss Orrincourt gave a long whistle. Millamant dropped on her knees and began to pick up backgammon pieces.

Pauline Kentish, gazing with something like terror at her son, gabbled incoherently: 'No darling! No, please! No, Paul, don't be naughty. No! Fenella!'

Cedric, his mouth open, his eyes glistening, rubbed his hands and made his crowing noise. But he, too, looked frightened.

And all the Ancreds, out of the corners of their eyes, watched Sir Henry.

He was the first man Troy had ever seen completely given over to rage. She found the exhibition formidable. If he had not been an old man his passion would have been less disquieting because less pitiable. Old lips, shaking with rage; old eyes, whose fierceness was glazed by rheum; old hands, that jerked in uncoordinated fury; these were intolerable manifestations of emotion.

Troy got up and attempted an inconspicuous retreat to the door.

'*Come back*,' said her host violently. Troy returned. 'Hear how these people conspire to humiliate me. Come back, I say.' Troy sat on the nearest chair.

'Papa!' whispered Pauline, weaving her hands together, and 'Papa!' Millamant echoed, fumbling with the dice. 'Please! So bad for you. Upsetting yourself! Please!'

He silenced them with a gesture and struggled to his feet. Paul, holding Fenella by the arm, waited until his grandfather stood before him and then said rapidly: 'We're sorry to make a scene. I persuaded Fen that this was the only way to handle the business. We've discussed it with you in private, Grandfather, and you've told us what you feel about it. We don't agree. It's our show, after all, and we've made up our minds. We could have gone off and got married without saying anything about it, but neither of us wanted to do that. So we thought —'

'We thought,' said Fenella rather breathlessly, 'we'd just make a general announcement.'

'Because,' Paul added, 'I've sent one already to the papers and we wanted to tell you before you read it.'

'But Paul darling—' his mother faintly began.

'You damned young puppy,' Sir Henry roared out, 'what do you mean by standing up with that god-damned conceited look on your face and talking poppycock to ME?'

'Aunt Pauline,' said Fenella, 'I'm sorry if you're not pleased, but—'

'Ssh!' said Pauline.

'Mother *is* pleased,' said Paul. 'Aren't you, Mother?'

'Ssh!' Pauline repeated distractedly.

'Be silent!' Sir Henry shouted. He was now in the centre of the hearth-rug. It seemed to Troy that his first violence was being rapidly transmuted into something more histrionic and much less disturbing. He rested an elbow on the mantelpiece. He pressed two fingers and a thumb against his eyelids, removed his hand slowly, kept his eyes closed, frowned as if in pain, and finally sighed deeply and opened his eyes very wide indeed.

'I'm an old fellow,' he said in a broken voice. 'An old fellow. It's easy to hurt me. Very easy. You have dealt me a shrewd blow. Never mind. Let me suffer. Why not? It won't be for long. Not for long, now.'

'Papa, *dearest*,' cried Pauline, sweeping up to him and clasping her hands. 'You make us utterly miserable. Don't speak like that, don't. Not for the world would my boy cause you a moment's unhappiness. Let me talk quietly to these children. Papa, I implore you.'

'This,' a voice whispered in Troy's ear, 'is perfect Pinero.' She jumped violently. Cedric had slipped round behind his agitated relations and now leant over the back of her chair. 'She played the name part, you know, in a revival of *The Second Mrs Tanqueray*.'

'It's no use, Pauline. Let them go. They knew my wishes. They have chosen the cruellest way. Let them,' said Sir Henry with relish, 'dree their weird.'

'Thank you, Grandfather,' said Fenella brightly, but with a shake in her voice. 'It's our weird and we shall be delighted to dree it.'

Sir Henry's face turned an uneven crimson. 'This is insufferable,' he shouted, and his teeth, unable to cope with the violence of his diction, leapt precariously from their anchorage and were clamped angrily home. Fenella giggled nervously. 'You are under age,' Sir Henry pronounced suddenly. 'Under age, both of you. Pauline, if you have the smallest regard for your old father's wishes, you will forbid this lunacy. I shall speak to your mother, miss. I shall cable to your father.'

'Mother won't mind,' said Fenella.

'You know well, you know perfectly well, why I cannot countenance this nonsense.'

'You think, don't you, Grandfather,' said Fenella, 'that because we're cousins we'll have loopy young. Well, we've asked about that and it's most unlikely. Modern medical opinion—'

'Be silent! At least let some semblance of decency—'

'I *won't* be silent,' said Fenella, performing with dexterity the feat known by actors as topping the other man's lines. 'And if we're to talk about decency, Grandfather, I should have thought it was a damn sight more decent for two people who are young and in love to say they're going to marry each other than for an old man to make an exhibition of himself—'

'*Fenella!*' shouted Pauline and Millamant in unison.

'—doting on a peroxide blonde fifty years younger than himself, and a brazen gold-digger into the bargain.'

Fenella then burst into tears and ran out of the room, followed rigidly by Paul.

Troy, who had once more determined to make her escape, heard Fenella weeping stormily outside the door and stayed where she was. The remaining Ancreds were all talking at once. Sir Henry beat his fist on the mantelpiece until the ornaments danced again, and roared out: 'My God, I'll not have her under my roof another hour! My God—!' Millamant and Pauline, on either side of him like a distracted chorus, wrung their hands and uttered plaintive cries. Cedric chattered noisily behind the sofa, where Miss Orrincourt still lay. It was she who put a stop to this ensemble by rising and confronting them with her hands on her hips.

'I am not remaining here,' said Miss Orrincourt piercingly, 'to be insulted. Remarks have been passed in this room that no self-respecting girl in my delicate position can be expected to endure. Noddy!'

Sir Henry, who had continued his beating of the mantelpiece during this speech, stopped short and looked at her with a kind of nervousness.

'Since announcements,' said Miss Orrincourt, 'are in the air, Noddy, haven't we got something to say ourselves in that line? Or,' she added ominously, 'have we?'

She looked lovely standing there. It was an entirely plastic loveliness, an affair of colour and shape, of line and texture. It was so complete in its kind, Troy thought, that to bring a consideration of character or vulgarity to bear upon it would be to labour at an irrelevant synthesis. In her kind she was perfect. 'What about it, Noddy?' she said.

Sir Henry stared at her, pulled down his waistcoat, straightened his back and took her hand. 'Whenever you wish, my dear,' he said, 'whenever you wish.'

Pauline and Millamant fell back from them, Cedric drew in his breath and touched his moustache. Troy saw, with astonishment, that his hand was shaking.

'I had intended,' Sir Henry said, 'to make this announcement at The Birthday. Now, however, when I realize only too bitterly that my family cares little, cares nothing for my happiness' (*'Papa!'* Pauline wailed), 'I turn, in my hour of sorrow, to One who does Care.'

'Uh-huh!' Miss Orrincourt assented. 'But keep it sunny-side-up, Petty-pie.'

Sir Henry, less disconcerted than one would have thought possible by this interjection, gathered himself together.

'This lady,' he said loudly, 'has graciously consented to become my wife.'

Considering the intensity of their emotions, Troy felt that the Ancreds really behaved with great aplomb. It was true that Pauline and Millamant were, for a moment, blankly silent, but Cedric almost immediately ran out from cover and seized his grandfather by the hand.

'Dearest Grandpapa—couldn't be more delighted—too marvellous. Sonia, *darling*,' he babbled, '*such* fun,' and he kissed her.

'Well, Papa,' said Millamant, following her son's lead but not kissing Miss Orrincourt, 'we can't say that it's altogether a surprise, can we? I'm sure we all hope you'll be very happy.'

Pauline was more emotional. 'Dearest,' she said, taking her father's hands and gazing with wet eyes into his face, 'dearest, dearest Papa. Please, please believe my only desire is for your happiness.'

Sir Henry inclined his head. Pauline made an upward pounce at his moustache. 'Oh, Pauline,' he said with an air of tragic resignation, 'I have been wounded, Pauline! Deeply wounded!'

'No,' cried Pauline. 'No!'

'Yes,' sighed Sir Henry. 'Yes.'

Pauline turned blindly from him and offered her hand to Miss Orrincourt. 'Be good to him,' she said brokenly. 'It's all we ask. Be good to him.'

With an eloquent gesture, Sir Henry turned aside, crossed the room, and flung himself into a hitherto unoccupied armchair. It made a loud and extremely vulgar noise.

Sir Henry, scarlet in the face, leapt to his feet and snatched up the loose cushioned seat. He exposed a still partially inflated bladder-like object, across which was printed a legend, 'The Raspberry. Makes your Party go off with a Bang.' He seized it, and again, through some concealed orifice, it emitted its dreadful sound. He hurled it accurately into the fire and the stench of burning rubber filled the room.

'Well, I mean to say,' said Miss Orrincourt, 'fun's fun, but I think that kid's getting common in her ways.'

Sir Henry walked in silence to the door, where, inevitably, he turned to deliver an exit line. 'Millamant,' he said, 'in the morning you will be good enough to send for my solicitor.'

The door banged. After a minute's complete silence Troy was at last able to escape from the drawing-room.

Troy was not much surprised in the morning to learn that Sir Henry was too unwell to appear, though he hoped in the afternoon to resume the usual sitting. A note on her early tea-tray informed her that Cedric would be delighted to pose in the costume if this would be of any service. She thought it might. There was the scarlet cloak to be attended to. She had half-expected a disintegration of the family forces, at least the disappearance, possibly in opposite directions, of Fenella and Paul. She had yet to learn of the Ancreds' resilience in inter-tribal warfare. At breakfast they both appeared—Fenella, white and silent; Paul, red and silent. Pauline arrived a little later. Her attitude to her son suggested that he was ill of some not entirely respectable disease. With Fenella she adopted an air of pained antipathy and would scarcely speak to her. Millamant presided. She was less jolly than usual, but behind her anxiety, if she was indeed anxious, Troy detected a hint of complacency. There was more than a touch of condolence in her manner towards her sister-in-law, and this, Troy felt, Pauline deeply resented.

'Well, Milly,' said Pauline after a long silence, 'do you propose to continue your role under new management?'

'I'm always rather lost, Pauline, when you adopt theatrical figures of speech.'

'Are you going to house-keep, then, for the new châtelaine?'

'I hardly expect to do so.'

'Poor Milly,' said Pauline. 'It's going to be difficult for you, I'm afraid.'

'I don't think so. Cedric and I have always thought we'd like to have a little *pied-à-terre* together in London.'

'Yes,' Pauline agreed, much too readily, 'Cedric will have to draw in his horns a bit too, one supposes.'

'Perhaps Paul and Fenella would consider allowing me to house-keep for them,' said Millamant, with her first laugh that morning. And with an air of genuine interest she turned to them. 'How *are* you going to manage, both of you?' she asked.

'Like any other husband and wife without money,' said Fenella. 'Paul's got his pension and I've got my profession. We'll both get jobs.'

'Oh, well,' said Millamant comfortably, 'perhaps after all, your grandfather—'

'We don't want Grandfather to do anything, Aunt Milly,' said Paul quickly. 'He wouldn't anyway, of course, but we don't want him to.'

'Dearest!' said his mother. 'So hard! So bitter! I don't know you, Paul, when you talk like that. Something'—she glanced with extraordinary distaste at Fenella—'has changed you so dreadfully.'

'Where,' asked Millamant brightly, 'is Panty?'

'Where should she be if not in school?' Pauline countered with dignity. 'She is not in the habit of breakfasting with us, Milly.'

'Well, you never know,' said Millamant. 'She seems to get about quite a lot, doesn't she? And, by the way, Pauline, I've a bone to pick with Panty myself. Someone has interfered with My Work. A large section of embroidery has been deliberately unpicked. I'd left it in the drawing-room and—'

'Panty never goes there,' cried Pauline.

'Well, I don't know about that. She must, for instance, have been in the drawing-room last evening during dinner.'

'Why?'

'Because Sonia, as I suppose we must call her, says she sat in that chair before dinner, Pauline. She says it was perfectly normal.'

'I can't help that, Milly. Panty did not come into the drawing-room last night at dinner-time for the very good reason that she and the other children were given their medicine then and sent early to bed. You told me yourself, Milly, that Miss Able found the medicine in the flower-room and took it straight in for Dr Withers to give the children.'

'Oh, yes,' said Millamant. 'Would you believe it, the extraordinary Sonia didn't trouble to take it in to Miss Able, or to give Papa's bottle to me. She merely went to the flower-room, where it seems,' said Millamant with a sniff, 'orchids had been brought in for her; and dumped the lot. Miss Able hunted everywhere before she found it, and so did I.'

'T'uh,' said Pauline.

'All the same,' said Paul. 'I don't mind betting that Panty—'

'It has yet to be proved,' Pauline interrupted with spirit rather than conviction, 'that Panty had anything to do with—with—'

'With the Raspberry?' said Paul, grinning. 'Mother, of course she did.'

'I have reason to believe—' Pauline began.

'No, really, Mother. It's Panty all over. Look at her record.'

'Where did she get it? I've never given her such a thing.'

'Another kid, I suppose, if she didn't buy it. I've seen them in one of the village shops; haven't you, Fen? I remember thinking to myself that they ought to have been sent to a rubber dump.'

'I've had a little talk with Panty,' said Panty's mother, obstinately, 'and she promised me on her word of honour she didn't know anything about it. I know when that child is speaking the truth, Milly. A mother always knows.'

'*Honestly*, Mother!' said Paul.

'I don't care what anyone says—' Pauline began, but was interrupted by the entrance of Cedric, very smooth and elegant, and with more than a touch of smugness in his general aspect.

'Good morning, dearest Mrs Alleyn. Good morning, my sweets,' he said. 'Planning how to lay out the proverbial shilling to advantage, Paul dear? I've been so excited thinking up a scheme for a double wedding. It's a teeny bit involved. The Old Person, you see, in Uncle Claude's absence, must give Fenella away and then whisk over to the other side as First Bridegroom. I thought I might be joint Best Man and Paul could double Second Bridegroom and Sonia's papa. It's like a rather intricate ballet. Uncle Thomas is to be a page and Panty a flower-girl, which will give her wonderful opportunities for throwing things. And you, dearest Mama, and all the aunts shall be Dowagers-in-Waiting. I've invented such marvellously intimidating gowns for you.'

'Don't be naughty,' said Millamant.

'No, but truly,' Cedric went on, bringing his plate to the table. 'I *do* feel, you two, that you've managed your affairs the least bit clumsily.'

'It's not given to all of us,' said Paul dryly, 'to be quite as nimble after the main chance as you.'

'Well, I do rather flatter myself I've exhibited a pretty turn of low cunning,' Cedric agreed readily. 'Sonia's going to let me do her trousseau, and the Old Person said that I at least showed some family feeling. But I'm afraid, dearest Auntie Pauline, that Panty has lost ground almost irretrievably. Such a very robust sense of comedy.'

'I have already told your mother, Cedric, that I have reason to believe that Panty was not responsible for that incident.'

'Oh, Gracious!' said Cedric. 'So touching. Such faith.'

'Or for the writing on your grandfather's looking-glass.'

Cedric made one of his ingratiating wriggles at Troy. 'Panty has another champion,' he said.

Pauline turned quickly to Troy, who, with a sense of stepping from the stalls up to the stage, murmured: 'I didn't think Panty wrote on the glass. I thought her protests rang true.'

'There!' cried Pauline emotionally, and stretched out her hand to Troy. 'There, all of you! *Thank* you, Mrs Alleyn. *Someone* has faith in *my poor old Panty.*'

But Troy's faith in Panty Kentish, already slightly undermined, was to suffer a further jolt.

She went from the dining-room to the little theatre. Her canvas was leaning, face to the wall, where she had left it. She dragged it out, tipped it up on one corner, set it on the lowered tray of her easel and stepped back to look at it.

Across the nose and eyes of the completed head somebody had drawn in black paint an enormous pair of spectacles.

For perhaps five seconds alternate lumps of ice and red-hot coal chased each other down her spine and round her stomach. She then touched the face. It was hard dry. The black spectacles were still wet. With a sense of relief that was so violent that it came upon her like an attack of nausea, Troy clipped a rag in oil and gingerly wiped off the addition. She then sat down and pressed her shaking hands together. Not a stain, not a blur on the bluish shadows that she had twisted under the eyes, not a trace of dirt across the strange pink veil that was the flesh under his frontal bone. 'Oh, Golly!' Troy whispered. 'Oh, Golly! Thank God! Oh, Golly!'

'Good morning,' said Panty, coming in by the side door. 'I'm allowed to do another picture. I want some more board and lots more paint. Look, I've finished the cows and the aeroplane. Aren't they good?'

She dumped her board on the floor against the foot of the easel, and, with a stocky imitation of Troy, fell back a pace and looked at it, her hands clasped behind her back. Her picture was of three vermilion cows in an emerald meadow. Above them, against a sky for which Panty had used neat New Blue, flew an emerald aeroplane in the act of secreting a black bomb.

'Damn good,' said Panty, 'isn't it?' She tore her gaze away from her picture and allowed it to rest on Troy's.

'That's good too,' she said. 'It's nice. It gives me a nice feeling inside. I think you paint good pictures.'

'Somebody,' said Troy, watching her, 'thought it would be better if I put in a pair of spectacles.'

'Well, they must have been pretty silly,' said Panty. 'Kings don't wear spectacles. That's a king.'

'Whoever it was, painted them on the face.'

'If anybody puts spectacles on my cows,' Panty said, 'I'll kill them.'

'Who do you think could have done it?'

'I dunno,' said Panty without interest. 'Did Noddy?'

'I hardly think so.'

'I suppose it was whoever put whatever it was on Noddy's glass. Not me, anyway. Now can I have another board and more paint? Miss Able likes me to paint.'

'You may go up to my room and get yourself one of the small boards in the cupboard.'

'I don't know where your room is.'

Troy explained as best she could. 'Oh, well,' said Panty, 'if I can't find it I'll just yell till somebody comes.'

She stumped away to the side door. 'By the way,' Troy called after her, 'would you know a Raspberry if you saw one?'

'You bet,' said Panty with interest.

'I mean a rubber thing that makes a noise if you sit on it.'

'What sort of noise?'

'Never mind,' said Troy wearily. 'Forget about it.'

'You're mad,' said Panty flatly and went out.

'If I'm not,' Troy muttered, 'there's somebody in this house who is.'

All that morning she painted solidly through the background. In the afternoon Sir Henry posed for an hour and a half with two rests. He said nothing, but sighed a great deal. Troy worked at the hands, but he was restless, and kept making small nervous movements so that she did little more than lay down the general tone and shape of them. Millamant came in just before the end of the sitting, and, with a word of apology, went to him and murmured something indistinguishable. 'No, no,' he said angrily. 'It must be tomorrow. Ring up again and tell them so.'

'He says it's very inconvenient.'

'That be damned. Ring up again.'

'Very well, Papa,' said the obedient Millamant.

She went away, and Troy, seeing that he was growing still more restless, called an end to the sitting, telling him that Cedric had offered to pose for the cloak. He left with evident relief. Troy grunted disconsolately, scraped down the hands, and turned again to the background. It was a formalized picture of a picture. The rooky wood, a wet mass, rimmed with boldly stated strokes of her brush, struck sharply across a coldly luminous night sky. The monolithic forms in the middle distance were broadly set down as interlocking masses. Troy had dragged a giant brush down the canvas, each stroke the summing-up of painful thinking that suddenly resolved itself in form. The background was right, and the Ancreds, she reflected, would think it very queer and unfinished. All of them, except, perhaps, Cedric and Panty. She had arrived at this conclusion when on to the stage pranced Cedric himself, heavily and most unnecessarily made-up, moving with a sort of bouncing stride, and making much of his grandfather's red cloak.

'Here I am,' he cried, 'feeling so keyed up with the mantle of high tragedy across my puny shoulders. Now, what *precisely* is the pose?'

There was no need to show him, however. He swept up his drape, placed himself, and, with an expert wriggle, flung it into precisely the right sweep. Troy eyed it, and, with a sense of rising excitement, spread unctuous bands of brilliant colour across her palette.

Cedric was an admirable model. The drape was frozen in its sculptured folds. Troy worked in silence for an hour, holding her breath so often that she became quite stuffy in the nose.

'Dearest Mrs Alleyn,' said a faint voice, 'I have a tiny cramp in my leg.'

'Lord, I'm sorry!' said Troy. 'You've been wonderful. Do have a rest.'

He came down into the auditorium, limping a little but still with an air, and stood before her canvas.

'It's so piercingly *right*,' he said. 'Too exciting! I mean, it really is theatre, and the Old Person and that devastating Bard all synthesized and made eloquent and everything. It terrifies me.'

He sank into a near-by stall, first spreading his cloak over the back, and fanned himself. 'I can't tell you how I've died to prattle,' he went on, 'all the time I was up there. This house is simply *seething* with intrigue.'

Troy, who was herself rather exhausted, lit a cigarette, sat down, and eyed her work. She also listened with considerable interest to Cedric.

'First I must tell you,' he began, 'the Old Person has positively sent for his solicitor. Imagine! Such lobbyings and whisperings! One is reminded of Papal elections in the seventeenth century. First the marriage settlement, of course. What do you suppose darling Sonia will have laid down as the minimum? I've tried *piteously* hard to wheedle it out of her, but she's turned rather secretive and *grande dame*. But, of course, however much it is it's got to come from *somewhere*. Panty was known to be first favourite. He's left her some fabulous sum to make her *à parti* when she grows up. But we all feel her little pranks will have swept her right out of the running. So perhaps darling Sonia will have that lot. Then there's Paul and Fenella, who have undoubtedly polished themselves off. I rather *hope*,' said Cedric with a modest titter and a very sharp look in his eye, 'that I *may* reap something there. I *think* I'm all right, but you never know. He simply detests me, really, and the entail is quite ridiculous. Somebody broke it up or something ages ago, and I *may* only get this awful house and nothing whatever to keep it up with. Still, I really have got Sonia on my side.'

He touched his moustache and pulled a small pellet of cosmetic off his eyelashes. 'I made up,' he explained in parentheses, 'because I felt it was so essential to get the feeling of the Macsoforth *seeping* through into every fold of the mantle. And partly because it's such fun painting one's face.'

He hummed a little air for a moment or two and then continued: 'Thomas and Dessy and the Honourable Mrs A. are all pouring in on Friday night. The Birthday is on Saturday, did you realize? The Old Person and the Ancient of Days will spend Sunday in bed, the one suffering from gastronomic excess, the other from his exertions as Ganymede. The family will no doubt pass the day in mutual recrimination. The general feeling is that the *pièce-de-résistance* for the Birthday will be an announcement of the new Will.'

'But, good Lord—!'" Troy ejaculated. Cedric talked her down. 'Almost certain, I assure you. He has always made public each new draft. He can't resist the dramatic *mise-en-scène.*'

'But how often does he change his Will?'

'I've never kept count,' Cedric confessed after a pause, 'but on an average I should say once every two years, though for the last three years Panty has held firm as first favourite. While she was still doing baby-talk and only came here occasionally he adored her, and she, most unfortunately, was crazy about him. Pauline must curse the day when she manoeuvred the school to Ancreton. Last time I was *grossly* unpopular and down to the bare bones of the entail. Uncle Thomas was second to Panty with the general hope that he would marry and have a son, and I remain a celibate with Ancreton as a millstone round my poor little neck. *Isn't* it all too tricky?'

There was scarcely a thing that Cedric did or said of which Troy did not wholeheartedly disapprove, but it was impossible to be altogether bored by him. She found herself listening quite attentively to his recital, though after a time his gloating delight in Panty's fall from grace began to irritate her.

'I still think,' she said, 'that Panty didn't play these tricks on her grandfather.' Cedric, with extraordinary vehemence, began to protest, but Troy insisted. 'I've talked to her about it. Her manner, to my mind, was conclusive. Obviously she didn't know anything about last night's affair. She'd never heard of the squeaking cushion.'

'That child,' Cedric announced malevolently, 'is incredibly, terrifyingly subtle. She is not an Ancred for nothing. She was acting. Depend upon it, she was acting.'

'I don't believe it. And what's more, she didn't know her way to my room.'

Cedric, who was biting his nails, paused and stared at her. After a long pause he said: 'Didn't know her way to your room? But, dearest Mrs Alleyn, what has that got to do with it?'

It was on the tip of her tongue to relate the incident of the painted banister. She had even begun: 'Well, if you promise—' And then, catching sight of his face with its full pouting mouth and pale eyes, she suddenly changed her mind. 'It doesn't matter,' Troy said; 'it wouldn't convince you. Never mind.'

'Dearest Mrs Alleyn,' Cedric tittered, pulling at his cloak, 'you are mysterious. Any one would suppose you didn't trust me.'

CHAPTER SEVEN

Fiesta

ON FRIDAY, A WEEK AFTER her arrival at Ancreton,
Troy dragged her canvas out of the property room, where she
now kept it locked up, and stared at it with mixed sensations
of which the predominant was one of astonishment. How
in the world had she managed it? Another two days would
see its completion. Tomorrow night Sir Henry would lead
his warring celebrants into the little theatre and she would
stand awkwardly in the background while they talked about
it. Would they be very disappointed? Would they see at once
that the background was not the waste before Forres Castle
but a theatrical cloth presenting this, that Troy had painted,
not Macbeth himself, but an old actor looking backwards into
his realization of the part? Would they see that the mood was
one of relinquishment?

Well, the figure was completed. There were some
further places she must attend to—a careful balancing stroke
here and here. She was filled with a great desire that her

husband should see it. It was satisfactory, Troy thought, that of the few people to whom she wished to show her work her husband came first. Perhaps this was because he said so little yet was not embarrassed by his own silence.

As the end of her work drew near her restlessness increased and her fears for their reunion. She remembered phrases spoken by other women: 'The first relationship is never repeated.' 'We were strangers again when we met.' 'It wasn't the same.' 'It feels extraordinary. We were shy and had nothing to say to each other.' Would her reunion also be inarticulate? 'I've no technique,' Troy thought, 'to see me through. I've no marital technique at all. Any native adroitness I possess has gone into my painting. But perhaps Roderick will know what to say. Shall I tell him at once about the Ancreds?'

She was cleaning her palette when Fenella ran in to say a call had come through for her from London.

It was the Assistant Commissioner at the Yard. Troy listened to him with a hammer knocking at her throat. He thought, he said with arch obscurity, that she might enjoy a run up to London on Monday. If she stayed the night, the Yard might have something of interest to show her on Tuesday morning. A police car would be coming in by way of Ancreton Halt early on Monday and would be delighted to give her a lift. 'Thank you,' said Troy in an unrecognizable voice. 'Yes, I see. Yes, of course. Yes, very exciting. Thank you.'

She fled to her room, realizing as she sat breathless on her bed that she had run like a madwoman up three flights of stairs. 'It's as well,' she thought, 'that the portrait's finished. In this frame of mind I'd be lucky if I reached Panty's form.'

She began distractedly to imagine their meeting. 'But I can't see his face,' she thought in a panic. 'I can't remember his voice. I've forgotten my husband.'

She felt by turns an unreasonable urge for activity and a sense of helpless inertia. Ridiculous incidents from the Ancred repertoire flashed up in her mind. 'I must remember to tell him that,' she would think, and then wonder if, after all, the Ancreds in retrospect would sound funny. She remembered with a jolt that she must let Katti Bostock know about Tuesday. They had arranged for Alleyn's old servant to go to London and open the flat.

'I should have done it at once,' she cried, and returned downstairs. While she waited, fuming, in a little telephone-room near the front doors, for her call to go through, she heard wheels on the drive, the sound of voices, and finally the unmistakable rumpus of arrival in the hall. A charming voice called gaily: 'Milly, where are you? Come down. It's Dessy and Thomas and me. Dessy found a Colonel, and the Colonel had a car, and we've all arrived together.'

'Jenetta!' Millamant's disembodied voice floated down from the gallery. Still more distantly Pauline's echoed her: 'Jenetta!'

Was there an overtone of disapproval, not quite of dismay, in this greeting, Troy wondered, as she quietly shut the door?

Jenetta, the Hon Mrs Claude Ancred, unlike Millamant, had caught none of the overtones of her relations-in-law. She was a nice-looking woman, with a gay voice, good clothes, an intelligent face, and an air of quietly enjoying herself. Her conversation was unstressed and crisp. If she sensed internecine warfare she gave no hint of doing so, and seemed to be equally pleased with, and equally remote from, each member of that unlikely clan.

Desdemona, on the other hand, was, of all the Ancreds after Sir Henry, most obviously of the theatre. She was startlingly good looking, of voluptuous build, and had a warm ringing voice that seemed to be perpetually uttering important lines of climax from a West-End success. She ought really, Troy thought, to be surrounded by attendant figures: a secretary, an author, an agent, perhaps a doting producer. She had an aura of richness and warmth, and a knack of causing everybody else to subscribe to the larger-than-life atmosphere in which she herself moved so easily. Her Colonel, after a drink, drove away to his lawful destination, with Dessy's magnificent thanks no doubt ringing in his ears. Troy, emerging from the telephone-room, found herself confronted by the new arrivals. She was glad to see Thomas: already she thought of him as 'old Thomas', with his crest of faded hair and his bland smile. 'Oh, hallo,' he said, blinking at her, 'so here you are! I hope your carbuncle is better.'

'It's gone,' said Troy.

'We're all talking about Papa's engagement,' said Thomas. 'This is my sister-in-law, Mrs Claude Ancred, and this is my sister, Desdemona. Milly and Pauline are seeing about rooms. Have you painted a nice picture?'

'Not bad. Are you producing a nice play?'

'It's quite good, thank you,' said Thomas primly.

'Darling Tommy,' said Desdemona, 'how *can* it be quite good with that woman? What were you thinking about when you cast it!'

'Well, Dessy, I told the management you wanted the part.'

'I didn't want it. I could play it, but I didn't want it, thank you.'

'Then everybody ought to be pleased,' said Thomas mildly. 'I suppose, Jenetta,' he continued, 'you are anxious to see Fenella and Paul. Papa's engagement has rather swamped theirs, you may feel. Are you as angry as he is about them?'

'I'm not a bit angry,' she said, catching Troy's eye and smiling at her. 'I'm fond of Paul and want to talk to him.'

'That's all very nice,' said Dessy restlessly, 'but Milly says it was Paul and Fenella who exploded the bomb.'

'Oh, well,' said Thomas comfortably, 'I expect it would have gone off anyway. Did you know Mr Rattisbon has been sent for to make a new Will? I suppose Papa'll tell us all about it at the Birthday Dinner tomorrow. Do you expect to be cut out this time, Dessy?'

'My dear,' cried his sister, sinking magnificently into the sofa and laying her arms along the back of it, 'I've said so often exactly what I think of the Orrincourt that he can't possibly do anything else. I don't give a damn, Tommy. If Papa expects me to purr round congratulating them, he's never been more mistaken. I can't do it. It's been a hideous shock to me. It hurts me, *here*,' she added, beating a white fist on her striking bosom. 'All my respect, my love, my *ideal*—shattered.' She flashed her eyes at her sister-in-law. 'You think I exaggerate, Jen. You're lucky. You're not easily upset.'

'Well,' said Jenetta lightly, 'I've yet to meet Miss Orrincourt.'

'He's not your father,' Dessy pointed out with emotion.

'No more he is,' she agreed.

'T'uh!' said Dessy bitterly.

This conversation was interrupted by Fenella, who ran downstairs, flew across the hall, and, with an inarticulate cry, flung herself into her mother's arms.

'Now, then,' said Jenetta softly, holding her daughter for a moment, 'no high strikes.'

'Mummy, you're not furious? Say you're not furious!'

'Do I look furious, you goat? Where's Paul?'

'In the library. Will you come? Mummy, you're Heaven. You're an angel.'

'Do pipe down, darling. And what about Aunt Dessy and Uncle Thomas?'

Fenella turned to greet them. Thomas kissed her carefully. 'I hope you'll be happy,' he said. 'It ought to be all right, really. I looked up genetics in a medical encyclopedia after I read the announcement. The chap said the issue of first cousins was generally quite normal, unless there was any marked insanity in the family which was common to both.'

'Tommy!' said his sister. 'Honestly, you *are*!'

'Well,' said Jenetta Ancred, 'with that assurance to fortify us, Fen, suppose you take me to see Paul.'

They went off together. Millamant and Pauline came downstairs. 'Such a nuisance,' Millamant was saying, 'I really don't quite know how to arrange it.'

'If you're talking about rooms, Milly,' said Desdemona, 'I tell you flatly that unless something has been done about the rats I won't go into *Bracegirdle*.'

'Well, but Dessy—' Pauline began.

'Has something been done about the rats?'

'Barker,' said Millamant unhappily, 'has lost the arsenic. I think he did Miss Orrincourt's rooms some time ago, and after that the tin disappeared.'

'Good God!' said Thomas quietly.

'Pity he didn't put some in her tooth-glass,' said Desdemona vindictively.

'What about *Ellen Terry*?'

'I was putting Jenetta into *Terry*.'

'Come into *Bernhardt* with me, Dess,' Pauline suggested richly. 'I'd love to have you. We can talk. Let's.'

'The only thing against that,' said Millamant, knitting her brows, 'is that since Papa had all those large Jacobean pieces put in *Bernhardt*, there really isn't anywhere for a second bed. I can put one in my room, Desdemona. I wondered if you'd mind...*Lady Bancroft*, you know. Quite spacious and plenty of hanging room.'

'Well, Milly, if it isn't turning you upside down.'

'Not at all,' said Millamant coldly.

'And you can still talk to me,' said Pauline. 'I'll be next door.'

On Friday night the weather broke and a deluge of rain beat down on the tortuous roofs of Ancreton. On Saturday morning Troy was awakened by a regular sequence of sharp percussionlike notes: Ping, ping, ping.

On going to her bath she nearly fell into a basin that had been placed on the landing. Into it fell a continuous progression of water-drops from a spreading patch in the roof. All day it rained. At three o'clock it had grown too dark to paint in the little theatre, but she had worked through the morning, and, having laid her last touch against the canvas, walked away from it and sat down. She felt that curious blankness which follows the completion of a painting. It was over. Her house was untenanted. It did not long remain so, for now, unchecked by the discipline of her work, Troy's thoughts were filled with the anticipation of reunion. 'The day after tomorrow I shall be saying: "Tomorrow."' The Ancreds and their machinations now seemed unreal. They were two-dimensional figures gesticulating on a ridiculously magnificent stage. This reaction was to colour all memories of her last two days at Ancreton, blurring their edges, lending a tinge of fantasy to commonplace events, and causing her to doubt the integrity of her recollections when, in a little while, it would be imperative for her to recount them accurately.

She was to remember that Sir Henry was invisible all day, resting in preparation for his Birthday Dinner; that there was an air of anticipation in his enormous house, that his presents were set out in the library, a dark no-man's-land in the east wing, and that the members of his family visited this Mecca frequently, eyeing each other's gifts with intense partiality. Troy herself, in readiness for The Birthday, had made a lively and diverting sketch of Panty, which she had mounted and placed among the other gifts, wondering if, in view of Panty's fall from grace, it was too preposterously inept. The sketch was viewed with wholehearted favour by Panty herself and her mother, and by nobody else except Cedric, who chose to regard it as an acid comment on the child's character, which it was not.

Troy remembered afterwards how she had looked at the long dresses she had brought with her and decided that they were nothing like grand enough for the occasion. She remembered how the air of festivity had deepened as evening came, and how Barker and his retinue of elderly maids were in a continuous state of controlled bustle. Most often, though still with a feeling of incredulity, would it seem to her that there had been a sense of impending climax in the house, an impression of something drawing to its close. At the time Troy said to herself: 'It's because Rory's coming. It's because I've finished an intensive bit of work done at concert pitch.' But in retrospect these answers sounded unconvincing, and she wondered if the thoughts of one malevolent creature could have sent out a thin mist of apprehension.

Troy had cleaned her palette, shut her paint-box on ranks of depleted tubes, and washed her brushes for the last time at Ancreton. The portrait had been set up on the stage and framed in crimson velvet curtains that did their best to kill it. 'If it was springtime,' Troy thought, 'I believe they'd have festooned it in garlands.' The act-drop had been lowered in front of the portrait and there it waited on a dark stage for the evening's ceremony. She couldn't glower at it. She couldn't walk in that deluge. She was unendurably restless. The dinner itself was at nine; she had three hours to fill in. Taking a book with her, she wandered uncertainly from one vast room to another, and wherever she went there seemed to be two Ancreds in private conversation. Having disclosed Paul and Fenella tightly embraced in the study, disturbed Desdemona and Pauline hissing together in the drawing-room, and interrupted Millamant in what appeared to be angry parley with Barker under the stairs, she made her way to a room next the library, known as the Great Boudoir (the Little Boudoir was upstairs). Unnerved by her previous encounters, Troy paused outside the door and listened. All was still. She pushed open the door, and was confronted by Cedric and Miss Orrincourt side by side on a sofa, doubled up in an ecstasy of silent laughter.

She was well into the room before they saw her. Their behaviour was extraordinary. They stared at her with their mouths open, the laughter drying out on their faces as if she had scorched it. Cedric turned an ugly red, Miss Orrincourt's eyes were as hard as blue glass marbles. She was the first to speak.

'Well, for crying out loud,' she said in a flat voice, 'look who's here.'

'Dearest Mrs Alleyn,' said Cedric breathlessly, 'do come in. We've been having a dreadfully naughty giggle over everything. The Birthday, you know, and all the wheels within wheels and so on. Do join us. Or are you too grand and upright? Dear me, that sounds as if you were a piano, doesn't it?'

'It's all right,' said Troy, 'I won't come in, thank you. I'm on my way upstairs.'

She went out, closing the door on their silence.

In the hall she found a completely strange elderly gentleman reading a newspaper before the fire. He wore London clothes, an old-fashioned wing collar and a narrow black tie. His face was thin and his hands blue-veined and knotty. When he saw Troy he dropped his newspaper, snatched off his pince-nez, and ejaculating 'M-m-m-mah!' rose nimbly to his feet.

'Are you waiting to see somebody?' Troy asked.

'Thank yer, thank yer, no thank-yer,' said the elderly gentleman rapidly. 'Make myself known. Haven't had the pleasure—Introduce myself. M-mah. Rattisbon.'

'Oh, yes, of course,' said Troy. 'I knew you were coming. How do you do?' She introduced herself.

Mr Rattisbon vibrated the tip of his tongue between his lips and wrung his hands. 'How d'do,' he gabbled. 'Delighted. Take it, fellow-guests. If I may so designate myself. Professional visit.'

'So's mine,' said Troy, picking the sense out of this collection of phrases. 'I've been doing a job here.'

He glanced at the painting-smock she had not yet removed. 'Surely,' he clattered, 'Mrs Roderick Alleyn? Née Troy?'

'That's it.'

'Pleasure of your husband's acquaintance,' Mr Rattisbon explained. 'Professional association. Twice. Admirable.'

'Really?' said Troy, at once delighted. 'You know Roderick? Do let's sit down.'

Mr Rattisbon sucked in his breath and made a crowing sound. They sat before the fire. He crossed his knees and joined his gnarled fingers. 'He's a drawing by Cruikshank,' Troy thought. She began to talk to him about Alleyn, and he listened exactly as if she was making a series of statements which he would presently require his clerk to come in and witness. Troy was to remember vividly this quiet encounter, and how in the middle of her recital she broke off apologetically to say: 'But I don't know why I should bore you with these stories about Roderick.'

'Bore?' he said. 'On the contrary. Entirely so. May I add, strictly *in camera*, that I—ah—had contemplated this call with some misgivings as—ah—a not altogether propitious necessity. I find myself unexpectedly received, and most charmingly so, by a lady for whose remarkable talents I have long entertained the highest regard. M-m-mah!' Mr Rattisbon added, dipping like a sparrow towards Troy. 'Entirely so.'

At this juncture Pauline and Desdemona appeared in the hall and bore down rapidly upon Mr Rattisbon.

'We are so sorry,' Pauline began. 'Leaving you so long. Papa's only just been told—a little upset. The great day, of course. He will be ready for you in a few minutes, dear Mr Rattisbon. Until then Dessy and I would be so glad if you— we feel we'd like to—'

Troy was already on her way out. They were waiting for her to get out of earshot.

She heard Desdemona's rich voice: 'Just a tiny talk, Mr Rattisbon. Just to warn you.' And Mr Rattisbon suddenly very dry and brittle: 'If you desire it, certainly.'

'But,' thought Troy, plodding along the passage, 'they won't get much change out of Mr Rattisbon.'

'It's the big scene from a film script,' thought Troy, looking down the table, 'and I'm the bit-part lady.' The analogy was unavoidable. How often had one not seen Sir Aubrey Smith at the head of such a table? Where else but on the screen was such opulence to be found? Where else such a welter of flowers, such sumptuously Edwardian epergnes, or such incredibly appropriate conversation? Never out of a film studio had characters been so well typed. Even the neighbouring squire and the parson, the one lean and monocled, the other rubicund and sleek, who apparently were annual fixtures for the event; even they were carefully selected cameo parts, too like themselves to be credible. And Mr Rattisbon? The absolute in family solicitors. As for the Ancreds themselves, to glance at them or to hear their carefully modulated laughter, their beautifully articulated small-talk, was to realize at once that this was an all-star vehicle. Troy began to make up titles. 'Homage to Sir Henry.' 'The Astonishing Ancreds.'

'Going quite nicely, so far, don't you consider?' said Thomas at her left elbow. She had forgotten Thomas, although he had taken her in. Cedric, on her right hand, had directed at her and at his partner, Desdemona, a number of rather spasmodic and intensely artificial remarks, all of which sounded as if they were designed for the ears of his grandfather. Thomas, presumably, had been silent until now.

'Very nicely,' Troy agreed hurriedly.

'I mean,' Thomas continued, lowering his voice, 'you wouldn't think, if you didn't know, how terrified everyone is about the Will, would you? Everybody except me, that is, and perhaps Cedric.'

'Ssh!' said Troy. 'No, you wouldn't.'

'It's because we're putting on the great Family Act, you know. It's the same on the stage. People that hate each other's guts make love like angels. You'd be surprised, I dare say. Outsiders think it very queer. Well,' Thomas continued, laying down his soup-spoon and gazing mildly at her. 'What, after all, *do* you think of Ancreton?'

'I've found it absorbing.'

'I'm so glad. You've come in for a set-piece, haven't you? All the intrigues and fights. Do you know what will happen after dinner?' And without waiting for her reply he told her. 'Papa will propose the King's health and then I shall propose Papa's. I'm the eldest son present so I shall have to, but it's a pity. Claude would be much better. Last year Panty was brought in to do it. I coached her in the "business" and she managed very nicely. Papa cried. This year, because of ringworm and the practical jokes, she hasn't been invited. Gracious,' Thomas continued, as Troy helped herself from a dish that had appeared over her shoulder, 'that's never New Zealand crayfish! I thought Millamant had decided against it. Has Papa noticed? There'll be trouble if he has.'

Thomas was right. Sir Henry, when offered this dish, glanced truculently at his daughter-in-law and helped himself to it. An instant silence fell upon the table, and Troy, who was opposite Millamant, saw her make a helpless deprecating grimace at Pauline, who, from the foot of the table, responded by raising her eyebrows.

'He insisted,' Millamant whispered to Paul on her left hand.

'What?' asked Sir Henry loudly.

'Nothing, Papa,' said Millamant.

'They call this,' said Sir Henry, addressing himself to Mr Rattisbon, 'rock lobster. No more like a lobster than my foot. It's some antipodean shell-fish.'

Furtively watched by his family, he took a large mouthful and at the same time pointed to his glass and added: 'One must drink something with it. I shall break my rule, Barker. Champagne.'

Barker, with his lips very slightly pursed, filled the glass.

'That's a big boy,' said Miss Orrincourt approvingly. The Ancreds, after a frightened second or two, burst simultaneously into feverish conversation.

'There,' said Thomas with an air of sober triumph. 'What did I tell you? Champagne and hot crayfish. We shall hear more of this, you may depend upon it.'

'Do be careful,' Troy murmured nervously, and then, seeing that Sir Henry was in gallant conversation with Jenetta on his left, she added cautiously: 'Is it so very bad for him?'

'I promise you,' said Thomas, 'disastrous. I don't think it tastes very nice, anyway,' he continued after a pause. 'What do you think?' Troy had already come to this conclusion. The crayfish, she decided, were dubious.

'Hide it under your toast,' said Thomas, 'I'm going to. It's the Birthday turkey next, from the home farm. We can fill up on that, can't we?'

But Sir Henry, Troy noticed, ate all his crayfish.

Apart from this incident, the dinner continued in the same elevated key up to the moment when Sir Henry, with the air of a Field Marshal in Glorious Technicolor, rose and proposed the King.

A few minutes later Thomas, coughing modestly, embarked upon his speech.

'Well, Papa,' said Thomas, 'I expect you know what I'm going to say, because, after all, this is your Birthday dinner, and we all know it's a great occasion and how splendid it is for us to be here again as usual in spite of everything. Except Claude, of course, which is a pity, because he would think of a lot of new things to say, and I can't.' At this point a slight breeze of discomfort seemed to stir among the Ancreds. 'So I shall only say,' Thomas battled on, 'how proud we are to be gathered here, remembering your past achievements and wishing you many more Birthday dinners in the time that is to come. Yes,' said Thomas, after a thoughtful pause, 'that's all, I think. Oh, I almost forgot! We all, of course, hope that you will be very happy in your married life. I shall now ask everybody to drink Papa's health, please.'

The guests, evidently accustomed to a very much longer speech and taken unawares by the rapidity of Thomas's peroration, hurriedly got to their feet.

'Papa,' said Thomas.

'Papa,' echoed Jenetta, Millamant, Pauline and Desdemona.

'Grandpapa,' murmured Fenella, Cedric and Paul.

'Sir Henry,' said the Rector loudly, followed by Mr Rattisbon, the Squire and Troy.

'Noddy!' said Miss Orrincourt, shrilly. 'Cheers. Oodles of juice in your tank.'

Sir Henry received all this in the traditional manner. He fingered his glass, stared deeply at his plate, glanced up at Thomas, and, towards the end, raised his hand deprecatingly and let it fall. There was evidence of intense but restrained feeling. When they had all settled down he rose to reply. Troy had settled herself for resounding periods and a great display of rhetoric. She was not prepared, in view of the current family atmosphere, for touching simplicity and poignant emotion. These, however, were the characteristics of Sir Henry's speech. It was also intensely manly. He had, he said, taken a good many calls in the course of his life as a busker, and made a good many little speeches of gratitude to a good many audiences. But moving as some of these occasions had been, there was no audience as near and dear to an old fellow as his own kith and kin and his few tried and proven friends. He and his dear old Tommy were alike in this: they had few words in which to express their dearest thoughts. Perhaps they were none the worse for it. (Pauline, Desdemona and the Rector made sounds of fervent acquiescence.) Sir Henry paused and glanced first at Paul and then at Fenella. He had intended, he said, to keep for this occasion the announcement of the happy change he now contemplated. But domestic events had, should he say, a little forced his hand, and they were now all aware of his good fortune. (Apparently the Squire and Rector were not aware of it, as they looked exceedingly startled.) There was however, one little ceremony to be observed.

He took a small morocco box from his pocket, opened it, extracted a dazzling ring, and, raising Miss Orrincourt, placed it on her engagement finger and kissed the finger. Miss Orrincourt responded by casting one practised glance at the ring and embracing him with the liveliest enthusiasm. His hearers broke into agitated applause, under cover of which Cedric muttered: 'That's the Ranee's Solitaire re-set. I swear it is. Stay me with flagons, playmates.'

Sir Henry, with some firmness, reseated his fiancée and resumed his speech. It was, he said, a tradition in his family that the head of it should be twice married. The Sieur d'Ancred—he rambled on genealogically for some time. Troy felt embarrassment give place to boredom. Her attention was caught, however, by a new development. It had also been the custom, Sir Henry was saying, on these occasions, for the fortunate Ancred to reveal to his family the manner in which he had set his house in order. (Mr Rattisbon raised his eyebrows very high and made a little quavering noise in his throat.) Such frankness was perhaps out of fashion nowadays, but it had an appropriate Shakespearian precedent. King Lear—But glancing at his agonized daughters Sir Henry did not pursue the analogy. He said that he proposed to uphold this traditional frankness. 'I have today,' he said, 'executed—my old friend Rattisbon will correct me if this is not the term'—('M-m-mah!' said Mr Rattisbon confusedly)—'thank you—executed My Will. It is a simple little document, conceived in the spirit that actuated my ancestor, the Sieur d'Ancred when'—A fretful sigh eddied round the table. This time, however, Sir Henry's excursion into antiquity was comparatively brief. Clearing his throat, and speaking on a note so solemn that it had an almost ecclesiastical timbre, he fired point-blank and gave them a résumé of his Will.

Troy's major concern was to avoid the eyes of everybody else seated at that table. To this end she stared zealously at a detail of the epergne immediately in front of her. For the rest of her life, any mention of Sir Henry Ancred's last Will and Testament will immediately call up for her the image of a fat silver cupid who, in a pose at once energetic and insouciant, lunged out from a central globe, to which he was affixed only by his great toe, and, curving his right arm, supported on the extreme tip of his first finger a cornucopia three times his own size, dripping with orchids.

Sir Henry was speaking of legacies. Five thousand pounds to his devoted daughter-in-law, Millamant, five thousand pounds to his ewe lamb, Desdemona. To his doctor and his servants, to the hunt club, to the Church there were grand seigneurial legacies. Her attention wandered, and was again arrested by a comparison he seemed to be making between himself and some pentateuchal patriarch. 'Into three parts. The residue divided into three parts.' This, then, was the climax. To his bride-to-be, to Thomas, and to Cedric, he would leave, severally, a life interest in a third of the residue of his estate. The capital of this fund to be held in trust and ultimately devoted to the preservation and endowment of Ancreton as a historical museum of drama to be known as The Henry Ancred Memorial.

'Tra-hippit!' Cedric murmured at her elbow. 'Honestly, I exult. It might have been so much worse.'

Sir Henry was now making a brief summary of the rest of the field. His son, Claude, he thanked God, turning slightly towards Jenetta, had inherited a sufficient portion from his maternal grandmother, and was therefore able through this and through his own talents to make provision for his wife and (he momentarily eyed Fenella) daughter. His daughter Pauline (Troy heard her make an incoherent noise) had been suitably endowed at the time of her marriage and generously provided for by her late husband. She had her own ideas in the bringing up of her children and was able to carry them out. 'Which,' Cedric muttered with relish, 'is a particularly dirty crack at Paul and Panty, don't you feel?'

'Ssh!' said Desdemona on the other side of him.

Sir Henry drifted into a somewhat vague and ambiguous diatribe on the virtues of family unity and the impossibility, however great the temptation, of ever entirely forgetting them. For the last time her attention wandered, and was jerked sharply back by the sound of her own name: 'Mrs Agatha Troy Alleyn…her dramatic and, if I as the subject may so call it, magnificent canvas, which you are presently to see—'

Troy, greatly startled, learned that the portrait was to be left to the Nation.

❀ ❀ ❀

'It's not the money, Milly. It's not the money, Dessy,' wailed Pauline in the drawing-room. 'I don't mind about the money, Jen. It's the cruel, cruel wound to my love. That's what hurts me, girls. That's what hurts.'

'If I were you,' said Millamant with her laugh, 'I think I should feel a bit hipped about the money, too.'

Miss Orrincourt, according to her custom, had gone away to do her face. The ladies were divided into two parties—the haves and the have-nots. Dessy, a not altogether delighted legatee, had a foot in each camp. 'It's damn mean,' she said; 'but after the things I've said about the Orrincourt, I suppose I'm lucky to get anything. What do you think of her, Jen?'

'I suppose,' said Jenetta Ancred thoughtfully, 'she *is* real, isn't she? I mean, I catch myself wondering, quite seriously, if she could be somebody who has dressed up and is putting on the language and everything as a colossal practical joke. I didn't think people ever were so shatteringly true to type. But she's much too lovely, of course, to be a leg-pull.'

'Lovely!' cried Desdemona. 'Jen! Straight out of the third row of the chorus and appallingly common at that.'

'I dare say, but they *are* generally rather lovely in the chorus nowadays, aren't they, Fenella?'

Fenella had withdrawn entirely from the discussion. Now, when they all turned to her, she faced them rigidly, two bright red spots burning over her cheek-bones.

'I want to say,' she began in a loud, shaky voice, 'that I'm very sorry, Aunt Pauline and Mummy, that because of Paul and me you've been treated so disgracefully. We don't mind for ourselves. We'd neither of us, after the things he's said, touch a penny of his money. But we are sorry about you and Panty.'

'Well, darling,' said her mother, putting an arm through hers, 'That's very handsome of you and Paul, but don't let's have any more speeches, shall we?'

'Yes, but Mummy—'

'Your two families are very anxious for both of you to be happy. It's like that, isn't it, Pauline?'

'Well, Jenetta, that, of course, goes without saying, but—'

'There you are, Fen,' said Jenetta. 'It goes, and without saying, which is such a blessing.'

Pauline, looking extremely vexed, retired into a corner with Desdemona.

Jenetta offered Troy a cigarette. 'I suppose,' she muttered in a friendly manner, 'that was not a very good remark for me to make, but, to tell you the truth, I take a pretty gloomy view of all these naked wounds. Mr Rattisbon tells me your husband's coming back. What fun for you.'

'Yes,' said Troy, 'it's all of that.'

'Does everything else seem vague and two-dimensional? It would to me.'

'It does with me, too. I find it very muddling.'

'Of course the Ancreds are on the two-dimensional side anyway, if it comes to that. Especially my father-in-law. Did it make painting him easier or more difficult?'

Before Troy could answer this entertaining question, Cedric, flushed and smirking, opened the door, and stood against it in a romantic attitude waving his handkerchief.

'Darlings,' he said, '*Allez-houp!* The great moment. I am to bid you to the little theatre. Dearest Mrs Alleyn, you and the Old Person should be jointly feted. A cloud of little doves with gilded wings should be lowered by an ingenious device from the flies, and, with pretty gestures, crown you with laurels. Uncle Thomas could have arranged it. I should so adore to see Panty as an aerial coryphée. Will you all come?'

They found the men assembled in the little theatre. It was brilliantly lit, and had an air of hopefully waiting for a much larger audience. Soft music rumbled synthetically behind the front curtain, which (an inevitable detail) was emblazoned with the arms of Ancred. Troy found herself suddenly projected into a star role. Sir Henry led her up the aisle to a seat beside himself. The rest of the party settled behind them. Cedric, with a kind of consequential flutter, hurried backstage.

Sir Henry was smoking a cigar. When he inclined gallantly towards Troy she perceived that he had taken brandy. This circumstance was accompanied by a formidable internal rumbling.

'I shall,' he murmured gustily, 'just say a few words.'

They were actually few, but as usual they were intensely embarrassing. Her reluctance to undertake the portrait was playfully outlined. His own pleasure in the sittings was remorselessly sketched.

Some rather naïve quotations on art from *Timon of Athens* were introduced, and then: 'But I must not tantalize my audience any longer,' said Sir Henry richly. 'Curtain, my boy. Curtain!'

The house lights went down: the front drop slid upwards. Simultaneously four powerful floodlamps poured down their beams from the flies. The scarlet tabs were drawn apart, and there, in a blaze of highly unsuitable light, the portrait was revealed.

Above the sombre head and flying against a clear patch of night sky, somebody had painted an emerald green cow with vermilion wings. It was in the act of secreting an object that might or might not have been a black bomb.

CHAPTER EIGHT

Big Exit

THIS TIME TROY FELT only a momentary sensation of panic. That particular area of background was hard-dry, and almost at once she remembered this circumstance. She did, however, feel overwhelmingly irritated. Above the automatic burst of applause that greeted the unveiling and only petered out when the detail of the flying cow was observed, she heard her own voice saying loudly: 'No, really, this is too much.'

At the same moment Cedric, who had evidently operated the curtains, stuck his head round the proscenium, stared blindly into the front of the house, turned, saw the portrait, clapped his hand over his mouth and ejaculated: 'Oh, God! Oh, Dynamite!'

'*Darling!*' said his mother from the back row 'Ceddie, *dear*! What's the matter?'

Sir Henry, on Troy's left, breathed stertorously, and contrived to let out a sort of hoarse roaring noise.

'It's all right,' said Troy. 'Please don't say anything. Wait.'

She strode furiously down the aisle and up the steps. Sacrificing her best evening handkerchief, she reduced the cow to a green smear. 'I think there's a bottle of turpentine somewhere,' she said loudly. 'Please give it to me.'

Paul ran up with it, offering his own handkerchief. Cedric flew out with a handful of rag. The blemish was removed. Meantime the auditorium rang with Miss Orrincourt's hysterical laughter and buzzed with the sound of bewildered Ancreds. Troy threw the handkerchief and rag into the wings, and, with hot cheeks, returned to her seat. 'I wouldn't have been so cross,' she thought grimly, 'if the damn thing hadn't looked so funny.'

'I *demand*,' Sir Henry was shouting, 'I *demand* to know the author of this outrage.'

He was answered by a minor uproar topped by Pauline: 'It was *not* Panty. I tell you, Millamant, once and for all, that Panty is in bed, and has been there since five o'clock. Papa, I protest. It was *not* Panty.'

'Nuts!' said Miss Orrincourt. 'She's been painting green cows for days. I've seen them. Come off it, dear.'

'Papa, I give you my solemn word—'

'Mother, wait a minute—'

'I shall not wait a second. Papa, I have reason to believe—'

'Look here, *do* wait,' Troy shouted, and at once they were silent. 'It's gone,' she said. 'No harm's been done. But there's one thing I must tell you. Just before dinner I came in here. I was worrying about the red curtains. I thought they might touch the canvas where it's still wet. It was all right then. If Panty's been in bed and is known to have been there since ten to nine, she didn't do it.'

Pauline instantly began to babble. 'Thank you, thank you, Mrs Alleyn. You hear that, Papa. Send for Miss Able. I insist that Miss Able be sent for. My child shall be vindicated.'

'I'll go and ask Caroline,' said Thomas unexpectedly. 'One doesn't send for Caroline, you know. I'll go and ask.'

He went out. The Ancreds were silent. Suddenly Millamant remarked: 'I thought perhaps it was just the modern style. What do they call it? Surrealism?'

'Milly!' screamed her son.

Jenetta Ancred said: 'What particular symbolism, Milly, did you read into the introduction of a flying cow behaving like a rude seagull over Papa's head?'

'You never know,' Millamant said, 'in these days,' and laughed uncertainly.

'Papa,' said Desdemona, who had been bending over him, 'is dreadfully upset. Papa, dearest, may I suggest—'

'I'm going to bed,' said Sir Henry. 'I am indeed upset. I am unwell. I am going to bed.'

They all rose. He checked them with a gesture. 'I am going alone,' he said, 'to bed.'

Cedric ran to the door. Sir Henry, without a backward glance, walked down the aisle, a shadowy figure looking larger than life against the glowing stage, and passing magnificently from the theatre.

The Ancreds at once began to chatter. Troy felt that she couldn't endure the inevitable revival of Panty's former misdemeanours, Pauline's indignant denials, Cedric's giggles, Millamant's stolid recital of the obvious. She was profoundly relieved when Thomas, slightly ruffled, returned with Caroline Able.

'I've asked Caroline to come,' he said, 'because I thought you mightn't exactly believe me. Panty's been in the sick-bay with all the other ringworms. Dr Withers wanted them to be kept under observation because of the medicine he's given them, so Caroline has been sitting there reading since half-past seven. So Panty, you see, didn't do it.'

'Certainly she didn't do it,' said Miss Able brightly. 'How could she? It's quite impossible.'

'So you see,' Thomas added mildly.

❀ ❀ ❀

Troy stayed behind in the little theatre with Paul and Fenella. Paul switched on the working lights, and together they examined Troy's painting gear, which had been stacked away behind the wings.

The paint-box had been opened. A dollop of Emerald Oxide of Chromium and one of Ivory Black had been squeezed out on the protective under-lid that separated the paints from a compartment designed to hold sketching-boards. A large brush had been used, and had been dipped first in the green and then in the black.

'You know,' said Paul, 'this brush ought to have finger-prints on it.' He looked rather shyly at Troy. 'Oughtn't it?' he added.

'Well, I suppose Roderick would say so,' she agreed.

'I mean, if it has and if we could get everybody's to compare, that would be pretty conclusive, wouldn't it? What's more, it'd be damned interesting.'

'Yes, but I've a notion fingerprints are not as easy as all that.'

'I know. The hand would move about and so on. But look! There is some green paint smeared up the handle. I've read about it. Suppose we asked them to let us take their prints. They couldn't very well refuse.'

'Oh, Paul, let's!' cried Fenella.

'What do you think, Mrs Alleyn?'

'My dear chap, you mustn't imagine I know anything about it. But I agree it would be interesting. I do know more or less how they take official prints.'

'I've read it up quite a bit,' said Paul. 'I say. Suppose we did get them to do it, and suppose we kept the brush and the box intact —well—well, would—do you think—?'

'I'd show them to him like a shot,' said Troy.

'I say, that's perfectly splendid,' said Paul. 'Look here, I'll damn well put it to them in the morning. It ought to be cleared up. It's all bloody rum, the whole show, isn't it? What d'you say, Mrs Alleyn?'

'I'm on,' said Troy.

'Glory!' said Fenella. 'So'm I. Let's.'

'OK,' said Paul, gingerly wrapping the brush in rag. 'We'll lock up the brush and box.'

'I'll take them up with me.'

'Will you? That's grand.'

They locked the portrait in the property-room, and said goodnight conspiratorially. Troy felt she could not face another session with the Ancreds, and sending her excuses, went upstairs to her room.

She could not sleep. Outside, in the night, rain drove solidly against the wall of her tower. The wind seemed to have got into the chimney and be trying uneasily to find its way out again. A bucket had replaced the basin on the landing, and a maddening and irregular progression of taps compelled her attention and played like castanets on her nerves. Only one more night here, she thought, and then the comfort of her familiar things in the London flat and the sharing of them with her husband. Illogically she felt a kind of regret for the tower-room, and in this mood fell to revising in their order the eccentricities of her days and nights at Ancreton. The paint on the banister. The spectacles on the portrait. The legend in grease-paint on Sir Henry's looking-glass. The incident of the inflated bladder. The flying cow.

If Panty was not the authoress of these inane facetiae, who was? If one person only was responsible for them all, then Panty was exonerated. But might not Panty have instituted them with the smearing of paint on the banister and somebody else have carried them on? Undoubtedly Panty's legend and past record included many such antics. Troy wished that she knew something of modern views on child psychology. Was such behaviour characteristic of a child who wished to become a dominant figure and who felt herself to be obstructed and repressed? But Troy was positive that

Panty had spoken the truth when she denied having any hand in the tricks with paint. And unless Miss Able had told a lie, Panty, quite definitely, had not been the authoress of the flying cow, though she undoubtedly had a predilection for cows and bombs. Troy turned uneasily in her bed, and fancied that beyond the sound of wind and rain she heard the voice of the Great Clock. Was there any significance in the fact that in each instance the additions to her canvas had been made on a dry area and so had done no harm? Which of the adults in the house would realize this? Cedric. Cedric painted, though probably in water-colours. She fancied his aesthetic fervour was, in its antic way, authentic. He would, she thought, instinctively recoil from this particular kind of vandalism. But suppose he knew that no harm would be done? And where was a motive for Cedric? He appeared to have a kind of liking for her; why should he disfigure her work? Bleakly Troy surveyed the rest of the field, and one by one dismissed them until she came to Miss Orrincourt.

The robust vulgarity of these goings-on was not out of character if Miss Orrincourt was considered. Was it, Troy wondered with an uneasy grin, remotely possible that Miss Orrincourt resented the somewhat florid attentions Sir Henry had lavished upon his guest? Could she have imagined that the sittings had been made occasions for even more marked advances, more ardent pattings of the hand, closer pilotings by the elbow? 'Crikey,' Troy muttered, writhing uncomfortably, '*what* an idea to get in the middle of the night!' No, it was too far-fetched. Perhaps one of the elderly maids had lost her wits and taken to this nonsense. 'Or Barker,' thought the now sleepy Troy. In the drumming of rain and wind about her room she began to hear fantastical things. Presently she dreamed of flying bombs that came out of the night, converging on her tower. When they were almost upon her they changed into green cows, that winked broadly, and with a Cedric-like flirt dropped soft bombs, at the same time saying very distinctly: 'Plop, plop, *dearest* Mrs Alleyn.'

'*Mrs Alleyn. Dearest Mrs Alleyn, do please wake up.*'

Troy opened her eyes. Fenella, fully dressed, stood at her bedside. In the thin light of dawn her face looked cold and very white. Her hands opened and shut aimlessly. The corners of her mouth turned down like those of a child about to cry. 'What now, for pity's sake?' cried Troy.

'I thought I'd better come and tell you. Nobody else would. They're all frantic. Paul can't leave his mother, and Mummy's trying to stop Aunt Dessy having hysterics. I feel so ghastly, I had to talk to someone.'

'But why? What is it? What's happened?'

'Grandfather. When Barker went in with his tea. He found him. Lying there. Dead.'

There is no more wretched lot than that of the comparative stranger in a house of grief. The sense of loneliness, the feeling that one constantly trespasses on other people's sorrow, that they would thankfully be rid of one; all these circumstances reduce the unwilling intruder to a condition of perpetual apology that must remain unexpressed. If there is nothing useful to be done this misery is the more acute, and Troy was not altogether sorry that Fenella seemed to find some comfort in staying with her. She hurriedly made a fire on top of last night's embers, set Fenella, who shivered like a puppy, to blow it up while she herself bathed and dressed, and, when at last the child broke down, listened to a confused recital which harked back continually to the break between herself and her grandfather. 'It's so awful that Paul and I should have made him miserable. We'll never be able to forgive ourselves—never,' Fenella sobbed.

'Now, look here,' said Troy, 'that just doesn't make sense. You and Paul did what you have every right to do.'

'But we did it brutally. You can't say we didn't. We grieved him frightfully. He said so.'

Sir Henry had said so a great many times and with extreme emphasis. It was impossible to suggest that anger rather than grief had moved him. Troy went off on another tack. 'He seemed to have got over it,' she said.

'Last night!' Fenella wailed. 'When I think of what we said about him last night. In the drawing-room after you'd gone up. Everybody except Mummy and Paul. Aunt Milly said he'd probably have an attack, and I said I didn't care if it was fatal. Actually! And he *did* feel it. He cut Aunt Pauline and Mummy and me and Paul out of his Will because of our engagement and the way we announced it. So he did feel it deeply.'

'The Will,' thought Troy. 'Good heavens, yes. The Will!' She said: 'He was an old man, Fenella. I don't think, do you, that the future was exactly propitious? Isn't it perhaps not so very bad that he should go now when everything seemed to him to be perfectly arranged. He'd had his splendid party.'

'And look how it ended.'

'Oh, dear!' said Troy. 'That. Well, yes.'

'And it was probably the party that killed him,' Fenella continued. 'That hot crayfish. It's what everybody thinks. Dr Withers had warned him. And nobody was there. He just went up to his room and died.'

'Has Dr Withers—?'

'Yes. He's been. Barker got Aunt Milly and she rang up. He says it was a severe attack of gastro-enteritis. He says it— it happened—it must have been—soon after he went up to bed. It's so awful when you think of all the frightful things we were saying about him down there in the drawing-room. All of us except Cedric, and he was simply gloating over us. Little beast, he's still gloating, if it comes to that.'

The gong rumbled distantly. 'You go down to breakfast,' said Fenella. 'I can't face it.'

'That won't do at all. You can at least choke down some coffee.'

Fenella took Troy's arm in a nervous grip. 'I think I like you so much,' she said, 'because you're so unlike all of us. All right, I'll come.'

The Ancreds in sorrow were a formidable assembly. Pauline, Desdemona and Millamant, who were already in the dining-room, had all found black dresses to wear, and Troy was suddenly conscious that she had without thinking pulled on a scarlet sweater. She uttered those phrases of sympathy that are always inadequate. Desdemona silently gripped her hand and turned aside. Pauline dumbfounded her by bursting into tears and giving her an impulsive kiss. And it was strange to find an unsmiling and pallid Millamant. Thomas came in, looking bewildered. 'Good morning,' he said to Troy. 'Isn't it awful? I really can't realize it a bit, you know. Everybody seems to realize it. They're all crying and everything, but I don't. Poor Papa.' He looked at his sisters. 'You're not eating anything,' he said. 'What can I get you, Pauline?'

Pauline said: 'Oh, Thomas!' and made an eloquent gesture. 'I suppose,' Thomas continued, 'that later on I shan't want to eat anything, but at the moment I am hungry.'

He sat down beside Troy. 'It's lucky you finished the portrait, isn't it?' he said. 'Poor Papa!'

'Tommy!' breathed his sister.

'Well, but it is,' he insisted gently. 'Papa would have been pleased too.'

Paul came in, and, a moment later, Jenetta Ancred, wearing tweeds. It was a relief to Troy that, like Thomas, neither of them spoke in special voices.

Presently Millamant began to speak of the manner in which Barker had discovered Sir Henry. At eight o'clock, it appeared, he had gone in as usual with Sir Henry's cup of milk and water. As he approached the room he heard the cat Carabbas wailing inside, and when he opened the door it darted out and fled down the passage. Barker supposed that Sir Henry had forgotten to let his cat out, and wondered that Carabbas had not waked him.

He entered the room. It was still very dark. Barker was shortsighted, but he could make out the figure lying across the bed.

He turned on the lights, and after one horrified glance, rushed down the corridor and beat on the door of Millamant's room. When she and Pauline answered together, he kept his head, remained outside, and, in an agitated whisper, asked Millamant if he might speak to her. She put on her dressing-gown and went out into the cold passage.

'And I knew,' Pauline interjected at this point. 'Something told me. I knew at once that something had happened.'

'Naturally,' said Millamant. 'Barker doesn't go on like that every morning.'

'I knew it was The Great Visitor,' Pauline insisted firmly. 'I knew.'

Millamant had gone with Barker to the room. She sent Barker to rouse Thomas and herself telephoned Dr Withers. He was out, but finally arrived in about an hour. It had been, he said, a severe attack of gastro-enteritis, probably brought on by his indiscretions at dinner. Sir Henry's heart had been unable to survive the attack and he had collapsed and died.

'What I can't understand,' said Pauline, 'is why he didn't ring. He always rang if he felt ill in the night. There was a special bell in the corridor, Dessy. The cord hung beside his bed.'

'He tried,' said Thomas. 'He must have grasped at it across the bed, we think, and fallen. It had come away from the cord. And I don't think, after all, I want very much to eat.'

Troy spent most of that last day between her room and the little theatre, lingering over her packing, which in any case was considerable. Carabbas, the cat, elected to spend the day in her room. Remembering where he had spent the night, she felt a little shudder at the touch of his fur. But they had become friendly, and after a time she was glad of his company. At first he watched her with some interest, occasionally sitting on such garments as she had laid out on the bed and floor. When she removed him he purred briefly, and at last, with a faint mew, touched her hand with his nose. It was hot. She noticed that his fur was staring. Was he, she wondered, actually distressed by the loss of his master? He grew restless and she opened the door. After a fixed look at her he went out, his tail drooping. She thought she heard him cry again on the stairs. She returned uneasily to her packing, broke off from time to time to wander restlessly about the room or stare out of the tower window at the rain-laced landscape. She came across a sketch-book and found herself absently making drawings of the Ancreds. Half an hour went past, and there they all were, like antics on the page, for her to show her husband. Guiltily she completed her packing.

Thomas had undertaken to send by rail such heavy baggage as the Yard car could not accommodate.

She was oppressed by the sensation of unreality. She felt more strongly than ever that she was held in suspension between two phases of experience. She was out of touch, not only with her surroundings, but with herself. While her hands folded and bestowed garment after garment, her thoughts ranged aimlessly between the events of the past twenty-four hours and those that were to come. 'It is I,' she thought in dismay, 'who will resemble the traveller who can speak of nothing but his fellow-passengers and the little events of his voyage, and it is Rory who will listen unhappily to anecdotes of these Ancreds whom he is never likely to meet.'

Lunch seemed to be an uncanny extension of breakfast. There, again, were the Ancreds, still using their special voices, still expressing so eloquently that sorrow whose authenticity Troy was not quite willing to discredit. She was half-aware of their conversation, catching only desultory pieces of information: Mr Rattisbon had been transferred to the rectory. Thomas had been dictating obituary notices over the telephone. The funeral would be held on Tuesday. The voices murmured on. Momentarily she was consulted, drawn in. A weekly paper had got wind of the portrait ('Nigel Bathgate,' thought Troy), and would like to send down a photographer. She made suitable rejoinders and suggestions. Cedric, whose manner was fretfully subdued, brightened a little over this subject, and then, unaccountably, reverted to a kind of nervous acquiescence. The conversation drifted towards Miss Orrincourt, who had expressed her inability to make a public appearance and was having her meals in her own rooms. 'I saw her breakfast-tray,' said Millamant with a ghost of her usual laugh. 'Her appetite doesn't seem to have suffered.'

'T'uh!' said the Ancreds softly.

'Are we to be told,' Pauline asked, 'how long she proposes to—?'

'I should imagine,' said Desdemona, 'no longer than it takes for the Will to become effective.'

'Well, but I mean to say,' Cedric began, and they all turned their heads towards him. 'If it's not *too* inappropriate and premature, one wonders rather, or doesn't one, if darling Sonia is in *quite* the same position *unmarried* as she would have been as the Old—as dearest Grandpapa's widow? Or not?'

An attentive stillness fell upon the table. It was broken by Thomas: 'Yes—well, of course,' he said, looking blandly about him, 'won't that depend on how the Will is made out. Whether her share is left to "Sonia Orrincourt," you know, or to "my wife, Sonia," and all that.'

Pauline and Desdemona stared for a moment at Thomas. Cedric smoothed his hair with two unsteady fingers. Fenella and Paul looked stolidly at their plates. Millamant, with a muffled attempt at easiness, said: 'There's no need to jump *that* fence, surely, till we meet it.' Pauline and Desdemona exchanged glances. Millamant had used the sacred 'we'.

'I think it's pretty ghastly,' said Fenella abruptly, 'to begin talking about Grandfather's Will when he's up there—lying there—' She broke off, biting her lip. Troy saw Paul reach for her hand. Jenetta Ancred, who had been silent throughout luncheon, gave her daughter a smile, half-deprecating, half-anxious. 'How she dislikes it,' Troy thought, 'when Fenella behaves like an Ancred.'

'Darling Fen,' Cedric murmured, 'you, of course, can afford to be grand and virtuous over the Will. I mean, you are so definitely *out* of that party, aren't you?'

'That's a pretty offensive remark, Cedric,' said Paul.

'Has everyone finished?' asked Pauline in a hurry. 'If so, Mrs Alleyn, shall we—?'

Troy excused herself from the post-prandial gathering in the drawing-room.

As she entered the hall a car drew up outside. Barker, who seemed to have been expecting it, was already in the outer porch. He admitted three pale men, dressed in London clothes of a particularly black character. They wore wide black ties. Two of them carried black cases. The third, glancing at Troy, spoke in a muted and inaudible voice.

'This way, if you please,' said Barker, ushering them into a small waiting-room across the hall. 'I will inform Sir Cedric.'

After the newcomers had been shut away and Barker had gone on his errand, Troy stood digesting the official recognition of Cedric's ascendancy. Her glance strayed to a table where, as she had observed, the senior of the three men, with a practised modesty, suggestive almost of sleight of hand, had dropped or slid a card. He had, indeed, given it a little push with his forefinger, so that it lay, partly concealed, under a book which Troy herself had brought from the library to solace her afternoon. The card was engraved in a type slightly heavier and more black than that of a normal visiting card:

MORTIMER, SON & LOAME
Undertakers—

Troy lifted her book, exposing the hidden corner of the card, '—and Embalmers,' she read.

CHAPTER NINE

Alleyn

BY AN ALTERATION IN THE rhythm of the ship's progress, suggestive almost of a physiological change, her passengers became aware of the end of their long voyage. Her pulse died. It was replaced by sounds of blind waves washing along her sides; of gulls, of voices, of chains, and, beyond these, of movement along the wharves and in the city beyond them.

At early dawn the Port of London looked as wan and expectant as an invalid already preparing for a return to vigour. Thin mist still hung about sheds and warehouses. Muffled lights were strung like a dim necklace along the waterfront. Frost glinted on roofs and bollards and ropes. Alleyn had gripped the rail for so long that its cold had bitten through his gloves into the palms of his hands. Groups of people stood about the wharves, outward signs of a life from which the passengers were, for a rapidly diminishing period, still remote. These groups, befogged by their own breath, were composed for the main part of men.

There were three women, and one wore a scarlet cap. Inspector Fox had come out in the pilot's boat. Alleyn had not hoped for this, and had been touched and delighted to meet him; but now it was impossible to talk to Fox.

'Mrs Alleyn,' said Fox, behind him, 'is wearing a red cap. If you'll excuse me, Mr Alleyn, I ought to have a word with a chap—The car's just behind the Customs shed. I'll meet you there.'

When Alleyn turned to thank him, he was already walking away, squarely overcoated, tidy, looking just like his job.

Now only a dark channel, a ditch, a gutter lay between the ship and the wharf. Bells rang sharply. Men moved forward to the bollards and stared up at the ship. One raised his hand and shouted a greeting in a clear voice. Ropes were flung out, and a moment later the final stoppage was felt dully throughout the ship.

That was Troy down there. She walked forward. Her hands were jammed down in the pockets of her overcoat. She looked along the deck, scowling a little, her gaze moving towards him. In these last seconds, while he waited for her to discover him, Alleyn knew that, like himself, she was nervous. He lifted his hand. They looked at each other, and a smile of extraordinary intimacy broke across her face.

'Three years seven months and twenty-four days,' said Alleyn that afternoon. 'It's a hell of a time to be without your wife.' He looked at Troy sitting on the hearth-rug hugging her knees. 'Or rather,' he added, 'to be away from you, Troy. From you, who, so astonishingly happens to be my wife. I've been getting myself into such a hullabaloo about it.'

'Wondering,' Troy asked, 'if we'd run short of conversation and feel shy?'

'You too, then?'

'It does happen, they say. It might easily happen.'

'I even considered the advisability of quoting Othello on his arrival at Cyprus. How would you have reacted, my darling, if I had laid hold upon you under letter A in the Customs shed and begun: "Oh, my fair warrior!"'

'I should probably have made a snappy come-back with something from *Macbeth*.'

'Why *Macbeth*?'

'To explain that would be to use up all the conversation I'd saved up on my own account. Rory—'

'My love?'

'I've been having a very queer time with Macbeth.'

She was looking doubtfully at him from under her ruffled forelock. 'You may not care to hear about it,' she mumbled. 'It's a long story.'

'It won't be too long,' Alleyn said, 'if it's you who tells it.'

Watching her, he thought: 'That's made her shy again. We are to re-learn each other.' Alleyn's habit of mind was accurate and exhaustive. He had recognized and examined in himself thoughts that another man might have preferred to ignore. During the long voyage home, he had many times asked himself if, when they met again, he and Troy might not find that the years had dropped between them a transparent barrier through which they would stare, without love, at each other. The possibility had occurred to him, strangely enough, at moments when he most desired and missed her. When she had moved forward on the quay, without at first seeing him, his physical reaction had been so sharp that it had blotted out his thoughts. It was only when she gave him the look of intimacy, which so far had not been repeated, that he knew, without question, he was to love her again.

Now, when she was before him in the room whose very familiarity was a little strange, his delight was of a virgin kind that anticipates a trial of its temper. Were Troy's thoughts at this moment comparable with his own? Could he be as certain of her as he was of himself? She had entered into an entirely different mode of life during his absence. He knew nothing of her new associates beyond the rather sparse phrases she had allowed them in her letters. Now, evidently, he was to hear a little more.

'Come over here,' he said, 'and tell me.'

She moved into her old place, leaning against his chair, and he looked down at her with a more tranquil mind, yet with such intense pleasure that the beginning of her story escaped him. But he had been ruthlessly trained to listen to statements and the habit asserted itself. The saga of Ancreton was unfolded.

Troy's account was at first tentative, but his interest stimulated her. She began to enjoy herself, and presently hunted out her sketch-book with the drawings she had made in her tower-room. Alleyn chuckled over the small lively figures with their enormous heads. 'Like the old-fashioned Happy Families cards,' he said, and she agreed that there was something Victorian and fantastic about the originals. After the eccentricities of the Ancreds themselves, the practical jokes turned out to be a dominant theme in her story. Alleyn heard of this with growing concern. 'Here,' he interrupted, 'did this blasted kid ruin your thing in the end or didn't she?'

'No, no! But it wasn't the blasted kid at all. Listen.'

He did, with a chuckle for her deductive methods. 'She might conceivably, you know, write "grandfarther" at one moment and "grandfather" the next, but it's a point of course.'

'It was her manner more than anything. I'm quite positive she didn't do it. I know she's got a record for practical jokes—but wait till I get to the end. Don't fluster the witness.'

'Why not?' said Alleyn, stooping his head.

'To continue,' said Troy after a moment or two, and this time he let her go on to the end. It was an odd story. He wondered if she realized quite how odd it was.

'I don't know whether I've conveyed the general dottiness of that monstrous house,' she said. 'I mean, the queer little things that turned up. Like the book on embalming amongst the *objets d'art* and the missing rat bane.'

'Why do you put them together?'

'I dunno. I suppose because there's arsenic in both of them.'

'You are *not* by any chance, my angel, attempting to land me with a suspected poisoning case on my return to your arms?'

'Well,' said Troy after a pause, 'you would think that one up, wouldn't you?' She screwed round and looked at him. 'And he's been embalmed, you know. By the Messrs Mortimer and Loame. I met them in the hall with their black bags. The only catch in it is the impossibility of regarding any of the Ancreds in the light of a slow poisoner. But it would fit.'

'A little too neatly, I fancy.' With a trace of reluctance he added: 'What were some of the other queer little things that happened?'

'I'd like to know what Cedric and the Orrincourt were giggling about on the sofa, and whether the Orrincourt was coughing or laughing in the governess-cart. I'd even like to know what it was she bought in the chemist's shop. And I'd like to know more about Millamant. One never knew what Millamant was thinking, except that she doted perpetually on her ghastly Cedric. It would have been in her Cedric's interest, of course, to sicken Sir Henry of poor old Panty, who, by the way, has a complete alibi for the flying cow. Her alibi's a dangerous drug. For ringworm.'

'Has this odious child been taking thallium?'

'Do you know about thallium?'

'I've heard of it.'

'It establishes her alibi for the flying cow,' said Troy. 'I'd better explain.'

'Yes,' Alleyn agreed when she had finished, 'that lets her out for the flying cow.'

'She didn't do any of them,' said Troy firmly. 'I wish now that Paul and Fenella and I had gone on with our experiment.'

'What was that to be?'

'It involved your collaboration,' said Troy, looking at him out of the corners of her eyes.

'Like hell it did!'

'Yes. We wrapped up the paint-brush that had been used for the flying cow and we were going to ask all of them to let us take their finger-prints for you to compare with it. Would you have minded?'

'My darling heart, I'd compare them with the Grand Cham of Tartary's if it would give you any fun.'

'But we never got them. Death, as you and Mr Fox would say, intervened. Sir Henry's death. By the way, the person who painted my banister left finger-prints on the stone wall above it. Perhaps after a decent interval I could hint for an invitation to Ancreton and you could come down with your insufflator and black ink. But honestly, it *is* a queer story, don't you think?'

'Yes,' he agreed, rubbing his nose. 'It's queer enough. We heard about Ancred's death on the ship's wireless. Little did I imagine you were in at it.'

'I liked him,' said Troy after a pause. 'He was a terrific old exhibitionist, and he made one feel dreadfully shy at times, but I did like him. And he was grand to paint.'

'The portrait went well?'

'I think so.'

'I'd like to see it.'

'Well, so you shall one of these days. He said he was leaving it to the Nation. What does the Nation do under those circumstances? Hang it in a dark corner of the Tate, do you imagine? Some paper or another, I suspect Nigel Bathgate's, is going to photograph it. We might get a print.'

But Alleyn was not to wait long for the photograph. It appeared that evening in Nigel's paper over a notice of Sir Henry's funeral. He had been buried in the family vault at Ancreton with as much ceremony as the times allowed.

'He hoped,' said Troy, 'that the Nation would wish otherwise.'

'The Abbey?'

'I'm afraid so. Poor Sir Henry, I wish it had. Ah, well,' said Troy, dropping the newspaper, 'that's the end of the Ancreds as far as I'm concerned.'

'You never know,' Alleyn said, vaguely. Then, suddenly impatient of the Ancreds and of anything that prolonged beyond this moment the first tentative phase of their reunion, he stretched out his hands towards Troy.

This story is concerned with Alleyn and Troy's reunion only in so far as it affected his attitude towards her account of the Ancreds. If he had heard it at any other time it is possible that, however unwillingly, he might have dwelt longer on its peculiarities. As it was, he welcomed it as a kind of interlude between their first meeting and its consummation, and then dismissed it from his conscious thoughts.

They had three days together, broken only by a somewhat prolonged interview between Alleyn and his chief at the Special Branch. He was to resume, for the time being at least, his normal job at the Yard. On the Thursday morning when Troy returned to her job, he walked part of the way with her, watched her turn off, and with an odd feeling of anxiety, himself set out for the familiar room and the old associates.

It was pleasant, after all, to cross that barren back hall, smelling of linoleum and coal, to revisit an undistinguished office where the superintendent of CI, against a background of crossed swords, commemorative photographs and a horseshoe, greeted him with unmistakable satisfaction. It was oddly pleasant to sit again at his old desk in the chief inspectors' room and contemplate the formidable task of taking up the threads of routine.

He had looked forward to a preliminary gossip with Fox, but Fox had gone out on a job somewhere in the country and would not be back before the evening. In the meantime here was an old acquaintance of Alleyn's, one Squinty Donovan, who, having survived two courts-martial, six months' confinement in Broadmoor, and a near-miss from a flying bomb, had left unmistakable signs of his ingenuity upon a lock-up antique shop in Beachamp Place, Chelsea. Alleyn set in motion the elaborate police machinery by which Squinty might be hunted home to a receiver. He then turned again to his file.

There was nothing exciting; a series of routine jobs. This pleased him. There had been enough of excursions and alarums, the Lord knew, in his three years' hunting for the Special Branch. He had wanted his return to CI to be uneventful.

Presently Nigel Bathgate rang up. 'I say,' he said, 'has Troy seen about the Will?'

'Whose Will?'

'Old Ancred's. She's told you about the Ancreds, of course.'

'Of course.'

'It's in this morning's *Times*. Have a look at it. It'll rock them considerably.'

'What's he done?' Alleyn asked. But for some reason he was unwilling to hear more about the Ancreds.

He heard Nigel chuckling. 'Well, out with it,' he said. 'What's he done?'

'Handed them the works.'

'In what way?'

'Left the whole caboosh to the Orrincourt.'

Nigel's statement was an over-simplification of the facts, as Alleyn discovered when, still with that sense of reluctance, he looked up the Will. Sir Henry had cut Cedric down to the bare bones of the entail, and had left a legacy of one thousand pounds to Millamant, to each of his children and to Dr Withers. The residue he had willed to Sonia Orrincourt.

'But—what about the dinner speech and the other Will!' Troy cried when he showed her the evening paper. 'Was that just a complete have, do you suppose? If so, Mr Rattisbon must have known. Or—Rory,' she said, 'I believe it was the flying cow that did it! I believe he was so utterly fed up with his family he marched upstairs, sent for Mr Rattisbon and made a new Will there and then.'

'But didn't he think the *enfant terrible* had done the flying cow? Why take it out of the whole family?'

'Thomas or somebody may have gone up and told him about Panty's alibi. He wouldn't know who to suspect, and would end up by damning the whole crew.'

'Not Miss Orrincourt, however.'

'She'd see to that,' said Troy with conviction.

She was, he saw, immensely taken up with this news, and at intervals during the evening returned to the Ancreds and their fresh dilemma. 'What will Cedric do, can you imagine? Probably the entail is hopelessly below the cost of keeping up Katzenjammer Castle. That's what he called it, you know. Perhaps he'll give it to the Nation. Then they could hang my portrait in its alloted place, chequered all over with coloured lights and everybody would be satisfied. *How* the Orrincourt will gloat.'

Troy's voice faded on a note of uncertainty. Alleyn saw her hands move nervously together. She caught his eye and turned away. 'Let's not talk about the poor Ancreds,' she said.

'What are you munching over in the back of your mind?' he asked uneasily.

'It's nothing,' she said quickly. He waited, and after a moment she came to him. 'It's only that I'd like you to tell me: Suppose you'd heard from somebody else, or read, about the Ancreds and all the unaccountable odds and ends—what would you think? I mean—' Troy frowned and looked at her clasped hands. 'Doesn't it sound rather horribly like the beginning of a chapter in *Famous Trials*?'

'Are you really worried about this?' he said after a pause.

'Oddly enough,' said Troy, 'I am.'

Alleyn got up and stood with his back turned to her. When he spoke again his voice had changed.

'Well,' he said, 'we'd better tackle it, then.'

'What's the matter?' he heard Troy saying doubtfully. 'What's happened?'

'Something quite ridiculous and we'll get rid of it. A fetish I nurse. I've never fancied coming home and having a

nice cosy chat about the current homicide with my wife. I've
never talked about such cases when they did crop up.'

'I wouldn't have minded, Rory.'

'It's a kind of fastidiousness. No, that's praising it.
It's illogical and indefensible. If my job's not fit for you, it
shouldn't be my job.'

'You're being too fancy. I've got over my squeamishness.'

'I didn't want you to get over it,' he said. 'I tell you I'm a
fool about this.'

She said the phrase he had hoped to hear. 'Then do you
think there's something in it—about the Ancreds?'

'Blast the Ancreds! Here, this won't do. Come on, let's
tackle the thing and scotch it. You're thinking like this,
aren't you? There's a book about embalming in their ghastly
drawing-room. It stresses the use of arsenic. Old Ancred went
about bragging that he was going to have himself mummi-
fied. Any one might have read the book. Sonia Orrincourt was
seen doing so. Arsenic, used for rat poison, disappeared in the
house. Old Ancred died immediately after altering his Will in
the Orrincourt's favour. There wasn't an autopsy. If one were
made now, the presence of arsenic would be accounted for by
the embalming. That's the thing, isn't it?'

'Yes,' said Troy, 'that's it.'

'And you've been wondering whether the practical jokes
and all the rest of the fun and games can be fitted in?'

'It sounds less possible as you say it.'

'Good!' he said quickly turning to her. 'That's better.
Come on, then. You've wondered if the practical jokes were
organized by the Orrincourt to put the old man off his favourite grandchild?'

'Yes. Or by Cedric, with the same motive. You see, Panty
was hot favourite before the Raspberry and Flying Cow
Period set in.'

'Yes. So, in short, you're wondering if one of the Ancreds,
particularly Cedric, or Miss Orrincourt, murdered old Ancred,
having previously, in effect, hamstrung the favourite.'

'This is like talking about a nightmare. It leaves off being horrid and turns silly.'

'All the better,' he said vigorously. 'All right. Now, if the lost arsenic was the lethal weapon, the murder was planned long before the party. You understood Millamant to say it had been missing for some time?'

'Yes. Unless—'

'Unless Millamant herself is a murderess and was doing an elaborate cover-up.'

'Because I said one didn't know what Millamant thought about it, it doesn't follow that she thought about murder.'

'Of course it doesn't, bless your heart. Now, if any one of the Ancreds murdered Sir Henry, it was on the strength of the announcement made at the dinner-party and without any knowledge of the effective Will he made that night. If he made it that night.'

'Unless one of the legatees thought they'd been cheated and did it out of pure fury.'

'Or Fenella and Paul, who got nothing? Yes. There's that.'

'Fenella and Paul,' said Troy firmly, 'are not like that.'

'And if Desdemona or Thomas or Jenetta—'

'Jenetta and Thomas are out of the question—'

'—did it, the practical jokes don't fit in, because they weren't there for the earlier ones.'

'Which leaves the Orrincourt, Cedric, Millamant and Pauline.'

'I can see it's the Orrincourt and Cedric who are really bothering you.'

'More particularly,' said Troy unhappily, 'the Orrincourt.'

'Well, darling, what's she like? Has she got the brains to think it up? Would she work out the idea from reading the book on embalming that arsenic would be found in the body anyway?'

'I shouldn't have thought,' said Troy cheerfully, 'that she'd make head or tail of the book. It was printed in very dim italics with the long "s" like an "f". She's not at all the type to pore over literary curiosa unless she thought they were curious in the specialized sense.'

'Feeling better?' he asked.

'Yes, thank you. I'm thinking of other things for myself. Arsenic takes effect pretty quickly, doesn't it? And tastes beastly? He couldn't have had it at dinner, because, apart from being in a foul rage, he was still all right when he left the little theatre. And—if Sonia Orrincourt had put it in his Ovaltine, or whatever he has in his bedside Thermos, could he have sipped down enough to kill him without noticing the taste?'

'Unlikely,' Alleyn said. Another silence fell between them. Alleyn thought: 'I've never been able to make up my mind about telepathy. Think of something else. Is she listening to my thoughts?'

'Rory,' said Troy. 'It is all right, isn't it?'

The telephone rang and he was glad to answer it. Inspector Fox was speaking from the Yard.

'Where have you been, you old devil?' said Alleyn, and his voice held that cordiality with which we greet a rescuer.

'Good evening, Mr Alleyn,' said Fox. 'I was wondering if it would inconvenience you and Mrs Alleyn very much if—'

'Come along!' Alleyn interrupted. 'Of course it won't. Troy will be delighted; won't you, darling? It's Fox.'

'Of course I shall,' said Troy loudly. 'Tell him to come.'

'Very kind, I'm sure,' Fox was saying in his deliberate way. 'Perhaps I ought to explain though. It's Yard business. You might say very unusual circumstances, really. Quite a contretemps.'

'The accent's improving, Fox.'

'I don't get the practice. About this business, though. In a manner of speaking, sir, I fancy you'll want to consult Mrs Alleyn. She's with you, evidently.'

'What is it?' Troy asked quickly. 'I can hear him. What is it?'

'Well, Fox,' said Alleyn after a pause, 'what is it?'

'Concerning the late Sir Henry Ancred, sir. I'll explain when I see you. There's been an Anonymous Letter.'

❧ ❧ ❧

'Coincidence,' said Fox, putting on his spectacles and flattening out a sheet of paper on his knee, 'is one of the things you get accustomed to in our line of business, as I think you'll agree, sir. Look at the way one of our chaps asked for a lift in the Gutteridge case. Look at the Thompson-Bywaters case—'

'For the love of heaven!' Alleyn cried, 'let us admit coincidence without further parley. It's staring us in the face. It's a bloody quaint coincidence that my wife should have been staying in this wretched dump, and there's an end of it.'

He glanced at Fox's respectable, grave, and attentive face. 'I'm sorry,' he said. 'It's no good expecting me to be reasonable over this business. Troy's had one bad enough experience of the nastiest end of our job. She'll never altogether forget it, and—well, there you are. One doesn't welcome anything like a reminder.'

'I'm sure it's very upsetting, Mr Alleyn. If I could have—'

'I know, I know.' And looking at Fox, Alleyn felt a spasm of self-distaste.

'Fox,' he said suddenly, 'I'm up against a silly complexity in my own attitude to my job. I've tried to shut it off from my private life. I've adopted what I suppose the Russians would call an unrealistic approach: Troy in one compartment, the detection of crime in another. And now, by way of dotting me one on the wind, the fates have handed Troy this little affair on a platter. If there's anything in it she'll be a witness.'

'There may not be anything in it, Mr Alleyn.'

'True enough. That's precisely the remark I've been making to her for the last hour or so.'

Fox opened his eyes very wide. 'Oh, yes,' said Alleyn, 'she's already thought there was something off-colour about the festivities at Ancreton.'

'Is that so?' Fox said slowly. 'Is that the case?'

'It is indeed. She's left us alone to talk it over. I can give you the story when you want it and so can she. But I'd better have your end first. What's that paper you've got there?'

Fox handed it to him. 'It came in to us yesterday, went through the usual channels, and finally the Chief got on to it and sent for me this evening. You'd gone by then, sir, but he asked me to have a word with you about it. White envelope to match, addressed in block capitals "CID, Scotland Yard, London." Postmark, Victoria.'

Alleyn took the paper. It appeared to be a sheet from a block of faintly ruled notepaper. The lines were, unusually, a pale yellow, and a margin was ruled down the side. The message it contained was flatly explicit:

THE WRITER HAS REASON TO BELIEVE THAT SIR HENRY ANCRED'S DEATH WAS BROUGHT ABOUT BY THE PERSON WHO HAS RECEIVED THE MOST BENEFIT FROM IT.

'Water-mark, "Crescent Script". People write these things,' said Fox. 'You know yourself there may be nothing in it. But we've got to take the usual notice. Talk to the super at the local station, I suppose. And the doctor who attended the old gentleman. He may be able to put the matter beyond doubt. There's an end of it.'

'He will if he can,' said Alleyn grimly. 'You may depend upon that.'

'In the meantime, the AC suggested I should report to you and see about a chat with Mrs Alleyn. He remembered Mrs Alleyn had been at Ancreton before you came back.'

'*Report* to me? If anything comes of this, does he want me to take over?'

'Well, sir, I fancy he will. He mentioned, jokingly-like, that it'd be quite unusual if the investigating officer got his first statement on a case from his wife.'

'Facetious ass!' said Alleyn with improper emphasis.

Fox looked demurely down his nose.

'Oh, well,' said Alleyn, 'let's find Troy and we'll hag over the whole blasted set up. She's in the studio. Come on.'

Troy received Fox cheerfully. 'I know what it's all about, Mr Fox,' she said, shaking hands with him.

'I'm sure I'm very sorry—' Fox began.

'But you needn't be,' Troy said quickly, linking her arm through Alleyn's. 'Why on earth should you be? If I'm wanted, here I am. What happens?'

'We sit down,' Alleyn said, 'and I go over the whole story as you've told it to me. When I go wrong, you stop me, and when you think of anything extra, you put it in. That's all, so far. The whole thing may be a complete washout, darling. Anonymous letter writers have the same affection for the Yard that elderly naturalists have for *The Times*. Now then. Here, Fox, to the best of my ability, is the Ancred saga.'

He went methodically through Troy's account, correlating the events, tracing the several threads in and out of the texture of the narrative and gathering them together at the end.

'How's that?' he asked her when he had finished. He was surprised to find her staring at him as if he had brought off a feat of sleight of hand.

'Amazingly complete and tidy,' she said.

'Well, Fox? What's it amount to?'

Fox wiped his hand over his jaw. 'I've been asking myself, sir,' he said, 'whether you mightn't find quite a lot of circumstances behind quite a lot of sudden demises that might sound funny if you strung them together. What I mean to say, a lot of big houses keep rat-bane on the premises, and a lot of people can't lay their hands on it when they want it. Things get mislaid.'

'Very true, Foxkin.'

'And as far as this old-fashioned book on embalming goes, Mr Alleyn, I ask myself if perhaps somebody mightn't have picked it up since the funeral and got round to wondering about it like Mrs Alleyn has. You say these good people weren't very keen on Miss Sonia Orrincourt and are probably feeling rather sore about the late old gentleman's Will. They seem to be a highly-strung, excitable lot.'

'But I don't think I'm a particularly highly-strung, excitable lot, Mr Fox,' said Troy. 'And I got the idea too.'

'There!' said Fox, clicking his tongue. 'Putting my foot in it as usual, aren't I, sir?'

'Tell us what else you ask yourself,' said Alleyn.

'Why, whether one of these disappointed angry people hasn't let his imagination, or more likely hers, get the upper hand, and written this letter on the spur of the moment.'

'But what about the practical jokes, Mr Fox?' said Troy.

'Very silly, mischievous behaviour. Committing a nuisance. If the little girl didn't do them, and it looks as if she *couldn't* have done them at all, then somebody's brought off an unpleasant trick. Spiteful,' Fox added severely. 'Trying to prejudice the old gentleman against her, as you suggest, I dare say. But that doesn't necessarily mean murder. Why should it?'

'Why, indeed!' said Alleyn, taking him by the arm. 'You're exactly what we needed in this house, Br'er Fox. Let's all have a drink.' He took his wife on his other arm, and together they returned to the sitting-room. The telephone rang as Troy entered and she answered it. Alleyn held Fox back and they stared at each other.

'Very convincing performance, Fox. Thank you.'

'Rum go, sir, all the same, don't you reckon?'

'Too bloody rum by half. Come on.'

When they went into the room Troy put her hand over the mouthpiece of the telephone and turned to them. Her face was white.

'Rory,' she said, 'it's Thomas Ancred. He wants to come and see you. He says they've all had letters. He says he's made a discovery. He wants to come. What shall I say?'

'I'll speak to him,' said Alleyn. 'He can see me at the Yard in the morning, damn him.'

CHAPTER TEN

Bombshell from Thomas

THOMAS ANCRED ARRIVED punctually at nine o'clock, the hour Alleyn had appointed. Fox was present at the interview, which took place in Alleyn's room.

Troy had the painter's trick of accurate description, and she had been particularly good on Thomas. Alleyn felt he was already familiar with that crest of fine hair, those eyes wide open and palely astonished, that rather tight, small mouth, and the mild meandering voice.

'Thank you very much,' said Thomas, 'for letting me come. I didn't much want to, of course, but it's nice of you to have me. It was knowing Mrs Alleyn that put it into their heads.'

'Whose heads?' asked Alleyn.

'Well, Pauline's and Dessy's, principally. Paul and Fenella were quite keen too. I suppose Mrs Alleyn has told you about my people?'

'I think,' said Alleyn, 'that it might be best if we adopt the idea that I know nothing about anybody.'

'Oh, dear!' said Thomas, sighing. 'That means a lot of talking, doesn't it?'

'What about these letters?'

'Yes, to be sure,' said Thomas, beginning to pat himself all over. 'The letters. I've got them somewhere. Anonymous, you know. Of course I've had them before in the theatre from disappointed patrons and angry actresses, but this is different—really. Now, where?' He picked up one corner of his jacket, looked suspiciously at a bulging pocket, and finally pulled out a number of papers, two pencils and a box of matches. Thomas beamed at Alleyn. 'And there, after all, they are,' he said. In mild triumph he laid them out on the desk—eight copies of the letter Alleyn had already seen, all printed with the same type of pen on the same type of paper.

'What about the envelopes?' Alleyn asked.

'Oh,' said Thomas, 'we didn't keep them. I wasn't going to say anything about mine,' Thomas continued after a pause, 'and nor were Jenetta and Milly, but of course everybody noticed everybody else had the same sort of letter, and Pauline (my sister, Pauline Kentish) made a great hallabaloo over hers, and there we were, you know.'

'Eight,' said Alleyn. 'And there are nine in the party at Ancreton?'

'Sonia didn't get one, so everybody says she's the person meant.'

'Do you take that view, Mr Ancred?'

'Oh, yes,' said Thomas, opening his eyes very wide. 'It seems obvious, doesn't it? With the Will and everything. Sonia's meant, of course, but for my part,' said Thomas with a diffident cough, 'I don't fancy she murdered Papa.'

He gave Alleyn a rather anxious smile. 'It would be such a beastly thing to do, you know,' he said. 'Somehow one can't quite—however. Pauline actually almost leapt at the idea. Dessy, in a way, too. They're both dreadfully upset. Pauline fainted at the funeral anyway, and then with those letters on top of it all she's in a great state of emotional upheaval. You can't imagine what it's like at Ancreton.'

'It was Mrs Kentish, wasn't it, who suggested you should come to the Yard?'

'And Dessy. My unmarried sister, Desdemona. We all opened our letters yesterday morning at breakfast. Can you imagine? I got down first and really—such a shock! I was going to throw it on the fire, but just then Fenella came in, so I folded it up very small under the table. You can see which is mine by the creases. Paul's is the one that looks as if it had been chewed. He crunched it up, don't you know, in his agitation. Well, then I noticed that there were the same kind of envelopes in front of everybody's plate. Sonia has breakfast in her room, but I asked Barker if there were any letters for her. Fenella was by that time looking rather odd, having opened hers. Pauline said: "What an extraordinary looking letter I've got. Written by a child, I should think," and Milly said: "Panty again, perhaps," and there was a row, because Pauline and Milly don't see eye to eye over Panty. And then everybody said: "I've got one too," and then you know they opened them. Well, Pauline swooned away, of course, and Dessy said: "O, my prophetic soul," and began to get very excitable, and Milly said: "I think people who write anonymous letters are the *end*," and Jenetta (my sister-in-law), Fenella's mother (who is married to my brother Claude), said: "I agree, Milly." Then the next thing was, let me see—the next thing was everybody suspecting everybody else of writing the letter, until Paul got the idea—you must excuse me—that perhaps Mrs Alleyn being married to—'

Alleyn, catching sight of Fox's scandalized countenance, didn't answer, and Thomas, rather pink in the face, hurried on. 'Of course,' he said, 'the rest of us pooh-poohed the notion; quite howled it down, in fact. "The very idea," Fenella, for instance, said, "of Mrs Alleyn writing anonymous letters is just *so* bloody silly that we needn't discuss it," which led directly into another row, because Pauline made the suggestion and Fenella and Paul are engaged against her wish. It ended by my nephew Cedric, who is now the head of the family, saying that he thought the letter sounded like Pauline herself. He mentioned that a favourite phrase of Pauline's is: "I have reason to believe." Milly, Cedric's mother, you know, laughed rather pointedly, so naturally there was another row.'

'Last night,' Alleyn said, 'you told me you had made a discovery at Ancreton. What was it?'

'Oh, yes. I was coming to that some time. Now, actually, because it happened after lunch. I really don't care at all for this part of the story. Indeed, I quite forgot myself, and said I would *not* go back to Ancreton until I was assured of not having to get involved in any more goings on.'

'I'm afraid—' Alleyn began, but Thomas at once interrupted him. 'You don't follow? Well, of course you wouldn't, would you, because I haven't told you? Still, I suppose I'd better.'

Alleyn waited without comment.

'Well,' said Thomas at last. 'Here, after all, we go.'

'All yesterday morning,' Thomas said, 'after reading the letters, the battle, as you might put it, raged. Nobody really on anybody else's side except Paul and Fenella and Jenetta wanting to burn the letters and Pauline and Desdemona thinking there was something in it and we ought to keep them. And by lunch-time, you may depend on it, feeling ran very high indeed. And then, you know—'

Here Thomas paused and stared meditatively at a spot on the wall somewhere behind Fox's head. He had this odd trick of stopping short in his narratives. It was as if a gramophone needle was abruptly and unreasonably lifted from the disc. It was impossible to discover whether Thomas was suddenly bereft of the right word or smitten by the intervention of a new train of thought, or whether he had merely forgotten what he was talking about. Apart from a slight glazing of his eyes, his facial expression remained uncannily fixed.

'And then,' Alleyn prompted after a long pause.

'Because, when you come to think of it,' Thomas's voice began, 'it's the last thing one expects to find in the cheese-dish. It was New Zealand cheese, of course. Papa was fortunate in his friends.'

'What,' Alleyn asked temperately, 'is the last thing, Fox, that one would expect to find in the cheese-dish?'

Before Fox could reply Thomas began again.

'It's an old piece of Devonport. Rather nice, really. Blue, with white swans sailing round it. Very large. In times of plenty we used to have a whole Stilton in it, but now, of course, only a tiny packet. Rather ridiculous, really, but it meant there was plenty of room.'

'For what?'

'It was Cedric who lifted the lid and discovered it. He gave one of his little screams, but beyond feeling rather irritated, I dare say nobody paid much attention. Then he brought it over to the table—did I forget to say it's always left on the sideboard?—and dropped it in front of Pauline, who is in a very nervous condition anyway, and nearly shrieked the place down.'

'Dropped the cheese-dish? Or the cheese?'

'The cheese? Good heavens,' cried the scandalized Thomas, 'what an idea! The book, to be sure.'

'What book?' Alleyn said automatically.

'*The* book, you know. The one out of the glass thing in the drawing-room.'

'Oh,' said Alleyn after a pause. 'That book. On embalming?'

'And arsenic and all the rest of it. Too awkward and beastly, because, you know, Papa, by special arrangement, was. It upset everybody frightfully. In such very bad taste, everybody thought, and, of course, the cry of "Panty" went up immediately on all sides, and there was Pauline practically in a dead faint for the second time in three days.'

'Yes?'

'Yes, and then Milly remembered seeing Sonia look at the book, and Sonia said she had never seen it before, and then Cedric read out some rather beastly bits about arsenic, and everybody began to remember how Barker couldn't find the rat poison when it was wanted for *Bracegirdle*. Then Pauline and Desdemona looked at each other in such a meaning sort of way that Sonia became quite frantic with rage, and said she'd leave Ancreton there and then, only she couldn't, because there wasn't a train, so she went out in the rain and the governess-cart, and is now in bed with bronchitis, to which she is subject.'

'Still at Ancreton?'

'Yes, still there. Quite,' said Thomas. His expression became dazed, and he went off into another of his silences.

'And that,' Alleyn said, 'is, of course, the discovery you mentioned on the telephone?'

'That? Discovery? What discovery? Oh, no!' cried Thomas. 'I see what you mean. Oh, no, indeed, *that* was nothing compared to what we found afterwards in her room!'

'What did you find, Mr Ancred, and in whose room?'

'Sonia's,' said Thomas. 'Arsenic.'

'It was Cedric and the girls' idea,' Thomas said. 'After Sonia had gone out in the governess-cart they talked and talked. Nobody quite liked to say outright that perhaps Sonia had put rat poison in Papa's hot drink, but even Milly remarked that Sonia had recently got into the way of making it. Papa said she made it better than any of the servants or even than Milly herself. She used to take it in and leave it at his bedside. Cedric remembered seeing Sonia with the Thermos flask in her hands. He passed her in the passage on his way to bed that very night.

'It was at about this stage,' Thomas continued, 'that somebody—I've forgotten quite whom—said that they thought

Sonia's room ought to be searched. Jenetta and Fenella and Paul jibbed at this, but Dessy and Cedric and Pauline were as keen as mustard. I had promised to lend Caroline Able a book so I went away rather gladly. Caroline Able teaches the Difficult Children, including Panty, and she is very worried because of Panty not going bald enough. So it might have been an hour later that I went back to our part of the house. And there was Cedric lying in wait for me. Well, he's the head of the house now, so I suppose I mustn't be beastly about him. All mysterious and whispering, he was.

'"Ssh," he said. "Come upstairs."'

'He wouldn't say anything more. I felt awfully bored with all this, but I followed him up.'

'To Miss Orrincourt's room?' Alleyn suggested as Thomas's eyes had glazed again.

'That's it. How did you guess? And there were Pauline and Milly and Dessy. I must tell you,' said Thomas delicately, 'that Sonia has a little sort of suite of rooms near Papa's for convenience. It wasn't called anything, because Papa had run out of famous actresses' names. So he had a new label done with "*Orrincourt*" on it, and that really infuriated everybody, because Sonia, whatever anybody may care to say to the contrary, is a very naughty actress. Well, not an actress at all, really. Absolutely dire, you might say.'

'You found your sisters and Mrs Henry Ancred in these rooms?'

'Yes. I must tell you that Sonia's suite is in a tower. Like the tower your wife had, only Sonia's tower is higher, because the architect who build Ancreton believed in quaintness. So Sonia has got a bedroom on top and then a bathroom, and at the bottom a boudoir. The bedroom's particularly quaint, with a little door and steps up into the pepper-pot roof which makes a box-room. They are milling about in this box-room and Dessy had found the rat poison in one of Sonia's boxes. It's a preparation of arsenic. It says so on the label. Well!'

'What have you done with it?'

'So awkward!' said Thomas crossly. 'They made me take it. To keep, they said, in case of evidence being needed. Cedric was very particular about it, having read detective books, and he wrapped it up in one of my handkerchiefs. So I've got it in my rooms here in London if you really want to see it.'

'We'll take possession of it, I think,' said Alleyn with a glance at Fox. Fox made a slight affirmative rumble. 'If it's convenient, Mr Ancred,' Alleyn went on, 'Fox or I will drop you at your rooms and collect this tin.'

'I hope I can find it,' Thomas said gloomily.

'Find it?'

'One does mislay things so. Only the other day—' Thomas fell into one of his trances and this time Alleyn waited for something to break through. 'I was just thinking, you know,' Thomas began rather loudly. 'There we all were in her room and I looked out of the window. It was raining. And away down below, like something out of a Noah's Ark, was the governess-cart creeping up the drive, and Sonia, in her fur coat, flapping the reins, I suppose, in the way she has. And when you come to think of it, there, according to Pauline and Dessy and Cedric and Milly, went Papa's murderess.'

'But not according to you?' said Alleyn. He was putting away the eight anonymous letters. Fox had risen, and now stared down at their visitor as if Thomas was some large unopened parcel left by mistake in the room.

'To *me*?' Thomas repeated, opening his eyes very wide. 'I don't know. How should I? But you wouldn't believe how uncomfortable it makes one feel.'

To enter Thomas's room was to walk into a sort of cross between a wastepaper basket and a workshop. Its principal feature was a large round table entirely covered with stacks of paper, paints, photographs, models for stage sets, designs for costumes, and books. In the window was an apparently unused desk. On the walls were portraits of distinguished players, chief among them Sir Henry himself.

'Sit down,' invited Thomas, sweeping sheafs of papers from two chairs on to the floor. 'I'll just think where—' He began to walk round his table, staring rather vacantly at it. 'I came in with my suitcase, of course, and then, you know, the telephone rang. It was *much* later than that when I wanted to find the letters, and I had put them carefully away because of showing them to you. And I *found* them. So I must have unpacked. And I can remember thinking: "It's poison, and I'd better be careful of my handkerchief in case—"'

He walked suddenly to a wall cupboard and opened it. A great quantity of papers instantly fell out. Thomas stared indignantly at them. 'I distinctly remember,' he said, turning to Alleyn and Fox with his mouth slightly open. 'I *distinctly* remember saying to myself—' But this sentence was also fated to remain unfinished, for Thomas pounced unexpectedly upon some fragment from the cupboard. 'I've been looking for that all over the place,' he said. 'It's *most* important. A cheque, in fact.'

He sat on the floor and began scuffling absently among the papers. Alleyn, who for some minutes had been inspecting the chaos that reigned upon the table, lifted a pile of drawings and discovered a white bundle. He loosened the knot at the top and a stained tin was disclosed. It bore a bright red label with the legend: 'Rat-X-it! Poison,' and, in slightly smaller print, the antidote for arsenical poisoning.

'Here it is, Mr Ancred,' said Alleyn.

'What?' asked Thomas. He glanced up. 'Oh, *that*,' he said. 'I *thought* I'd put it on the table.'

Fox came forward with a bag. Alleyn, muttering something about futile gestures, lifted the tin by the handkerchief. 'You don't mind,' he said to Thomas, 'if we take charge of this? We'll give you a receipt for it.'

'Oh, will you?' asked Thomas mildly. 'Thanks awfully.'

He watched them stow away the tin, and then, seeing that they were about to go, scrambled to his feet. 'You must have a drink,' he said. 'There's a bottle of Papa's whisky—I think.'

Alleyn and Fox managed to head him off a further search. He sat down, and listened with an air of helplessness to Alleyn's parting exposition.

'Now, Mr Ancred,' Alleyn said, 'I think I ought to make as clear as possible the usual procedure following the sort of information you have brought to us. Before any definite step can be taken, the police make what are known as "further inquiries." They do this as inconspicuously as possible, since neither their original informant, nor they, enjoy the public exploration of a mare's nest. If these inquiries seem to point to a suspicion of ill practice, the police then get permission from the Home Secretary for the next step to be taken. You know what that is, I expect?'

'I say,' said Thomas, 'that *would* be beastly, wouldn't it?' A sudden thought seemed to strike him. 'I say,' he repeated, 'would I have to be there?'

'We'd probably ask for formal identification by a member of his family.'

'Oh, Lor'!' Thomas whispered dismally. He pinched his lower lip between his thumb and forefinger. A gleam of consolation appeared to visit him.

'I say,' he said, 'it's a good job after all, isn't it, that the Nation didn't plump for the Abbey?'

CHAPTER ELEVEN

Alleyn at Ancreton

'IN OUR GAME,' said Fox as they drove back to the Yard, 'you get some funny glimpses into what you might call human nature. I dare say I've said that before, but it's a fact.'

'I believe you,' said Alleyn.

'Look at this chap we've just left,' Fox continued with an air of controversy. 'Vague! And yet he must be good at his job, wouldn't you say, sir?'

'Indisputably.'

'There! Good at his job, and yet to meet him you'd say he'd lose his play, and his actors, and his way to the theatre. In view of which,' Fox summed up, 'I ask myself if this chap's as muddle-headed as he lets on.'

'A pose, you think, do you, Fox?'

'You never know with some jokers,' Fox muttered, and, wiping his great hand over his face, seemed by that gesture to dispose of Thomas Ancred's vagaries. 'I suppose,' he said, 'it'll be a matter of seeing the doctor, won't it?'

'I'm afraid so. I've looked out trains. There's one in an hour. Get us there by midday. We may have to spend the night in Ancreton village. We can pick up our emergency bags at the Yard. I'll talk to the AC and telephone Troy. What a hell of a thing to turn up.'

'It doesn't look as if we'll be able to let it alone, do you reckon, Mr Alleyn?'

'I still have hopes. As it stands, there's not a case in Thomas's story to hang a dead dog on. They lose a tin of rat poison and find it in a garret. Somebody reads a book about embalming, and thinks up an elaborate theme based on an arbitrary supposition. Counsel could play skittles with it—as it stands.'

'Suppose we *did* get an order for exhumation. Suppose they found arsenic in the body. With this embalming business it'd seem as if it would prove nothing.'

'On the contrary,' said Alleyn, 'I rather think, Fox, that if they did find arsenic in the body it would prove everything.'

Fox turned slowly and looked at him. 'I don't get that one, Mr Alleyn,' he said.

'I'm not at all sure that I'm right. We'll have to look it up. Here we are. I'll explain on the way down to this accursed village. Come on.'

He saw his Assistant Commissioner, who, with the air of a connoisseur, discussed the propriety of an investigator handling a case in which his wife might be called as a witness. 'Of course, my dear Rory, if by any chance the thing should come into court and your wife be subpoenaed, we would have to reconsider our position. We've no precedent, so far as I know. But for the time being I imagine it's more reasonable for you to discuss it with her than for anybody else to do so—Fox, for instance. Now, you go down to this place, talk to the indigenous GP and come back and tell us what you think about it. Tiresome, if it comes to anything. Good luck.'

As they left, Alleyn took from his desk the second volume of a work on medical jurisprudence. It dealt principally with poisons. In the train he commended certain passages to Fox's notice. He watched his old friend put on his spectacles, raise his eyebrows, and develop the slightly catarrhal breathing that invariably accompanied his reading.

'Yes,' said Fox, removing his spectacles as the train drew into Ancreton Halt, 'that's different, of course.'

Doctor Herbert Withers was a short, tolerably plump man, with little of the air of wellbeing normally associated with plumpness. He came out into his hall as they arrived, admitting from some inner room the sound of a racing broadcast. After a glance at Alleyn's professional card he took them to his consulting-room, and sat at his desk with a movement whose briskness seemed to overlie a controlled fatigue.

'What's the trouble?' he asked.

It was the conventional opening. Alleyn thought it had slipped involuntarily from Dr Withers's lips.

'We hope there's no trouble,' he said. 'Would you mind if I asked you to clear up a few points about Sir Henry Ancred's death?'

The mechanical attentiveness of Dr Withers's glance sharpened. He made an abrupt movement and looked from Alleyn to Fox.

'Certainly,' he said, 'if there's any necessity. But why?' He still held Alleyn's card in his hand and he glanced at it again. 'You don't mean to say—' he began, and stopped short. 'Well, what are these few points?'

'I think I'd better tell you exactly what's happened,' Alleyn said. He took a copy of the anonymous letter from his pocket and handed it to Dr Withers. 'Mr Thomas Ancred brought eight of these to us this morning,' he said.

'Damn disgusting piffle,' said Dr Withers and handed it back.

'I hope so. But when we're shown these wretched things we have to do something about them.'

'Well?'

'You signed the death certificate, Dr Withers, and—'

'And I shouldn't have done so if I hadn't been perfectly satisfied as to the cause.'

'Exactly. Now will you, like a good chap, help us to dispose of these letters by giving us, in non-scientific words, the cause of Sir Henry's death?'

Dr Withers fretted a little, but at last went to his files and pulled out a card.

'There you are,' he said. 'That's the last of his cards. I made routine calls at Ancreton. It covers about six weeks.'

Alleyn looked at it. It bore the usual list of dates with appropriate notes. Much of it was illegible and almost all obscure to the lay mind. The final note, however, was flatly lucid. It read: 'Deceased. Between twelve-thirty and two a.m., Nov. 25th.'

'Yes,' said Alleyn. 'Thank you. Now will you translate some of this?'

'He suffered,' said Dr Withers angrily, 'from gastric ulcers and degeneration of the heart. He was exceedingly indiscriminate in his diet. He'd eaten a disastrous meal, had drunk champagne, and had flown into one of his rages. From the look of the room, I diagnosed a severe gastric attack followed by heart failure. I may add that if I had heard about the manner in which he'd spent the evening I should have expected some such development.'

'You'd have expected him to die?'

'That would be an extremely unprofessional prognostication. I would have anticipated grave trouble,' said Dr Withers stuffily.

'Was he in the habit of playing up with his diet?'

'He was. Not continuously, but in bouts.'

'Yet survived?'

'The not unusual tale of "once too often".'

'Yes,' said Alleyn, looking down at the card. 'Would you mind describing the room and the body?'

'Would you, in your turn, Chief Inspector, mind telling me if you have any reason for this interview beyond these utterly preposterous anonymous letters?'

'Some of the family suspect arsenical poisoning.'

'Oh, my God and the little starfish!' Dr Withers shouted and shook his fists above his head. 'That *bloody* family!'

He appeared to wrestle obscurely with his feelings. 'I'm sorry about that,' he said at last, 'inexcusable outburst. I've been busy lately and worried, and there you are. The Ancreds, collectively, have tried me rather high. Why, may one ask, do they suspect arsenical poisoning?'

'It's a long story,' said Alleyn carefully, 'and it involves a tin of rat poison. May I add also, very unprofessionally, that I shall be enormously glad if you can tell me that the condition of the room and the body precludes the smallest likelihood of arsenical poisoning?'

'I can't tell you anything of the sort. Why? (a) Because the room had been cleaned up when I got there. And (b) because the evidence as described to me, and the appearance of the body were entirely consistent with a severe gastric attack, and therefore *not* inconsistent with arsenical poisoning.'

'Damn!' Alleyn grunted. 'I thought it'd be like that.'

'How the hell could the old fool have got at any rat poison? Will you tell me that?' He jabbed his finger at Alleyn.

"They don't think,' Alleyn explained, 'that he got at it. They think it was introduced to him.'

The well-kept hand closed so strongly that the knuckles whitened. For a moment he held it clenched, and then, as if to cancel this gesture, opened the palm and examined his fingernails.

'That,' he said, 'is implicit in the letter, of course. Even that I can believe of the Ancreds. Who is supposed to have murdered Sir Henry? Am I, by any pleasant chance?'

'Not that I know,' said Alleyn comfortably. Fox cleared his throat and added primly: 'What an idea!'

'Are they going to press for an exhumation? Or are you?'

'Not without more reason than we've got at the moment,' Alleyn said. 'You didn't hold a post-mortem?'

'One doesn't hold a PM on a patient who was liable to go off in precisely this fashion at any moment.'

'True enough. Dr Withers, may I make our position quite clear? We've had a queer set of circumstances placed before us and we've got to take stock of them. Contrary to popular belief, the police do not, in such cases, burn to get a pile of evidence that points unavoidably to exhumation. If the whole thing turns out to be so much nonsense they are, as a general rule, delighted to write it off. Give us a sound argument against arsenical poisoning and we'll be extremely grateful to you.'

Dr Withers waved his hands. 'I can't give you, at a moment's notice, absolute proof that he didn't get arsenic. You couldn't do it for ninety-nine deaths out of a hundred, when there was gastric trouble with vomiting and purging and no analysis was taken of anything. As a matter of fact—'

'Yes?' Alleyn prompted as he paused.

'As a matter of fact, I dare say if there'd been anything left I might have done an analysis simply as a routine measure and to satisfy a somewhat pedantic medical conscience. But the whole place had been washed up.'

'By whose orders?'

'My dear man, by Barker's orders or Mrs Kentish's, or Mrs Henry Ancred's, or whoever happened to think of it. They didn't like to move him. Couldn't very well. Rigor was pretty well established, which gave me, by the way, a lead about the time of his death. When I saw him later in the day they'd fixed him up, of course, and a nice time Mrs Ancred must have had of it with all of them milling about the house in an advanced condition of hysteria and Mrs Kentish "insisting on taking a hand in the laying-out".'

'Good Lord!'

'Oh, they're like that. Well, as I was saying, there he was when they found him, hunched up on the bed, and the room in a pretty nauseating state. When I got there, two of those old housemaids were waddling off with their buckets and the whole place stank of carbolic. They'd even managed to change the bedclothes. I didn't get there, by the way, for an hour after they telephoned. Confinement.'

'About the children's ringworm——' Alleyn began.

'You know about them, do you? Yes. Worrying business. Glad to say young Panty's cleared up at last.'

'I understand,' Alleyn said pleasantly, 'that you are bold in your use of drugs.'

There was a long silence. 'And how, may I ask,' said Dr Withers very quietly, 'did you hear details of my treatment?'

'Why, from Thomas Ancred,' said Alleyn, and watched the colour return to Dr Withers's face. 'Why not?'

'I dislike gossip about my patients. As a matter of fact I wondered if you'd been talking to our local pharmacist. I'm not at all pleased with him at the moment, however.'

'Do you remember the evening the children were dosed—Monday, the nineteenth, I think it was?'

Dr Withers stared at him. 'Now, why——?' he began, and seemed to change his mind. 'I do,' he said. 'Why?'

'Simply because that evening a practical joke was played on Sir Henry and the child Panty has been accused of it. It's too elaborate a story to bother you about, but I'd like to know if she was capable of it. In the physical sense. Mentally, it seems, she certainly is.'

'What time?'

'During dinner. She would have visited the drawing-room.'

'Out of the question. I arrived at seven-thirty—Wait a moment.' He searched his filing cabinet and pulled out another card. 'Here! I superintended the weighing and dosing of these kids and noted the time. Panty got her quota at eight and was put to bed. I stayed on in the ante-room to their dormitory during the rest of the business and talked to Miss Able. I left her my visiting list for the next twenty-four hours so that she could get me quickly if anything cropped up. It was after nine when I left and this wretched kid certainly hadn't budged. I had a look at the lot of them. She was asleep with a normal pulse and so on.'

'That settles Panty, then,' Alleyn muttered.

'Look here, has this any bearing on the other business?'

'I'm not sure. It's a preposterous story. If you've the time and inclination to listen I'll tell it to you.'

'I've got,' said Dr Withers, glancing at his watch, 'twenty-three minutes. Case in half an hour, and I want to hear the racing results before I go out.'

'I shan't be more than ten minutes.'

'Go ahead, then. I should be glad to hear any story, however fantastic, that can connect a practical joke on Monday the nineteenth with the death of Sir Henry Ancred from gastro-enteritis after midnight on Saturday the twenty-fourth.'

Alleyn related all the stories of the practical jokes. Dr Withers punctuated this recital with occasional sounds of incredulity or irritation. When Alleyn reached the incident of the flying cow he interrupted him.

'The child Panty,' he said, 'is capable of every iniquity, but, as I have pointed out, she could not have perpetrated this offence with the blown-up bladder, nor could she have painted the flying cow on Mrs—' He stopped short. 'Is this lady—?' he began.

'My wife, as it happens,' said Alleyn, 'but let it pass.'

'Good Lord! Unusual that, isn't it?'

'Both unusual and bothering in this context. You were saying?'

'That the child was too seedy that night for it to be conceivable. And you tell me Miss Able (sensible girl that) vouches for her anyway.'

'Yes.'

'All right. Well, some other fool, the egregious Cedric in all likelihood, performed these idiocies. I fail to see how they can possibly be linked up with Sir Henry's death.'

'You have not,' Alleyn said, 'heard of the incident of the book on embalming in the cheese-dish.'

Dr Withers's mouth opened slightly, but he made no comment, and Alleyn continued his narrative. 'You see,' he added, 'this final trick does bear a sort of family likeness to the others, and, considering the subject matter of the book, and the fact that Sir Henry was embalmed—'

'Quite so. Because the damned book talks about arsenic they jump to this imbecile conclusion—'

'Fortified, we must remember, by the discovery of a tin of arsenical rat poison in Miss Orrincourt's luggage.'

'Planted there by the practical joker,' cried Dr Withers. 'I bet you. Planted!'

'That's a possibility,' Alleyn agreed, 'that we can't overlook.'

Fox suddenly said: 'Quite so.'

'Well,' said Dr Withers, 'I'm damned if I know what to say. No medical man enjoys the suggestion that he's been careless or made a mistake, and this would be a very awkward mistake. Mind, I don't for a split second believe there's a fragment of truth in the tale, but if the whole boiling of Ancreds are going to talk arsenic—Here! Have you seen the embalmers?'

'Not yet. We shall do so, of course.'

'I don't know anything about embalming,' Dr Withers muttered. 'This fossil book may not amount to a row of beans.'

'Taylor,' said Alleyn, 'has a note on it. He says that in such manipulations of a body, antiseptic substances are used (commonly arsenic), and might prevent detection of poison as the cause of death.'

'So, if we have an exhumation, where are we? Precisely nowhere.'

'I'm not sure of my ground,' said Alleyn, 'but I fancy that an exhumation should definitely show whether or not Sir Henry Ancred was poisoned. I'll explain.'

Fox and Alleyn lunched at the Ancreton Arms, on jugged hare, well cooked, and a tankard each of the local draught beer. It was a pleasant enough little pub, and the landlady, on Alleyn's inquiry, said she could, if requested, put them up for the night.

'I'm not at all sure we shan't be taking her at her word,' said Alleyn as they walked out into the village street. It was thinly bright with winter sunshine, and contained, beside the pub and Dr Withers's house, a post office shop, a chapel, a draper's, a stationer's, a meeting-hall, a chemist-cum-fancy-goods shop, and a row of cottages. Over the brow of intervening hills, the gothic windows, multiple towers and indefatigably varied chimney-pots of Ancreton Manor glinted against their background of conifers, and brooded, with an air of grand seigneury, faintly bogus, over the little village.

'And here,' said Alleyn, pausing at the chemist's window, 'is Mr Juniper's pharmacy. That's a pleasant name, Fox. E.M. Juniper. This is where Troy and Miss Orrincourt came in their governess-cart on a nasty evening. Let's call on Mr Juniper, shall we?'

But he seemed to be in no hurry to go in, and began to mutter to himself before the side window. 'A tidy window, Fox. I like the old-fashioned coloured bottles, don't you? Writing paper, you see, and combs and ink (that brand went off the market in the war) cheek-by-jowl with cough-lozenges and trusses in their modest boxes. Even some children's card games. Happy Families. That's how Troy drew the Ancreds. Let's give them a pack. Mr Juniper the chemist's window. Come on.'

He led the way in. The shop was divided into two sections. One counter was devoted to fancy goods, and one, severe and isolated, to Mr Juniper's professional activities. Alleyn rang a little bell, a door opened, and Mr Juniper, fresh and rosy in his white coat, came out, together with the cleanly smell of drugs.

'Yes, sir?' Mr Juniper inquired, placing himself behind his professional counter.

'Good morning,' said Alleyn. 'I wonder if by any chance you've got anything to amuse a small girl who's on the sick list?'

Mr Juniper removed to the fancy-goods department. 'Happy Families? Bubble-blowing?' he suggested.

'Actually,' Alleyn lied pleasantly. 'I've been told I must bring back some form of practical joke. Designed, I'm afraid, for Dr Withers.'

'Really? T't. Ha-ha!' said Mr Juniper. 'Well, now. I'm afraid we haven't anything much in that line. There were some dummy ink-spots, but I'm afraid—No. I know exactly the type of thing you mean, mind, but I'm just afraid—'

'Somebody said something about a thing you blow up and sit on,' Alleyn murmured vaguely. 'It sounded disgusting.'

'Ah! The Raspberry?'

'That's it.'

Mr Juniper shook his head sadly and made a gesture of resignation.

'I thought,' said Alleyn, 'I saw a box in your window that looked—'

'Empty!' Mr Juniper sighed. 'The customer didn't require the box, so I'm afraid I've just left it there. Now isn't that a pity,' Mr Juniper lamented. 'Only last week, or would it be a fortnight ago, I sold the last of that little line to a customer for exactly the same purpose. A sick little girl. Yes. One would almost think,' he hazarded, 'that the same little lady—'

'I expect so. Patricia Kentish,' said Alleyn.

'Ah, quite so. So the customer said! Up at the Manor. Quite a little tinker,' said Mr Juniper. 'Well, sir, I think you'll find that Miss Pant—Miss Pat—has already got a Raspberry.'

'In that case,' said Alleyn, 'I'll take a Happy Families. You want some toothpaste, don't you, Fox?'

'Happy Families,' said Mr Juniper, snatching a packet from the shelf. 'Dentifrice? Any particular make, sir?'

'For a plate,' said Fox stolidly.

'For the denture. Quite,' said Mr Juniper, and darted into the professional side of his shop.

'I wouldn't mind betting,' said Alleyn cheerfully to Fox, 'that it was Sonia Orrincourt who got in first with that thing.'

'Ah,' said Fox. Mr Juniper smiled archly. 'Well, now,' he said, 'I oughtn't to give the young lady away, ought I? Professional secrets. Ha-ha!'

'Ha-ha!' Alleyn agreed, putting Happy Families in his pocket. 'Thank you, Mr Juniper.'

'Thank you, sir. All well up at the Manor, I hope? Great loss, that. Loss to the Nation, you might say. Little trouble with the children clearing up, I hope?'

'On its way. Lovely afternoon, isn't it? Goodbye.'

'I didn't want any toothpaste,' said Fox, as they continued up the street.

'I didn't see why I should make all the purchases and you were looking rather too portentous. Put it down to expenses. It was worth it.'

'I don't say it wasn't that,' Fox agreed. 'Now, sir, if this woman Orrincourt took the Raspberry, I suppose we look to her for all the other pranks, don't we?'

'I hardly think so, Fox. Not all. We know, at least, that this ghastly kid tied a notice to the tail of her Aunt Millamant's coat. She's got a reputation for practical jokes. On the other hand, she definitely, it seems, did not perpetrate the Raspberry and the flying cow, and my wife is convinced she's innocent of the spectacles, the painted stair rail and the rude writing on Sir Henry's looking-glass. As for the book in the cheese-dish, I don't think either Panty or Miss Orrincourt is guilty of that flight of fancy.'

'So that if you count out the little girl for anything that matters, we've got Miss Orrincourt and another.'

'That's the cry.'

'And this other is trying to fix something on Miss Orrincourt in the way of arsenic and the old gentleman?'

'It's a reasonable thesis, but Lord knows.'

'Where are we going, Mr Alleyn?'

'Are you good for a two-mile walk? I think we'll call on the Ancreds.'

'It isn't,' said Alleyn as they toiled up the second flight of terraces, 'as if we can hope to keep ourselves dark, supposing that were advisable. Thomas will have rung up his family and told them that we have at least taken notice. We may as well announce ourselves and see what we can see. More especially, this wretched old fellow's bedroom.'

'By this time,' said Fox sourly, 'they'll probably have had it repapered.'

'I wonder if Paul Kentish is handy with electrical gadgets. I'll wager Cedric Ancred isn't.'

'What's that?' Fox demanded.

'What's what?'

'I can hear something. A child crying, isn't it, sir?'

They had reached the second terrace. At each end of this terrace, between the potato-field and the woods, were shrubberies and young copses. From the bushes on their left hand came a thin intermittent wailing; very dolorous. They paused uncertainly, staring at each other. The wailing stopped, and into the silence welled the accustomed sounds of the countryside—the wintry chittering of birds and the faint click of naked branches.

'Would it be some kind of bird, should you say?' Fox speculated.

'No bird!' Alleyn began and stopped short. 'There it is again.'

It was a thin piping sound, waving and irregular and the effect of it was peculiarly distressing. Without further speculation they set off across the rough and still frost-encrusted ground. As they drew nearer to it the sound became, not articulate, but more complex, and presently, when they had drawn quite close, developed a new character.

'It's mixed up,' Fox whispered, 'with a kind of singing.'

Goodbye poor pussy your coat was so warm,
And even if you did moult you did me no harm.
Goodbye poor pussy for ever and ever
And make me a good girl, amen.

'*For ever and ever,*' the thin voice repeated, and drifted off again into its former desolate wail. As they brushed against the first low bushes it ceased, and there followed a wary silence disrupted by harsh sobbing.

Between the bushes and the copse they came upon a little girl in a white cap, sitting by a newly-turned mound of earth. A child's spade was beside her. Stuck irregularly in the mound of earth were a few heads of geraniums. A piece of paper threaded on a twig stood crookedly at the head of the mound. The little girl's hands were earthy, and she had knuckled her eyes so that black streaks ran down her face. She crouched there scowling at them, rather like an animal that flattens itself near the ground, unable to obey its own instinct for flight.

'Hallo,' said Alleyn, 'this is a bad job!' And unable to think of a more satisfactory opening, he heard himself repeating Dr Withers's phrase. 'What's the trouble?' he asked.

The little girl was convulsed, briefly, by a sob. Alleyn squatted beside her and examined the writing on the paper. It had been executed in large shaky capitals.

KARABAS,

R.S.V.P.

LOVE FROM PANTY.

'Was Carabbas,' Alleyn ventured, 'your own cat?'

Panty glared at him and slowly shook her head.

Alleyn said quickly: 'How stupid of me; he was your grandfather's cat, wasn't he?'

'He loved me,' said Panty on a high note. 'Better than he loved Noddy. He loved me better than he loved anybody. I was his friend.' Her voice rose piercingly like the whistle of a small engine. 'And I didn't,' she screamed, 'I didn't, I didn't give him the ringworms. I hate my Auntie Milly. I wish she was dead. I wish they were all dead. I'll kill my Auntie Milly.' She beat on the ground with her fists, and, catching sight of Fox, screamed at him: 'Get out of here, will you? This is my place.'

Fox stepped back hastily.

'I've heard,' said Alleyn, cautiously, 'about Carabbas and about you. You paint pictures, don't you? Have you painted any more pictures lately?'

'I don't want to paint any more pictures,' said Panty.

'That's a pity, because we rather thought of sending you a box of paints for yourself from London.'

Panty sobbed dryly. 'Who did?' she said.

'Troy Alleyn,' said Alleyn. 'Mrs Alleyn, you know. She's my wife.'

'If I painted a picture of my Auntie Milly,' said Panty, 'I'd give her pig's whiskers, and she'd look like Judas Iscariot. They said my cat Carabbas had the ringworms, and they said I'd given them to him, and they're all, *all* liars. He hadn't, and I didn't. It was only his poor fur coming out.'

With the abandon which Troy had witnessed in the little theatre, Panty flung herself face forward on the ground and kicked. Tentatively Alleyn bent over her, and after a moment's hesitation picked her up. For a moment or two she fought violently, but suddenly, with an air of desolation, let her arms fall and hung limply in his hands.

'Never mind, Panty,' Alleyn muttered helplessly. 'Here, let's mop up your face.' He felt in his pocket and his fingers closed round a hard object. 'Look here,' he said. 'Look what I've got,' and pulled out a small packet. 'Do you ever play Happy Families?' he said. He pushed the box of cards into her hands and not very successfully mopped her face with his handkerchief. 'Let's move on,' he said to Fox.

He carried the now inert Panty across to the third flight of steps. Here she began to wriggle, and he put her down.

'I want to play Happy Families,' said Panty thickly. 'Here,' she added. She squatted down, and, still interrupting herself from time to time with a hiccuping sob, opened her pack of picture cards, and with filthy fingers began to deal them into three heaps.

'Sit down, Fox,' said Alleyn. 'You're going to play Happy Families.'

Fox sat uneasily on the second step.

Panty was a slow dealer, principally because she examined the face of each card before she put it down.

'Do you know the rules?' Alleyn asked Fox.

'I can't say I do,' he replied, putting on his spectacles. 'Would it be anything like euchre?'

'Not much, but you'll pick it up. The object is to collect a family. Would you be good enough,' he said, turning to Panty, 'to oblige me with Mrs Snips the Tailor's Wife?'

'You didn't say "Please," so it's my turn,' said Panty. 'Give me Mr Snips, the Tailor, and Master Snips and Miss Snips, please.'

'Damn,' said Alleyn. 'Here you are,' and handed over the cards, each with its cut of an antic who might have walked out of a Victorian volume of *Punch*.

Panty pushed these cards underneath her and sat on them. Her bloomers, true to her legend, were conspicuous. 'Now,' she said, turning a bleary glance on Fox, 'you give me—'

'Don't I get a turn?' asked Fox.

'Not unless she goes wrong,' said Alleyn. 'You'll learn.'

'Give me,' said Panty, 'Master Grit, the Grocer's Son.'

'Doesn't she have to say "please"?'

'Please,' yelled Panty. 'I said "please." Please.'

Fox handed over the card.

'And Mrs Grit,' Panty went on.

'It beats me,' said Fox, 'how she knows.'

'She knows,' said Alleyn, 'because she looked.'

Panty laughed raucously. 'And you give me Mr Bull, the Butcher,' she demanded, turning on Alleyn. 'Please.'

'Not at home,' said Alleyn triumphantly. 'And now, you see, Fox, it's my turn.'

'The game seems crook to me,' said Fox, gloomily.

'Master Bun,' Panty remarked presently, 'is azzakerly like my Uncle Thomas.' Alleyn, in imagination, changed the grotesque faces on all the cards to those of the Ancreds as Troy had drawn them in her notebook. 'So he is,' he said. 'And now I know you've got him. Please give me Master Ancred,

the Actor's Son.' This sally afforded Panty exquisite amuse-
ment. With primitive guffaws she began to demand cards
under the names of her immediate relations and to the utter
confusion of the game.

'There now,' said Alleyn at last, in a voice that struck
him as being odiously complacent. 'That was a lovely game.
Suppose you take us up to see the—ah—'

'The Happy Family,' Fox prompted in a wooden voice.

'Certainly,' said Alleyn.

'Why?' Panty demanded.

'That's what we've come for.'

Panty stood squarely facing him. Upon her stained face
there grew, almost furtively, a strange expression. It was
compounded, he thought, of the look of a normal child about to
impart a secret and of something less familiar, more disquieting.

'Here!' she said. 'I want to tell you something. Not him.
You.'

She drew Alleyn away, and with a sidelong glance pulled
him down until she could hook her arm about his neck. He
waited, feeling her breath uncomfortably in his ear.

'What is it?'

The whispering was disembodied but unexpectedly
clear. 'We've got,' it said, 'a murderer in our family.'

When he drew back and looked at her she was smiling
nervously.

CHAPTER TWELVE

The Bell and the Book

So ACCURATE AND LIVELY were Troy's draw-
ings that Alleyn recognized Desdemona Ancred as soon as
she appeared on the top step of the third terrace and looked
down upon the group, doubtless a curious one, made by
himself, Panty and Fox. Indeed, as she paused, she struck
precisely the attitude, histrionic and grandiose, with which
Troy had invested her caricature.

'Ah!' said Dessy richly. 'Panty! At last!'

She held out her hand towards Panty and at the same
time looked frankly at Alleyn. 'How do you do?' she said. 'Are
you on your way up? Has this terrible young person waylaid
you? Shall I introduce myself?'

'Miss Ancred?' Alleyn said.

'He's Mrs Alleyn's husband,' Panty said. 'We don't much
want you, thank you, Aunt Dessy.'

Dessy was in the act of advancing with poise down the steps.
Her smile remained fixed on her face. Perhaps she halted for a

fraction of time in her stride. The next second her hand was in his, and she was gazing with embarrassing intensity into his eyes.

'I'm so glad you've come,' she said in her deepest voice. 'So glad! We are terribly, terribly distressed. My brother has told you, I know.' She pressed his hand, released it, and looked at Fox.

'Inspector Fox,' said Alleyn. Desdemona was tragically gracious.

They turned to climb the steps. Panty gave a threatening wail.

'You,' said her aunt, 'had better run home as fast as you can. Miss Able's been looking everywhere for you. What *have* you been doing, Panty? You're covered in earth.'

Immediately they were confronted with another scene. Panty repeated her former performance, roaring out strange threats against her family, lamenting the cat Carabbas, and protesting that she had not infected him.

'Really, it's *too* ridiculous,' Dessy said in a loud aside to Alleyn. 'Not that we didn't all feel it. Poor Carabbas! And my father so attached always. But honestly, it was a menace to all our healths. Ringworm, beyond a shadow of doubt. Fur coming out in handfuls. Obviously it had given them the disease in the first instance. We did perfectly right to have it destroyed. Come *on*, Panty.'

By this time they had reached the top terrace, with Panty waddling lamentably behind them. Here they were met by Miss Caroline Able, who brightly ejaculated: 'Goodness, what a noise!' cast a clear sensible glance at Alleyn and Fox, and removed her still bellowing charge.

'I'm so distressed,' Desdemona cried, 'that you should have had this reception. Honestly, poor Panty is simply beyond everything. Nobody loves children more than I do, but she's got such a *difficult* nature. And in a house of tragedy, when one's nerves and emotions are lacerated—'

She gazed into his eyes, made a small helpless gesture, and finally ushered them into the hall. Alleyn glanced quickly at the space under the gallery, but it was still untenanted.

'I'll tell my sister and my sister-in-law,' Dessy began, but Alleyn interrupted her. 'If we might just have a word with you first,' he said. And by Dessy's manner, at once portentous and dignified, he knew that this suggestion was not unpleasing to her. She led them to the small sitting-room where Troy had found Sonia Orrincourt and Cedric giggling together on the sofa. Desdemona placed herself on this sofa. She sat down, Alleyn noticed, quite beautifully; not glancing at her objective, but sinking on it in one movement and then elegantly disposing her arms.

'I expect,' he began, 'that your brother has explained the official attitude to this kind of situation. We're obliged to make all sorts of inquiries before we can take any further action.'

'I see,' said Desdemona, nodding owlishly. 'Yes, I see. Go on.'

'To put it baldly, do you yourself think there is any truth in the suggestion made by the anonymous letter-writer?'

Desdemona pressed the palms of her hands carefully against her eyes. 'If I *could* dismiss it,' she cried. 'If I could!'

'You have no idea, I suppose, who could have written the letters?' She shook her head. Alleyn wondered if she had glanced at him through her fingers.

'Have any of you been up to London since your father's funeral?'

'How frightful!' she said, dropping her hands and gazing at him. 'I was afraid of this. How frightful!'

'What?'

'You think one of us wrote the letter? Someone at Ancreton?'

'Well, really,' said Alleyn, stifling his exasperation, 'it's not a preposterous conjecture, is it?'

'No, no. I suppose not. But what a disturbing thought.'

'Well, did any of you go to London—'

'Let me think, let me think,' Desdemona muttered, again covering her eyes. 'In the evening. After we had—had—after

Papa's funeral, and after Mr Rattisbon had—' She made another little helpless gesture.

'—had read the Will?' Alleyn suggested.

'Yes. That evening, by the seven-thirty. Thomas and Jenetta (my sister-in-law) and Fenella (her daughter) and Paul (my nephew, Paul Kentish) all went up to London.'

'And returned? When?'

'Not at all. Jenetta doesn't live here and Fenella and Paul, because of—However, Fenella has joined her mother in a flat and I think Paul's staying with them. My brother Thomas, as you know, lives in London.'

'And nobody else has left Ancreton?'

Yes, it seemed that the following day Millamant and Cedric and Desdemona herself had gone up to London by the early morning train. There was a certain amount of business to be done. They returned in the evening. It was by that evening's post, the Wednesday's, Alleyn reflected, that the anonymous letter reached the Yard. He found by dint of cautious questioning that they had all separated in London and gone their several ways to meet in the evening train.

'And Miss Orrincourt?' Alleyn asked.

'I'm afraid,' said Desdemona grandly, 'that I've really no knowledge at all of Miss Orrincourt's movements. She was away all day yesterday; I imagine in London.'

'She's staying on here?'

'You may well look astonished,' said Desdemona, though Alleyn, to his belief, had looked nothing of the sort. 'After everything, Mr Alleyn. After working against us with Papa! After humiliating and wounding us in every possible way. In the teeth, you might say, of the Family's feelings, she stays on. T'uh!'

'Does Sir Cedric—?'

'Cedric,' said Desdemona, 'is now the head of the Family, but I have no hesitation in saying that I think his attitude to a good many things inexplicable and revolting. Particularly where Sonia Orrincourt (you'll never get me to believe she was born Orrincourt) is concerned. What he's up to, what both of them—However!'

Alleyn did not press for an exposition of Cedric's behaviour. At the moment he was fascinated by Desdemona's. On the wall opposite her hung a looking-glass in a Georgian frame. He saw that Desdemona was keeping an eye on herself. Even as she moved her palms from before her eyes, her fingers touched her hair and she slightly turned her head while her abstracted yet watchful gaze noted, he thought, the effect. And as often as she directed her melting glance upon him, so often did it return to the mirror to affirm with a satisfaction barely veiled its own limpid quality. He felt as if he interviewed a mannequin.

'I understand,' he said, 'that it was you who found the tin of rat-bane in Miss Orrincourt's suitcase?'

'Wasn't it awful? Well, it was three of us, actually. My sister Pauline (Mrs Kentish), my sister-in-law, and Cedric and I. In her box-room, you know. A very common-looking suitcase smothered in Number Three Company touring labels. As I've pointed out to Thomas a thousand times, the woman is simply a squalid little ham actress. Well, *not* an actress. All eyes and teeth in the third row of the chorus when she's lucky.'

'Did you yourself handle it?'

'Oh, we all handled it. Naturally. Cedric tried to prise up the lid, but it wouldn't come. So he tapped the tin, and said he could tell from the sound that it wasn't full.' She lowered her voice. '"Only half-full," he said. And Milly (my sister-in-law, Mrs Henry Ancred) said—' She paused.

'Yes?' Alleyn prompted, tired of these genealogical parentheses. 'Mrs Henry Ancred said?'

'She said that to the best of her knowledge it had never been used.' She changed her position a little and added: 'I don't understand Milly. She's so off-hand. Of course I know she's frightfully capable but—well, she's not an Ancred and doesn't feel as we do. She's—well, let's face it, she's a bit MC, do you know?'

Alleyn did not respond to this appeal from blue blood to blue blood. He said: 'Was the suitcase locked?'

'We wouldn't have broken anything open, Mr Alleyn.'

'Wouldn't you?' he said vaguely. Desdemona glanced in the mirror. 'Well—Pauline might,' she admitted after a pause.

Alleyn waited for a moment, caught Fox's eye and stood up. He said: 'Now, Miss Ancred, I wonder if we may see your father's room?'

'Papa's *room*?'

'If we may.'

'I couldn't—you won't mind if I—? I'll ask Barker—'

'If he'd just show us in the general direction we could find our own way.'

Desdemona stretched out her hands impulsively. 'You *do* understand,' she said. 'You do understand how one feels. Thank you.'

Alleyn smiled vaguely, dodged the outstretched hands and made for the door. 'Perhaps Barker,' he suggested, 'could show us the room.'

Desdemona swept to the bell-push and in a moment or two Barker came in. With enormous aplomb she explained what he was to do. She contrived to turn Barker into the very quintessence of family retainers. The atmosphere in the little sitting-room grew more and more feudal. 'These gentlemen,' she ended, 'have come to help us, Barker. We, in our turn, must help them, mustn't we? You will help them, won't you?'

'Certainly, miss,' said Barker. 'If you would come this way, sir?'

How well Troy had described the great stairs and the gallery and the yards and yards of dead canvas in heavy frames. And the smell. The Victorian smell of varnish, carpet, wax, and mysteriously, paste. A yellow smell, she had said. Here was the first long corridor, and there, branching from it, the passage to Troy's tower. This was where she had lost herself that first night and these were the rooms with their ridiculous names. On his right, *Bancroft* and *Bernhardt*; on his left, *Terry* and

Bracegirdle; then an open linen closet and bathrooms. Barker's coattails jigged steadily ahead of them. His head was stooped, and one saw only a thin fringe of grey hair and a little dandruff on his back collar. Here was the cross-corridor, corresponding with the picture gallery, and facing them a closed door, with the legend, in gothic lettering, '*Irving.*'

'This is the room, sir,' said Barker's faded and breathless voice. 'We'll go in, if you please.'

The door opened on darkness and the smell of disinfectant. A momentary fumbling, and then a bedside lamp threw a pool of light upon a table and a crimson counterpane. With a clatter of rings Barker pulled aside the window curtains and then let up the blinds.

The aspect of the room that struck Alleyn most forcibly was the extraordinary number of prints and photographs upon the walls. They were so lavishly distributed that almost all the paper, a red flock powdered with stars, was concealed by them. Next he noticed the heavy richness of the appointments; the enormous looking-glass, the brocades and velvets, the massive and forbidding furniture.

Suspended above the bed was a long cord. He saw that it ended, not in a bell-push, but in raw strands of wire.

'Will that be all, sir?' said Barker, behind them.

'Stop for a minute, will you?' Alleyn said. 'I want you to help us, Barker.'

He was indeed very old. His eyes were filmy and expressed nothing but a remote sadness. His hands seemed to have shrunk away from their own empurpled veins, and were tremulous. But all these witnesses of age were in part disguised by a lifetime's habit of attentiveness to other people's wants. There was the shadow of alacrity still about Barker.

'I don't think,' Alleyn said, 'that Miss Ancred quite explained why we are here. It's at Mr Thomas Ancred's suggestion. He wants us to make fuller inquiries into the cause of Sir Henry's death.'

'Indeed, sir?'

'Some of his family believe that the diagnosis was too hastily given.'

'Quite so, sir.'

'Had you any such misgivings yourself?'

Barker closed and unclosed his hands. 'I can't say I had, sir. Not at first.'

'Not at first?'

'Knowing what he took to eat and drink at dinner, sir, and the way he was worked up, and had been over and over again. Dr Withers had warned him of it, sir.'

'But later? After the funeral? And now?'

'I really can't say, sir. What with Mrs Kentish and Mrs Henry and Miss Desdemona asking me over and over again about a certain missing article and what with us all being very put about in the servants' hall, I can't really say.'

'A tin of rat-bane was the missing article?'

'Yes, sir. I understand they've found it now.'

'And the question they want settled is whether it was an opened or unopened tin before it was lost. Is that it?'

'I understand that's it, sir. But we've had that stuff on the premises these last ten years and more. Two tins there were, sir, in one of the outside store-rooms and there was one opened and used up and thrown out. That I do know. About this one that's turned up, I can't say. Mrs Henry Ancred recollects, sir, that it was there about a year ago, unopened, and Mrs Bullivant, the cook, says it's been partly used since then, and Mrs Henry doesn't fancy so, and that's all I can say, sir.'

'Do you know if rat poison has ever been used in Miss Orrincourt's room?'

Barker's manner became glazed with displeasure.

'Never to my knowledge, sir,' he said.

'Are there no rats there?'

'The lady in question complained of them, I understand, to one of the housemaids, who set traps and caught several. I believe the lady said she didn't fancy the idea of poison, and for that reason it was not employed.'

'I see. Now, Barker, if you will, I should like you to tell me exactly what this room looked like when you entered it on the morning after Sir Henry's death.'

Barker's sunken hand moved to his lips and covered their trembling. A film of tears spread over his eyes.

'I know it's distressing for you,' Alleyn said, 'and I'm sorry. Sit down. No, please sit down.'

Barker stooped his head a little and sat on the only high chair in the room.

'I'm sure,' Alleyn said, 'that if there was anything gravely amiss you'd want to see it remedied.'

Barker seemed to struggle between his professional reticence and his personal distress. Finally, in a sudden flood of garrulity, he produced the classical reaction: 'I wouldn't want to see this house mixed up in anything scandalous, sir. My father was butler here to the former baronet, Sir Henry's second cousin—Sir William Ancred, that was—I was knife-boy and then footman under him. He was not,' said Barker, 'anything to do with theatricals, sir, the old gentleman wasn't. This would have been a great blow to him.'

'You mean the manner of Sir Henry's death?'

'I mean'—Barker tightened his unsteady lips—'I mean the way things were conducted lately.'

'Miss Orrincourt?'

'T'uh!' said Barker, and thus established his life-long service to the Ancreds.

'Look here,' Alleyn said suddenly, 'do you know what the family have got into their heads about this business?'

There was a long pause before the old voice whispered: 'I don't like to think. I don't encourage gossip below stairs, sir, and I don't take part in it myself.'

'Well,' Alleyn suggested, 'suppose you tell me about this room.'

It was, after all, only a slow enlargement of what he had already heard. The darkened room, the figure hunched on the bed, 'as if,' Barker said fearfully, 'he'd been trying to crawl down to the floor,' the stench and disorder and the broken bell-cord.

'Where was the end?' Alleyn asked. 'The bell-push itself?'

'In his hand, sir. Tight clenched round it, his hand was. We didn't discover it at first.'

'Have you still got it?'

'It's in his dressing-table drawer, sir. I put it there, meaning to get it mended.'

'Did you unscrew it or examine it in any way?'

'Oh, no, sir. No. I just put it away and disconnected the circuit on the board.'

'Right! And now, Barker, about the night before, when Sir Henry went to bed. Did you see anything of him?'

'Oh, yes, indeed, sir. He rang for me as usual. It was midnight when the bell went, and I came up to his room. I'd valeted him, sir, since his own man left.'

'Did he ring his room bell?'

'No, sir. He always rang the bell in the hall as he went through. By the time he reached his room, you see, I had gone up the servants' stairs and was waiting for him.'

'How did he seem?'

'Terrible. In one of his tantrums and talking very wild and angry.'

'Against his family?'

'Very hot against them.'

'Go on.'

'I got him into his pyjamas and gown and him raging all the while and troubled with his indigestion pain as well. I put out the medicine he took for it. He said he wouldn't take it just then so I left the bottle and glass by his bed. I was offering to help him into bed when he says he must see Mr Rattisbon. He's the family solicitor, sir, and always comes to us for The Birthday. Well, sir, I tried to put Sir Henry off, seeing he was tired and upset, but he wouldn't hear of it. When I took him by the arm he got quite violent. I was alarmed and tried to hold him but he broke away.'

Alleyn had a sudden vision of the two old men struggling together in this grandiose bedroom.

'Seeing there was nothing for it,' Barker went on, 'I did as he ordered, and took Mr Rattisbon up to his room. He called me back and told me to find the two extra helps we always get in for The Birthday. A Mr and Mrs Candy, sir, formerly on the staff here and now in a small business in the village. I understood from what Sir Henry said that he wished them to witness his Will. I showed them up, and he then told me to inform Miss Orrincourt that he would be ready for his hot drink in half an hour. He said he would not require me again. So I left him.'

'And went to give this message?'

'After I had switched over the mechanism of his bell, sir, so that if he required anything in the night it would sound in the passage outside Mrs Henry's door. It has been specially arranged like this, in case of an emergency, and, of course, sir, it must have broke off in his hand before it sounded, because even if Mrs Henry had slept through it, Miss Dessy was sharing her room and must have heard. Miss Dessy sleeps very light, I understand.'

'Isn't it strange that he didn't call out?'

'He wouldn't be heard, sir. The walls in this part of the house are very thick, being part of the original outer walls. The previous baronet, sir, added this wing to Ancreton.'

'I see. At this time where was Miss Orrincourt?'

'She had left the company, sir. They had all moved into the drawing-room.'

'*All* of them?'

'Yes, sir. Except her and Mr Rattisbon. And Mrs Alleyn, who was a guest. They were all there. Mrs Kentish said the young lady had gone to her room and that's where I found her. Mr Rattisbon was in the hall.'

'What was the business with the hot drink?'

The old man described it carefully. Until the rise of Sonia Orrincourt, Millamant had always prepared the drink. Miss Orrincourt had taken over this routine. The milk and ingredients were left in her room by the housemaid, who turned down her bed. She brewed the drink over a heater, put it in a Thermos flask, and, half an hour after he had retired, took it to his room. He slept badly and sometimes would not drink it until much later in the night.

'What happened to the Thermos flask and the cup and saucer?'

'They were taken away and washed up, sir. They've been in use since.'

'Had he drunk any of it?'

'It had been poured into the cup, sir, at all events, and into the saucer for that cat, as was always done, and the saucer set on the floor. But the cup and the flask and the medicine bottle had been overturned and there was milk and medicine soaked into the carpet.'

'Had he taken his medicine?'

'The glass was dirty. It had fallen into the saucer.'

'And has, of course, been washed,' said Alleyn. 'What about the bottle?'

'It had been knocked over, sir, as I mentioned. It was a new bottle. I was very much put out, sir, but I tried to tidy the room a bit, not knowing exactly what I was doing. I remember I took the dirty china and the bottle and Thermos downstairs with me. The bottle was thrown out, and the other things cleared up. The medicine cupboard has been cleaned out thoroughly. It's in the bathroom, sir, through that door. The whole suite,' said Barker conscientiously, 'has been turned out and cleaned.'

Fox mumbled inarticulately.

'Well,' said Alleyn. 'To go back to the message you took to Miss Orrincourt that night. Did you actually see her?'

'No, sir. I tapped on the door and she answered.' He moved uneasily.

'Was there anything else?'

'It was a queer thing—' His voice faded.

'What was a queer thing?'

'She must have been alone,' Barker mused, 'because, as I've said, sir, the others were downstairs, and afterwards, *just* afterwards, when I took in the grog-tray, there they all were. But before I knocked on her door, sir, I could have sworn that she was laughing.'

When Barker had gone, Fox sighed gustily, put on his spectacles and looked quizzically through them at the naked end of the bell-cord.

'Yes, Br'er Fox, exactly,' said Alleyn, and went to the dressing-table. 'That'll be the lady,' he said.

A huge photograph of Sonia Orrincourt stood in the middle of the dressing-table.

Fox joined Alleyn. 'Very taking,' he said. 'Funny, you know, Mr Alleyn. That's what they call a pin-up girl. Plenty of teeth and hair and limbs. Sir Henry put it in a silver frame, but that, you might say, is the only difference. Very taking.'

Alleyn opened the top drawer on the left.

'First pop,' Fox remarked.

Alleyn pulled on a glove and gingerly took out a pear-shaped wooden bell-push. 'One takes these pathetic precautions,' he said, 'and a hell of a lot of use they are. Now then.' He unscrewed the end of the bell-push and looked into it.

'See here, Fox. Look at the two points. Nothing broken. One of the holding-screws and its washer are tight. No bits of wire. The other screw and washer are loose. Got your lens? Have a look at that cord again.'

Fox took out a pocket lens and returned to the bed. 'One of the wires is unbroken,' he said presently. 'No shiny end, and it's blackened like they do get with time. The other's different, though. Been dragged through and scraped, I'd say. That's what must have happened. He put his weight on it and they pulled through.'

'In that case,' Alleyn said, 'why is one of the screws so tight, and only one wire shiny? We'll keep this bell-push, Fox.'

He had wrapped his handkerchief round it and dropped it in his pocket, when the door was opened and Sonia Orrincourt walked in.

She was dressed in black, but so dashingly that mourning was not much suggested. Her curtain of ashen hair and her heavy fringe were glossy, her eyelids were blue, her lashes incredible and her skin sleek. She wore a diamond clasp and bracelet and ear-rings. She stood just inside the room.

'Pardon the intrusion,' she said, 'but am I addressing the police?'

'You are,' said Alleyn. 'Miss Orrincourt?'

'That's the name.'

'How do you do? This is Inspector Fox.'

'Now listen!' said Miss Orrincourt, advancing upon them with a professional gait. 'I want to know what's cooking in this icehouse. I've got my rights to look after, same as anybody else, haven't I?'

'Undoubtedly.'

'Thank you. Very kind I'm sure. Then perhaps you'll tell me who asked you into my late fiancé's room and just what you're doing now you've got there.'

'We were asked by his family and we're doing a job of work.'

'*Work?* What sort of work? Don't tell me the answer to that one,' said Miss Orrincourt angrily. 'I seem to know it. They're trying to swing something across me. Is that right? Trying to pack me up. *What is it?* That's what I want to know. Come on. *What is it?*'

'Will you first of all tell me how you knew we were here and why you thought we were police officers?'

She sat on the bed, leaning back on her hands, her hair falling vertically from her scalp. Behind her was spread the crimson counterpane. Alleyn wondered why she had ever attempted to be an actress while there were magazine artists who needed models. She looked in a leisurely manner at Fox's feet. 'How do I know you're police? That's a scream! Take a look at your boy friend's boots.'

'Yours, partner,' Alleyn murmured, catching Fox's eye.

Fox cleared his throat. 'Er—*touché*,' he said carefully. 'Not much good me trying to get by with a sharp-eyed young lady, is it, sir?'

'Well, come on,' Miss Orrincourt demanded. 'What's the big idea? Are they trying to make out there's something funny in the Will? Or what? What are you doing, opening my late fiancé's drawers? Come on!'

'I'm afraid,' said Alleyn, 'you've got this situation the wrong way round. We're on a job, and part of that job is asking questions. And since you're here, Miss Orrincourt, I wonder if you'd mind answering one or two?'

She looked at him, he thought, as an animal or a completely unselfconscious child might look at a stranger. It was difficult to expect anything but perfect sounds from her. He experienced a shock each time he heard the Cockney voice with its bronchial overtones, and the phrases whose very idiom seemed shoddy, as if she had abandoned her native dialect for something she had half-digested at the cinema.

'All upstage and county!' she said. 'Fancy! And what were you wanting to know?'

'About the Will, for instance.'

'The Will's all right,' she said quickly. 'You can turn the place inside out. Crawl up the chimney if you like. You won't find another Will. I'm telling you, and I know.'

'Why are you so positive?'

She had slipped back until she rested easily on her forearm. 'I don't mind,' she said. 'I'll tell you. When I came in here last thing that night, my fiancé showed it to me. He'd had old Rattisbon up and a couple of witnesses and he'd signed it. He showed me. The ink was still wet. He'd burnt the old one in the fireplace there.'

'I see.'

'And he couldn't have written another one even if he'd wanted to. Because he was tired and his pain was bad and he said he was going to take his medicine and go to sleep.'

'He was in bed when you visited him?'

'Yes.' She waited for a moment, looking at her enamelled fingernails. 'People seem to think I've got no feelings, but I've been very upset. Honestly. Well, he was sweet. And when a girl's going to be married and everything's marvellous it's a terrible thing for this to happen, I don't care what any one says.'

'Did he seem very ill?'

'That's what everybody keeps asking. The doctor and old Pauline and Milly. On and on. Honestly, I could scream. He just had one of his turns and he felt queer. And with the way he'd eaten and thrown a temperament on top of it, no wonder. I gave him his hot drink and kissed him nighty-nighty and he seemed all right and that's all I know.'

'He drank his hot milk while you were with him?'

She swung over a little with a luxurious movement and looked at him through narrowed eyes. 'That's right,' she said. 'Drank it and liked it.'

'And his medicine?'

'He poured that out for himself. I told him to drink up like a good boy, but he said he'd wait a bit and see if his tummy wouldn't settle down without it. So I went.'

'Right. Now, Miss Orrincourt,' said Alleyn, facing her with his hands in his pockets, 'you've been very frank. I shall follow your example. You want to know what we're doing here. I'll tell you. Our job, or a major part of it, is to find out why you played a string of rather infantile practical jokes on Sir Henry Ancred and let it be thought that his granddaughter was responsible.'

She was on her feet so quickly that he actually felt his nerves jump. She was close to him now; her under-lip jutted out and her brows, thin hairy lines, were drawn together in a scowl. She resembled some drawing in a man's magazine of an infuriated baggage in a bedroom. One almost expected some dubious caption to issue in a balloon from her lips.

'Who says I did it?' she demanded.

'I do, at the moment,' Alleyn said. 'Come now. Let's start at Mr Juniper's shop. You bought the Raspberry there, you know.'

'The dirty little so-and-so,' she said meditatively. 'What a pal! *And* what a gentleman, I don't suppose.'

Alleyn ignored these strictures upon Mr Juniper. 'Then,' he said, 'there's that business about the paint on the banisters.'

Obviously this astonished her. Her face was suddenly bereft of expression, a mask with slightly dilated eyes. 'Wait a bit,' she said. 'That's funny!'

Alleyn waited.

'Here!' she said. 'Have you been talking to young Ceddie?'

'No.'

'That's what you say,' she muttered, and turned on Fox. 'What about you, then?'

'No, Miss Orrincourt,' said Fox blandly. 'Not me or the Chief Inspector.'

'Chief Inspector?' she said. 'Coo!'

Alleyn saw that she was looking at him with a new interest and had a premonition of what was to come.

'That'd be one of the high-ups, wouldn't it? Chief Inspector who? I don't seem to have caught the name.'

Any hopes he may have entertained that his connection with Troy was unknown to her vanished when she repeated his name, clapped her hand over her mouth and ejaculating 'Coo! That's a good one,' burst into fits of uncontrollable laughter.

'Pardon me,' she said presently, 'but when you come to think of it it's funny. You can't get away from it, you know, it's funny. Seeing it was her that—Well, of course! That's how you knew about the paint on the banisters.'

'And what,' Alleyn asked, 'is the connection between Sir Cedric Ancred and the paint on the banisters?'

'I'm not going to give myself away,' said Miss Orrincourt, 'nor Ceddie either, if it comes to that. Ceddie's pretty well up the spout anyway. If he's let me down he's crazy. There's a whole lot of things I want to know first. What's all this stuff about a book? What's the idea? Is it me, or is it everybody else in this dump that's gone haywire? Look! Somebody puts a dirty little book in a cheese-dish and serves it up for lunch. And when they find it, what do these half-wits do? Look at me as if I was the original hoodunit. Well, I mean to say, it's silly. And what a book! Written by somebody with a lisp and what about? Keeping people fresh after they're dead. Give you the willies. And when I say I never put it in the cheese-dish what do they do? Pauline starts tearing herself to shreds and Dessy says, "We're not so foolish as to suppose you'd want to run your head in a noose," and Milly says she happens to know I've read it, and they all go out as if I was something the cat'd brought in, and I sit there wondering if it's me or all of them who ought to be locked up.'

'And had you ever seen the book before?'

'I seem to remember,' she began, and then looking from Alleyn to Fox with a new wariness, she said sharply: 'Not to notice. Not to know what it was about.' And after a pause she added dully: 'I'm not much of a one for reading.'

Alleyn said: 'Miss Orrincourt, will you without prejudice tell me if you personally were responsible for any of the practical jokes other than the ones already under discussion?'

'I'm not answering any questions. I don't know what's going on here. A girl's got to look after herself. I thought I had one friend in this crazy-gang, now I'm beginning to think *he's* let me down.'

'I suppose,' said Alleyn, wearily, 'you mean Sir Cedric Ancred?'

'*Sir* Cedric Ancred,' Miss Orrincourt repeated with a shrill laugh. 'The bloody little baronet. Excuse my smile, but honestly it's a scream.' She turned her back on them and walked out, leaving the door open.

They could still hear her laughing with unconvincing virtuosity as she walked away down the corridor.

'Have we,' Fox asked blandly, 'got anywhere with that young lady? Or have we not?'

'Not very far, if anywhere at all,' Alleyn said, morosely. 'I don't know about you, Fox, but I found her performance tolerably convincing. Not that impressions of that sort amount to very much. Suppose she did put arsenic in the old man's hot milk, wouldn't this be the only line she could reasonably take? And at this stage of the proceedings, when I still have a very faint hope that we may come across something that blows their damn' suspicions to smithereens, I couldn't very well insist on anything. We'll just have to go mousing along.'

'Where to?' Fox asked.

'For the moment, in different directions. I've been carrying you about like a broody hen, Foxkin, and it's time you brought forth. Down you go and exercise the famous technique on Barker and his retinue of elderly maids. Find out all about the milk, trace its whole insipid history from cow to Thermos. Inspire gossip. Prattle. Seek out the paper-dump, the bottle-dump, the mops and the pails. Let us go clanking back to London like a dry canteen. Salvage the Thermos flask. We'll have to try for an analysis but what a hope! Get along with you, Fox. Do your stuff.'

'And where may I ask, Mr Alleyn, are you going?'

'Oh,' said Alleyn, 'I'm a snob. I'm going to see the baronet.'

Fox paused at the doorway. 'Taking it by and large, sir,' he said, 'and on the face of it as it stands, do you reckon there'll be an exhumation?'

'There'll be one exhumation at all events. Tomorrow, if Dr Curtis can manage it.'

'Tomorrow!' said Fox, startled. 'Dr Curtis? Sir Henry Ancred?'

'No,' Alleyn said, 'the cat, Carabbas.'

CHAPTER THIRTEEN

Spotlight on Cedric

ALLEYN INTERVIEWED CEDRIC in the library. It was a place without character or life. Rows of uniform editions stood coldly behind glass doors. There was no smell of tobacco, or memory of fires, only the darkness of an unused room.

Cedric's manner was both effusive and uneasy. He made a little dart at Alleyn and flapped at his hand. He began at once to talk about Troy. 'She was too marvellous, a perfect darling. So thrilling to watch her at work: that *magical* directness, almost intimidating, one felt. You must be madly proud of her, of course.'

His mouth opened and shut, his teeth glinted, his pale eyes stared and his voice gabbled on and on. He was restless too, and wandered about the room aimlessly, lifting lids of empty cigarette boxes and moving ornaments. He recalled acquaintance with Alleyn's nephews, with whom, he said, he had been at school. He professed a passionate interest in

Alleyn's work. He returned again to Troy, suggesting that he alone among the Philistines had spoken her language. There was a disquieting element in all this, and Alleyn, when an opportunity came, cut across it.

'One moment,' he said. 'Our visit is an official one. I'm sure you will agree that we should keep it so. May we simply think the fact of my wife having been commissioned to paint Sir Henry a sort of freakish coincidence and nothing to do with the matter in hand? Except, of course, in so far as her job may turn out to have any bearing on the circumstances.'

Cedric's mouth had remained slightly open. He turned pink, touched his hair, and said: 'Of course if you feel like that about it. I merely thought that a friendly atmosphere—'

'That was extremely kind,' said Alleyn.

'Unless your somewhat muscular sense of the official proprieties forbids it,' Cedric suggested acidly, 'shall we at least sit down?'

'Thank you,' said Alleyn tranquilly, 'that would be much more comfortable.'

He sat in a vast armchair, crossed his knees, joined his hands, and with what Troy called his donnish manner, prepared to tackle Cedric.

'Mr Thomas Ancred tells me you share the feeling that further inquiries should be made into the circumstances of Sir Henry's death.'

'Well, I suppose I do,' Cedric agreed fretfully. 'I mean, it's all pretty vexing, isn't it? Well, I mean one would like to know. All sorts of things depend...And yet again it's not very delicious...Of course, when one considers that I'm the one who's most involved...Well, *look* at me. *Incarcerated*, in this frightful house! And the entail a pittance. All those taxes too, and *rapacious* death duties. Never, never will anybody be found mad enough to rent it, and as for schools, Carol Able does nothing but exclaim how inconvenient and how damp. And now the war's over the problem children will be hurried away. One will be left to wander in rags down whispering corridors. So that you see,' he added, waving his hands, 'one does rather wonder—'

'Quite so.'

'And they *will* keep talking about me as Head of the Family. Before I know where I am I shall have turned into another Old Person.'

'There are one or two points,' Alleyn began, and immediately Cedric leant forward with an ineffable air of concentration, 'that we'd like to clear up. The first is the authorship of these anonymous letters.'

'Well, I didn't write them.'

'Have you any idea who did?'

'Personally I favour my Aunt Pauline.'

'Really? Why?'

'She prefaces almost every remark she makes with the phrase: "I have reason to believe."'

'Have you asked Mrs Kentish if she wrote the letters?'

'Yes, indeed. She denies it hotly. Then there's Aunt Dessy. Quite capable, in a way, but more likely, one would have thought, to tell us flatly what she suspected. I mean, why go in for all this hush-hush letter-writing? That leaves my cousins Paul and Fenella, who are, one imagines, too pleasurably engrossed in their amorous martyrdom for any outside activities; my Mama, who is much too common-sensical; my aunt-in-law, Jenetta, who is too grand; and all the servants led by the Ancient of Days. That, as they say in sporting circles, is the field. Unless you feel inclined to take in the squire and the parson and dear old Rattlebones himself. It couldn't be more baffling. No, on the whole I plump for Pauline. She's about somewhere. Have you encountered her? Since the Tragedy she is almost indistinguishable from Lady Macduff. Or perhaps that frightful Shakespearian dowager who curses her way up hill and down dale through one of the historical dramas. Constance? Yes, Pauline is now all compact of tragedy. Dessy's pretty bad, but wait till you meet Pauline.'

'Do you know if there's any paper in the house of the kind used for these letters?'

'Gracious, no! Exercise-book paper! The servants wouldn't have had it at any price. By the way, talking of exercise books, *do* you think Caroline Able might have done it? I mean, she's so wrapped up in id and isms and tracing everything back to the Oedipus Complex. Might it perhaps have all snapped back at her and made her a weeny bit odd? It's only an idea, of course. I merely throw it out for what it's worth.'

'About this tin of rat-bane,' Alleyn began. Cedric interrupted him with a shrill cry.

'My dear, what a party! Imagine! Milly, the complete hausfrau (my mama, you know)'—Cedric added the inevitable parentheses—'and Dessy steaming up the stairs and Pauline tramping at her heels like one of the Fates, and poor little me panting in the rear. We didn't know what we were looking for, really. Partly rat poison and partly they thought there might be compromising papers somewhere because Sonia's quite lovely, don't you think, and *really*—the Old Person! *Hardly* adequate, one couldn't help feeling. I pointed out that, constant or flighty, a Will was a Will, but nothing would stay them. I said in fun: "You don't expect, darlings, to find phials of poison in her luggage, do you?" and that put the idea of luggage into their heads. So up into the box-room they hounded me, and there, to use the language of the chase, we "found."'

'You yourself took the tin out of the suitcase?'

'Yes, indeed. I was petrified.'

'What was it like?'

'Like? But didn't dear Uncle Tom give it to you?'

'Was it clean or dirty?'

'My dear, *filthy*. They wanted me to prise open the lid, and such a struggle as I had. Little bits of rat-bane flying up and hitting me. I was terrified. And then it wouldn't come out.'

'Who first suggested this search?'

'Now, that *is* difficult. Did we, thinking of that beastly little brochure in the cheese-dish (and there, I must tell you, I see the hand of Panty), did we with one accord cry: "rat-bane" and let loose the dogs of war? I fancy Pauline, after coining the phrase "no smoke" (or is it "reek"?) "without heat," said: "But where would she get any arsenic?" and that Milly (my Mama), or it might have been me, remembered the missing rat-bane. Anyway, no sooner was it mentioned than Pauline and Dessy were in full cry for the guilty apartment. If you could see it, too. Darling Sonia! Well, "darling" with reservations. The bed-chamber a welter of piercing pink frills and tortured satin and dolls peering from behind cushions or squatting on telephones, do you know?'

'I would be very glad,' said Alleyn, 'if the suitcase could be produced.'

'Really? You wish, no doubt, to explore it for fingerprints? But of course you shall have it. Unbeknown, I suppose, to darling Sonia?'

'If possible.'

'I'll trip upstairs and get it myself. If she's there, I'll tell her there's a telephone call.'

'Thank you.'

'Shall I go now?'

'One moment, Sir Cedric,' Alleyn began, and again Cedric, with that winsome trick of anxiety, leant towards him. 'Why did you, with Miss Sonia Orrincourt, plan a series of practical jokes on your grandfather?'

It was not pleasant to watch the blood sink from Cedric's face. The process left his eyelids and the pouches under his eyes mauvish. Small grooves appeared beside his nostrils. His colourless lips pouted and then widened into an unlovely smile.

'Well, really!' he tittered. 'That just shows you, doesn't it? So darling Sonia has confided in you.' And after a moment's hesitation he added: 'As far as I'm concerned, dear Mr Alleyn, that's the end of darling Sonia.'

❀ ❀ ❀

'Perhaps I should explain,' Alleyn said after a pause, 'that Miss Orrincourt has not made any statement about the practical jokes.'

'She *hasn't?*' The ejaculation was so incisive that it was difficult to believe Cedric had uttered it. He now lowered his head and appeared to look at the carpet between his feet. Alleyn saw his hands slide over each other. 'How perfectly futile,' Cedric's voice said. 'Such a *very* old gag. Such an ancient wheeze! I didn't know but you've just told me! And in I go, as they say, boots and all.' He raised his face. Its pinkness had returned and its expression suggested a kind of boyish ruefulness. 'Now *do* promise you won't be lividly angry. It sounds too childish, I know. But I implore you, dear Mr Alleyn, to look about you. Observe the peculiar flavour of Katzenjammer Castle. The façade now. The utterly unnerving inequalities of the façade. The terrifying Victoriana within. The gloom. Note particularly the gloom.'

'I'm afraid,' Alleyn said, 'that I don't follow this. Unless you're going to tell me you hoped to enliven the architecture and decor of Ancreton by painting spectacles and flying cows on your grandfather's portrait.'

'But I didn't!' Cedric protested shrilly. 'That *miraculous* portrait! No, believe me, I didn't.'

'And the paint on the banister?'

'I didn't do that either. Darling Mrs Alleyn! I wouldn't have dreamed of it.'

'But at least you seem to have known about it.'

'I didn't do it,' he repeated.

'The message written in grease-paint on the mirror? And the grease-paint on the cat?'

Cedric gave a nervous giggle. 'Well—'

'Come,' said Alleyn. 'You had dark red grease-paint under your finger-nail, you know.'

'*What* sharp eyes!' cried Cedric. 'Dearest Mrs Alleyn! *Such* a help she must be to you.'

'You did, in fact—'

'The Old Person,' Cedric interrupted, 'had been particularly rococo. I couldn't resist. The cat, too. It was a kind of practical pun. The cat's whiskers!'

'And had you anything to do with the squeaking cushion in his chair?'

'Wasn't it too robust and Rabelaisian? Sonia bought it and I—I can't deny it—I placed it there. But why not? If I might make a tiny squeak of protest, dear Mr Alleyn, *has* all this got *anything* to do with the business in hand?'

'I think it might well have been designed to influence Sir Henry's Will, and with both his Wills we are, as I think you'll agree, very definitely concerned.'

'This is too subtle for my poor wits, I'm afraid.'

'It was common knowledge, wasn't it, that his youngest granddaughter was, at this time, his principal heir?'

'But one never knew. We bounced in and out of favour from day to day.'

'If this is true, wouldn't these tricks, if attributed to her, very much affect her position?' Alleyn waited but was given no answer. 'Why, in fact, did you allow him to believe she was the culprit?'

'That devilish child,' Cedric said, 'gets away with innumerable hideous offences. A sense of injured innocence must have been quite a change for her.'

'You see,' Alleyn went on steadily, 'the flying cow was the last trick of five, and, as far as we know, was the final reason for Sir Henry's changing his Will that night. It was fairly conclusively proved to him that Panty did not do it, and it's possible that Sir Henry, not knowing which of his family to suspect, took his revenge on all.'

'Yes, but—'

'Now whoever was a party to these tricks—'

'At least you'll admit that I wouldn't be very likely to try and cut myself out of the Will—'

'I think that result was unforeseen. You hoped, perhaps, to return to your former position with Panty out of the picture. To something, in fact, on the lines of the Will read at the dinner party, but rather better. You have told me that you and Miss Orrincourt were partners in one of these practical jokes. Indeed you've suggested to me that you at least had knowledge of them all.'

Cedric began to speak very rapidly. 'I resent all this talk of partnership. I resent the implication and deny it. You force me into an intolerable position with your hints and mysteries. I suppose there's nothing left but for me to admit I knew what she was doing and why she did it. It amused me and it enlivened the ghastly boredom of these wretched festivities. Panty I consider an abomination, and I don't in the least regret that she was suspected or that she was cut out of the Will. She probably wallowed in her borrowed glory. There!'

'Thank you,' said Alleyn. 'That clears up quite a lot of the fog. And now, Sir Cedric, are you quite sure you don't know who wrote the letters?'

'Absolutely.'

'And are you equally sure you didn't put the book on embalming in the cheese-dish?'

Cedric gaped at him. 'I?' he said. 'Why should I? Oh, no! I don't want Sonia to turn out to be a murderess. Or I didn't, then. I'd rather thought…I…I…we'd…it doesn't matter. But I must say I'd like to *know*.'

Looking at him, Alleyn was visited by a notion so extravagant that he found himself incapable of pressing Cedric any further on the subject of his relationship with Miss Orrincourt.

He was, in any case, prevented from doing so by the entrance of Pauline Kentish.

Pauline entered weeping: not loudly, but with the suggestion of welling tears held bravely back. She seemed to Alleyn to be an older and woollier version of her sister, Desdemona. She took the uncomfortable line of expressing thankfulness that Alleyn was his wife's husband. 'Like having a *friend* to help us.'

Italicized words and even phrases surged about in her conversation. There was much talk of Panty. Alleyn had been so kind, the child had taken a tremendous fancy to him. 'And I always think,' Pauline said, gazing at him, 'that they KNOW.' From here they were soon involved in Panty's misdoings. Pauline, if he had now wanted them, supplied good enough alibis for the practical jokes. 'How could she when the poor child was being watched; closely, anxiously watched? Dr Withers had given explicit orders.'

'And much good they've done, by the way!' Cedric interrupted. 'Look at Panty!'

'Dr Withers is extremely clever, Cedric. It's not his fault if Juniper's drugs have deteriorated. Your grandfather's medicines were always a great help to him.'

'Including rat-bane?'

'That,' said Pauline in her deepest voice, 'was not prescribed, Cedric, by Dr Withers.'

Cedric giggled.

Pauline ignored him and turned appealingly to Alleyn. 'Mr Alleyn, what are we to think? Isn't it all too tragically dreadful? The suspense! The haunting suspicion! The feeling that here in our midst...! What are we to do?'

Alleyn asked her about the events following Sir Henry's exit from the little theatre on the night of his death. It appeared that Pauline herself had led the way to the drawing-room, leaving Troy, Paul and Fenella behind. Miss Orrincourt had only remained a very short time in the drawing-room where, Alleyn gathered, a lively discussion had taken place as to the authorship of the flying cow. To this family wrangle the three guests had listened uncomfortably until Barker arrived, with Sir Henry's summons for Mr Rattisbon. The squire and the rector seized upon this opportunity to make their escape. Paul and Fenella came in on their way to bed. Troy had already gone upstairs. After a little more desultory haggling the Birthday party broke up.

Pauline, Millamant and Desdemona had forgathered in Pauline's room, *Bernhardt*, and had talked exhaustively. They went together to the bathrooms at the end of the passage and encountered Mr Rattisbon, who had evidently come out of Sir Henry's rooms. Alleyn, who knew him, guessed that Mr Rattisbon, skipped, with late Victorian coyness, past the three ladies in their dressing-gowns and hurriedly down the passage to his own wing. The ladies performed their nightly rites together and together returned to their adjacent rooms. At this juncture Pauline began to look martyred.

'Originally,' she said, '*Bernhardt* and *Bancroft* were one large room, a nursery, I think. The wall between is the merest partition. Milly and Dessy shared *Bancroft*. Of course, I know there was a great deal to be talked about and for a time I joined in. Milly's bed was just through the wall from mine, and Dessy's quite close. But it had been a long day and one was *exhausted*. They went on and on. I became quite frantic with sleeplessness. Really it *was* thoughtless.'

'Dearest Aunt Pauline, why didn't you beat on the wall and scream at them?' Cedric asked, with some show of interest.

'I wasn't going to do that,' Pauline rejoined with grandeur and immediately contradicted herself. 'As a matter of fact I did at last tap. I said wasn't it getting rather late. Dessy asked what time it was, and Milly said it couldn't be more than one. There was quite an argument, and at last Dessy said: "Well, if you're so certain, Pauline, look at your watch and see." And in the end I did, and it was five minutes to three. So at last they stopped and then it was only to snore. Your mother snores, Cedric.'

'I'm so sorry.'

'And to *think* that only a little way away, while Dessy and Milly gossiped and snored, a frightful tragedy was being enacted. To think that if only I had obeyed my instinct to go to Papa and tell him—'

'To tell him what, Aunt Pauline?'

Pauline shook her head slowly from side to side and boggled a little. 'Everything was so sad and dreadful. One seemed to see him rushing to his doom.'

'One also saw Paul and Panty rushing to theirs, didn't one?' Cedric put in. 'You could have pleaded with him for them perhaps?'

'I cannot expect, Cedric, that you would understand or sympathize with disinterested impulses.'

'No,' Cedric agreed with perfect candour. 'I don't think they exist.'

'T'uh!'

'And if Mr Alleyn has no further absorbing questions to ask me I think I should like to leave the library. I find the atmosphere of unread silent friends in half-morocco exceedingly gloomy. Mr Alleyn?'

'No, thank you, Sir Cedric,' Alleyn said cheerfully. 'No more questions. If I may go ahead with my job?'

'Oh, do. Please consider this house your own. Perhaps you would like to buy it. In any case I do hope you'll stay to dinner. And your own particular silent friend. What is his name?'

'Thank you so much, but Fox and I,' Alleyn said, 'are dining out.'

'Then in that case,' Cedric murmured, sidling towards the door, 'I shall leave Aunt Pauline to divert you with tales of Panty's innocence in the matter of cheese-dishes, and her own incapability of writing anonymous letters.'

He was prevented from getting to the door by Pauline. With a movement of whose swiftness Alleyn would have thought her incapable, she got there first, and there she stood in a splendid attitude, the palms of her hands against the door, her head thrown back. 'Wait!' she said breathlessly. 'Wait!'

Cedric turned with a smile to Alleyn. 'As I hinted,' he said, 'Lady Macduff. With all her pretty chickens concentrated in the persons of Panty and Paul. The hen (or isn't it oddly enough "dam"?) at bay.'

'Mr Alleyn,' said Pauline, 'I was going to say nothing of this to anybody. We are an ancient family—'

'On my knees,' said Cedric, 'on my knees, Aunt Pauline, not the Sieur d'Ancred.'

'—and perhaps wrongly, we take some pride in our antiquity. Until today no breath of dishonour has ever smirched our name. Cedric is now Head of the Family. For that reason and for the sake of my father's memory I would have spared him. But now, when he does nothing but hurt and insult me and try to throw suspicion on my child, now when I have no one to protect me—' Pauline stopped as if for some important peroration. But something happened to her. Her face crinkled and reminded Alleyn instantly of her daughter's. Tears gathered in her eyes. 'I have reason to believe,' she began and stopped short, looking terrified. 'I don't care,' she said, and her voice cracked piteously. 'I never could bear people to be unkind to me.' She nodded her head at Cedric. 'Ask him,' she said, 'what he was doing in Sonia Orrincourt's rooms that night. Ask him.'

She burst into tears and stumbled out of the room.

'Oh, *bloody* hell!' Cedric ejaculated shrilly and darted after her.

Alleyn, left alone, whistled disconsolately, and after wandering about the cold and darkening room went to the windows and there made a series of notes in his pocket-book. He was still at this employment when Fox came in.

'They said I'd find you here,' Fox said. 'Have you done any good, Mr Alleyn?'

'If stirring up a hive and finding foul-brood can be called good. What about you?'

'I've got the medicine bottle and three of the envelopes. I've had a cup of tea in Mr Barker's room.'

'That's more than I've had in the library.'

'The cook and the maids came in and we had quite a nice little chat. Elderly party, it was. Mary, Isabel and Muriel, the maids are. The cook's Mrs Bullivant.'

'And what did you and Mary, Isabel and Muriel talk about?'

'We passed the time of day and listened to the wireless. Mrs Bullivant showed me photographs of her nephews in the fighting forces.'

'Come *on*, Fox,' said Alleyn, grinning.

'By gradual degrees,' said Fox, enjoying himself, 'we got round to the late baronet. He must have been a card, the late old gentleman.'

'I believe you.'

'Yes. The maids wouldn't say much while Mr Barker was there, but he went out after a bit and then it was, as you might say, plain sailing.'

'You and your methods!'

'Well, we were quite cosy. Naturally, they were dead against Miss Orrincourt, except Isabel, and she said you couldn't blame the old gentleman for wanting a change from his family. It came as a bit of a surprise from Isabel, who's the oldest of the maids, I should say. She's the one who looks after Miss Orrincourt's rooms, and it seems Miss Orrincourt got quite friendly with her. Indiscreet, really, but you know the type.'

'It's evident, at least, that you do.'

'They seemed to be as thick as thieves, Miss O. and Isabel, and yet, you know, Isabel didn't mind repeating most of it. The garrulous sort, she is, and Mrs Bullivant egging her on.'

'Did you get anywhere with the history of the milk?'

'Isabel took it out of a jug in the refrigerator and left it in Miss Orrincourt's room. The rest of the milk in the jug was used for general purposes next day. Miss O. was in her room and undressing when Isabel brought it. It couldn't have been more than ten minutes or so later that Miss O. took it to the old gentleman. It was heated by Isabel in the kitchen and some patent food put in. The old gentleman fancied Miss O. did it, and said nobody else could make it to suit him. It was quite a joke between Isabel and Miss O.'

'So there's no chance of anybody having got at it?'

'Only if they doped the tin of patent food, and I've got that.'

'Good.'

'And I don't know if you're thinking she might have tampered with the medicine, sir, but it doesn't seem likely. The old gentleman never let anybody touch the bottle on account of Miss Desdemona Ancred having once given him embrocation in error. It was a new bottle, Isabel says, I've got it from the dump. Cork gone, but there's enough left for analysis.'

'Another job for Dr Curtis. What about the Thermos?'

'Nicely washed and sterilized and put away. I've taken it, but there's not a chance.'

'And the same goes, I imagine, for the pails and cloths?'

'The pails are no good, but I found some tag-ends of rag.'

'Where have you put these delicious exhibits?'

'Isabel,' said Fox primly, 'hunted out a case. I told her I had to buy pyjamas in the village, being obliged unexpectedly to stay the night, and I mentioned that a man doesn't like to be seen carrying parcels. I've promised to return it.'

'Didn't they spot you were taking these things?'

'Only the patent food. I let on that the police were a bit suspicious about the makers and it might have disagreed. I dare say they didn't believe me. Owing to the behaviour of the family I think they know what's up.'

'They'd be pretty dumb if they didn't.'

'Two other points came out that might be useful,' said Fox.

Alleyn had a clear picture of the tea-party. Fox, no doubt, had sipped and complimented, had joked and sympathized, had scarcely asked a question, yet had continually received answers. He was a past master at the game. He indulged his hostesses with a few innocuous hints and was rewarded with a spate of gossip.

'It seems, Mr Alleyn, that the young lady was, as Isabel put it, leading Sir Henry on and no more.'

'D'you mean—'

'Relationship,' said Fox sedately, 'according to Isabel, had not taken place. It was matrimony or nothing.'

'I see.'

'Isabel reckons that before this business with the letters came out, there was quite an understanding between Miss O. and Sir Cedric.'

'What sort of understanding, in the name of decency?'

'Well, sir, from hints Miss O. dropped, Isabel works it out that after a discreet time had elapsed Miss O. would have turned into Lady A. after all. So that what she lost on the swings she would, in a manner of speaking, have picked up on the roundabouts.'

'Good Lord!' said Alleyn. ' "What a piece of work is man!" That, if it's true, would explain quite a number of the young and unlovely baronet's antics.'

'Supposing Miss Orrincourt did monkey with the Thermos, Mr Alleyn, we might have to consider whether Sir Cedric knew what she was up to.'

'We might indeed.'

'I know it's silly,' Fox went on, rubbing his nose, 'but when a case gets to this stage I always seem to get round to asking myself whether such-and-such a character is a likely type for homicide. I know it's silly, because there isn't a type, but I ask myself the question just the same.'

'And at the moment you ask it about Sonia Orrincourt?'

'That's right, sir.'

'I don't see why you shouldn't. It's quite true, that beyond the quality of conceit, nobody's found a nice handy trait common to all murderers. But I'm not so sure that you should sniff at yourself for saying: "That man or woman seems to me to have characteristics that are inconceivable in a murderer!" They needn't be admirable characteristics either.'

'D'you remember what Mr Barker said about the rats in Miss Orrincourt's rooms?'

'I do.'

'He mentioned that Miss Orrincourt was quite put-about by the idea of using poison, and refused to have it at any price.

Now, sir, would a young woman who was at least, as you might say, toying with the idea of poison, behave like that? Would she? She wouldn't do it by accident. She might do it to suggest she had a dread of poison, though that'd be a very far-fetched kind of notion too. And would she have owned up as readily to those practical jokes? Mind, you caught her nicely, but she gave me the impression she was upset more on account of being found out for these pranks themselves than because she thought they'd lead us to suspect something else.'

'She was more worried about the Will than anything else,' Alleyn said. 'She and Master Cedric planned those damned stunts with the object of setting the old man against Panty. I fancy she was responsible for the portrait vandalism, Cedric having possibly told her to confine her daubs to dry canvas. We know she bought the Raspberry, and he admits he placed it. I *think* she started the ball rolling by painting the banister. They plotted the whole thing together. He practically admitted as much. Now, all that worries her may be merely an idea that the publication of these goings-on could upset the Will.'

'And yet—'

'I know. I know. That damn bell-push. All right, Fox. Good work. And now, I suppose, we'd better see Mrs Henry Ancred.'

Millamant was at least a change from her relations-by-marriage in that she was not histrionic, answered his questions directly, and stuck to the point. She received them in the drawing-room. In her sensible blouse and skirt she was an incongruous figure there. While she talked she stitched that same hideously involved piece of embroidery which Troy had noticed with horror and which Panty had been accused of unpicking. Alleyn heard nothing either to contradict or greatly to substantiate the evidence they had already collected.

'I wish,' he said, after a minute or two, 'that you would tell me your own opinion about this business.'

'About my father-in-law's death? I thought at first that he died as a result of his dinner and his temperament.'

'And what did you think when these letters arrived?'

'I didn't know what to think. I don't now. And I must say that with everybody so excited and foolish about it one can't think very clearly.'

'About the book that turned up in the cheese-dish...' he began.

Millamant jerked her head in the direction of the glass case. 'It's over there. Someone replaced it.'

He walked over to the case and raised the lid. 'If you don't mind, I'll take charge of it presently. You saw her reading it?'

'Looking at it. It was one evening before dinner. Some weeks ago, I think.'

'Can you describe her position and behaviour? Was she alone?'

'Yes. I came in and she was standing as you are now, with the lid open. She seemed to be turning over the leaves of the book as it lay there. When she saw me she let the lid fall. I was afraid it might have smashed, but it hadn't.'

Alleyn moved away to the cold hearth, his hands in his pockets, 'I wonder,' said Milly, 'if you'd mind putting a match to the fire. We light it at four-thirty, always.'

Glad of the fire, for the crimson and white room was piercingly cold, and faintly amused by her air of domesticity, he did as she asked. She moved, with her embroidery, to a chair before the hearth. Alleyn and Fox sat one on each side of her.

'Mrs Ancred,' Alleyn said, 'do you think any one in the house knew about this second Will?'

'She knew. She says he showed it to her that night.'

'Apart from Miss Orrincourt?'

'They were all afraid he might do something of the sort. He was always changing his Will. But I don't think any of them knew he'd done it.'

'I wondered if Sir Cedric—'

The impression that with Millamant all would be plain speaking was immediately dispelled. Her short hands closed on her work like traps. She said harshly: 'My son knew nothing about it. Nothing.'

'I thought that as Sir Henry's successor —'

'If he had known he would have told me. He knew nothing. It was a great shock to both of us. My son,' Millamant added, looking straight before her, 'tells me everything—everything.'

'Splendid,' murmured Alleyn after a pause. Her truculent silence appeared to demand comment. 'It's only that I should like to know whether this second Will was made that night when Sir Henry went to his room. Mr Rattisbon, of course, can tell us.'

'I suppose so,' said Millamant, selecting a strand of mustard-coloured silk.

'Who discovered the writing on Sir Henry's looking-glass?'

'I did. I'd gone in to see that his room was properly done. He was very particular and the maids are old and forget things. I saw it at once. Before I could wipe it away he came in. I don't think,' she said meditatively, 'that I'd ever before seen him so angry. For a moment he actually thought I'd done it, and then, of course, he realized it was Panty.'

'It was not Panty,' Alleyn said.

He and Fox had once agreed that if, after twenty years of experience, an investigating officer has learned to recognize any one manifestation, it is that of genuine astonishment. He recognized it now in Millamant Ancred.

'What are you suggesting?' she said at last. 'Do you mean—?'

'Sir Cedric has told me he was involved in one of the other practical jokes that were played on Sir Henry, and knew about all of them. He's responsible for this one.'

She took up her embroidery again. 'He's trying to shield somebody,' she said. 'Panty, I suppose.'

'I think not.'

'It was very naughty of him,' she said in her dull voice. 'If he played one of these jokes, and I don't believe he did, it was naughty. But I can't see—I may be very stupid, but I can't see why you, Mr Alleyn, should concern yourself with any of these rather foolish tricks.'

'Believe me, we shouldn't do so if we thought they were irrelevant.'

'No doubt,' she said, and after a pause, 'you've been influenced by your wife. She would have it that Panty was all innocence.'

'I'm influenced,' Alleyn said, 'by what Sir Cedric and Miss Orrincourt have told me.'

She turned to look at him, moving her torso stiffly. For the first time her alarm, if she felt alarm, coloured her voice. 'Cedric? And that woman? Why do you speak of them together like that?'

'It appears that they planned the practical jokes together.'

'I don't believe it. She's told you that. I can see it now,' said Millamant on a rising note. 'I've been a fool.'

'What can you see, Mrs Ancred?'

'She planned it all. Of course she did. She knew Panty was his favourite. She planned it, and when he'd altered the Will she killed him. She's trying to drag my boy down with her. I've watched her. She's a diabolical, scheming woman, and she's trying to entrap my boy. He's generous and unsuspecting and kind. He's been too kind. He's at her mercy,' Millamant cried sharply and twisted her hands together.

Confronted by this violence and with the memory of Cedric fresh in his mind, Alleyn was hard put to it to answer her. Before he could frame a sentence she had recovered something of her composure. 'That settles it,' she said woodenly. 'I've kept out of all this, as far as one can keep out of their perpetual scenes and idiotic chattering. I've thought all along that they were probably right but I left it to them. I've even felt sorry for her. Now I hope she suffers. If I can tell you anything that will help you, I'll do so. Gladly.'

'Oh, damn!' thought Alleyn. 'Oh, Freud! Oh, hell!' And he said: 'There may still be no case, you know. Have you any theory as to the writer of the anonymous letters?'

'Certainly,' she said with unexpected alacrity.

'You have?'

'They're written on the paper those children use for their work. She asked me some time ago to re-order it for them when I was in the village. I recognized it at once. Caroline Able wrote the letters.'

And while Alleyn was still digesting this, she added: 'Or Thomas. They're very thick. He spent half his time in the school wing.'

CHAPTER FOURTEEN

Psychiatry and a Churchyard

THERE WAS SOMETHING firmly coarse about Milly
Ancred. After performances by Pauline, Desdemona and
Cedric, this quality was inescapable. It was incorporate in her
solid body, her short hands, the dullness of her voice and her
choice of phrase. Alleyn wondered if the late Henry Irving
Ancred, surfeited with ancestry, fine feeling and sensibility,
had chosen his wife for her lack of these qualities—for her
normality. Yet was Milly, with her adoration of an impossible
son, normal?

'But there is no norm,' he thought, 'in human behaviour;
who should know this better than Fox and I?'

He began to ask her routine questions, the set of questions that crop up in every case and of which the investigating
officer grows tired. The history of the hot drink was traced
again with no amendments, but with clear evidence that Milly
had resented her dethronement in favour of Miss Orrincourt.
He went on to the medicine. It was a fresh bottle. Dr Withers

had suggested an alteration and had left the prescription at the chemist. Miss Orrincourt had picked it up at Mr Juniper's on the day she collected the children's medicine, and Milly herself had sent Isabel with it to Sir Henry's room. He was only to use it in the event of a severe attack, and until that night had not done so.

'She wouldn't put it in that,' said Milly. 'She wouldn't be sure of his taking a dose. He hated taking medicine and only used it when he was really very bad. It doesn't seem to have been much good, anyway. I've no faith in Dr Withers.'

'No?'

'I think he's careless. I thought at the time he ought to have asked more questions about my father-in-law's death. He's too much wrapped up in his horse racing and bridge and not interested enough in his patients. However,' she added, with a short laugh, 'my father-in-law liked him well enough to leave more to him than to some of his own flesh and blood.'

'About the medicine,' Alleyn prompted.

'She wouldn't have interfered with it. Why should she use it when she had the Thermos in her own hands?'

'Have you any idea where she could have found the tin of rat-bane?'

'She complained of rats when she first came here. I asked Barker to set poison and told him there was a tin in the storeroom. She made a great outcry and said she had a horror of poison.'

Alleyn glanced at Fox, who instantly looked extremely bland.

'So,' Milly went on, 'I told Barker to set traps. When we wanted rat-bane, weeks afterwards, for *Bracegirdle*, the tin had gone. It was an unopened tin, to the best of my knowledge. It had been in the store-room for years.'

'It must have been an old brand,' Alleyn agreed. 'I don't think arsenical rat-bane is much used nowadays.'

He stood up and Fox rose with him. 'I think that's all,' he said. 'No,' said Millamant strongly, 'it's not all. I want to know what the woman has said about my son.'

'She suggested they were partners in the practical jokes and he admitted it.'

'I warn you,' she said, and for the first time her voice was unsteady. 'I warn you, she's trying to victimize him. She's worked on his kindness and good nature and his love of fun. I warn you—'

The door at the far end of the room opened and Cedric looked in. His mother's back was turned to him, and, unconscious of his presence, she went on talking. Her shaking voice repeated over and over again that he had been victimized. Cedric's gaze moved from her to Alleyn, who was watching him. He sketched a brief grimace, deprecating, rueful, but his lips were colourless and the effect was of a distortion. He came in and shut the door with great delicacy. He carried a much be-labelled suitcase, presumably Miss Orrincourt's, which, after a further grimace at Alleyn, he placed behind a chair. He then minced across the carpet.

'Darling Milly,' he said, and his hands closed on his mother's shoulders. She gave a startled cry. 'There now! I made you jump. So sorry.'

Millamant covered his hands with her own. He waited for a moment, submissive to her restless and possessive touch. 'What is it, Milly?' he asked. 'Who's been victimizing little Me? Is it Sonia?'

'Ceddie?'

'I've been such a goose, you can't think. I've come to "fess up," like a good boy,' he said nauseatingly, and slid round to his familiar position on the floor, leaning against her knees. She held him there, strongly.

'Mr Alleyn,' Cedric began, opening his eyes very wide, 'I couldn't be more sorry about rushing away just now after Aunt Pauline. Really, it was too stupid. But one does like to tell people things in one's own way, and there she was, huffing and puffing and going on as if I'd been trying to conceal some dire skeleton in my, I assure you, too drearily barren cupboard.'

Alleyn waited.

'You see—(Milly, my sweet, this is going to be a faint shock to you, but never mind)—you see, Mr Alleyn, there's been a—what shall I call it?—a—well, an *understanding*, of sorts, between Sonia and me. It only really developed quite lately. After dearest Mrs Alleyn came here. She seems to have noticed quite a number of things; perhaps she noticed that.'

'If I understand you,' Alleyn said, 'she, I am sure, did not.'

'Really?'

'Are you trying to tell me why you visited Miss Orrincourt's rooms on the night of your grandfather's death?'

'Well,' Cedric muttered petulantly, 'after Aunt Pauline's announcement—and, by the way, she gleaned her information through a nocturnal visit to the *archaic* offices at the end of the passage—after that there seems to be nothing for it but an elaborate cleaning of the breast, does there?'

'Cedric,' Millamant said, 'what has this woman done to you?'

'My sweet, nothing, thank God. I'm trying to tell you. She really is too beautiful, Mr Alleyn, don't you think? I know you didn't like her, Milly dear, and how right you seem to have been. But I really was quite intrigued and she was so bored and it was only the teeniest flutter, truly. I merely popped in on my way to bed and had a good giggle with her about the *frightful* doings down below.'

'Incidentally,' Alleyn suggested, 'you may have hoped to hear the latest news about Sir Henry's Will.'

'Well, that among other things. You see, I did rather wonder if the flying cow hadn't been sort of once too often, as it were. Sonia did it before dinner, you know. And then at the dinner the Old Person announced a Will that was really quite satisfactory from both our points of view, and with the insufferable Panty not even a starter, one rather wished Sonia had left well alone.'

'Cedric,' said his mother suddenly, 'I don't think, dear, you should go on. Mr Alleyn won't understand. Stop.'

'But, Milly, my sweet, don't you see dear old Pauline has already planted a horrid little seed of suspicion, and one simply must tweak it up before it sprouts. Mustn't one, Mr Alleyn?'

'I think,' Alleyn said, 'you'll be well advised to make a complete statement.'

'There! Now, where was I? Oh, yes. Now, all would have been well if Carol Able, who is so scientific and "un-thing" that she's a sort of monster, hadn't made out a water-tight alibi for that septic child. This, of course, turned the Old Person's suspicious glare upon all of us equally, and so he wrote the second Will and so we were all done in the eye except Sonia. And to be *quite* frank, Milly and Mr Alleyn, I should so like to have it settled whether she's a murderess or not, rather quickly.'

'Of course she is,' Millamant said.

'Yes, but are you *positive*? It really is of mountainous significance for me.'

'What do you mean, Cedric? I don't understand—'

'Well—well, never mind.'

'I think I know what Sir Cedric means,' Alleyn said. 'Isn't it a question of marriage at some time in the future with Miss Orrincourt?'

Millamant, with a tightening of her hold on Cedric's shoulder, said, 'No!' loudly and flatly.

'Oh, Milly darling,' he protested, wriggling under her hand, 'please let's be civilized.'

'It's all nonsense,' she said. 'Tell him it's all nonsense. A disgusting idea! Tell him.'

'What's the use when Sonia will certainly tell him something else.' He appealed to Alleyn. 'You do understand, don't you? I mean, one can't deny she's decorative and in a way it would have been quite fun. Don't you think it would have worked, Mr Alleyn? I do.'

His mother again began to protest. He freed himself with ugly petulance and scrambled to his feet. 'You're idiotic, Milly. What's the good of hiding things.'

'You'll do yourself harm.'

'What harm? I'm in the same position, after all, as you. I don't know the truth about Sonia but I want to find out.' He turned to Alleyn with a smile. 'When I saw her that night she told me about the new Will. I knew then that if he died I'd be practically ruined. There's no collaboration where I'm concerned, Mr Alleyn. I didn't murder the Old Person. *Pas si bête!*"

'"*Pas si bête*,"' Fox quoted as they made their way to the school wing. 'Meaning, "not such a fool." I shouldn't say he was, either, would you, Mr Alleyn?'

'Oh, no. There are no flies on the egregious Cedric. But what a cold-blooded little worm it is, Fox! Grandpapa dies, leaving him encumbered with a large unwanted estate and an insufficient income to keep it up. Grandpapa, on the other hand, dies leaving his extremely dubious fiancée a fortune. What more simple than for the financially embarrassed Cedric to marry the opulent Miss O.? I could kick that young man,' said Alleyn thoughtfully, 'in fourteen completely different positions and still feel half-starved.'

'I reckon,' said Fox, 'it's going to be a case for the Home Secretary.'

'Oh, yes, yes, I'm afraid you're right. Down this passage, didn't they say? And there's the green baize door. I think we'll separate here, Fox. You to collect your unconsidered trifles in Isabel's case and, by the way, you might take charge of Miss Orrincourt's. Here it is. Then, secretly, Foxkin, exhume Carabbas, deceased, and enclose him in a boot-box. By the way, do we know who destroyed poor Carabbas?'

'Mr Barker,' said Fox, 'got Mr Juniper to come up and give him an injection. Strychnine, I fancy.'

'I hope, whatever it was, it doesn't interfere with the autopsy. I'll meet you on the second terrace.'

Beyond the green baize door the whole atmosphere
of Ancreton was charged. Coir runners replaced the heavy
carpets, passages were draughty and smelt of disinfectant, and
where Victorian prints may have hung there were pictures of
determined modernity that had been executed with a bright
disdain for comfortable, but doubtless undesirable, prettiness.

Led by a terrific rumpus, Alleyn found his way to a
large room where Miss Able's charges were assembled, with
building games, with modelling clay, with paints, hammers,
sheets of paper, scissors and paste. Panty, he saw, was
conducting a game with scales, weights and bags of sand, and
appeared to be in hot dispute with a small boy. When she saw
Alleyn she flung herself into a strange attitude and screamed
with affected laughter. He waved to her and she at once did a
comedy fall to the floor, where she remained, apeing violent
astonishment.

Miss Caroline Able detached herself from a distant
group and came towards him.

'We're rather noisy in here,' she said crisply. 'Shall we go
to my office? Miss Watson, will you carry on?'

'Certainly, Miss Able,' said an older lady, rising from
behind a mass of children.

'Come along, then,' said Caroline Able.

Her office was near at hand and was hung with charts
and diagrams. She seated herself behind an orderly desk,
upon which he at once noticed a pile of essays written on
paper with yellow lines and ruled margin.

'I suppose you know what all this is about,' he said.

Miss Able replied cheerfully that she thought she did.
'I see,' she said frankly, 'quite a lot of Thomas Ancred and
he's told me about all the trouble. It's been a pretty balanced
account, as a matter of fact. He's fairly well adjusted, and has
been able to deal with it quite satisfactorily so far.'

Alleyn understood this to be a professional opinion on
Thomas, and wondered if a courtship had developed and if it
was conducted on these lines. Miss Able was pretty. She had a

clear skin, large eyes and good teeth. She also had an intimidating air of utter sanity.

'I'd like to know,' he said, 'what you think about it all.'

'It's impossible to give an opinion that's worth much,' she
replied, 'without a pretty thorough analysis of one if not all of
them. Obviously the relationship with their father was unsat-
isfactory. I should have liked to know about his marriage. One
suspected, of course, that there was a fear of impotency, not
altogether sublimated. The daughters' violent antagonism to his
proposed second marriage suggests a rather bad father-fixation.'

'Does it? But it wasn't a particularly suitable alliance
from—from the ordinary point of view, was it?'

'If the relationship with the father,' Miss Able said firmly,
'had been properly adjusted, the children should not have
been profoundly disturbed.'

'Not even,' Alleyn ventured, 'by the prospect of Miss O.
as a mother-in-law and principal beneficiary in the Will?'

'Those may have been the reasons advanced to explain
their antagonism. They may represent an attempt to ratio-
nalize a basic and essentially sexual repulsion.'

'Oh, dear!'

'But, as I said before,' she added, with a candid laugh,
'one shouldn't pronounce on mere observation. Deep analysis
might lead to a much more complex state of affairs.'

'You know,' Alleyn said, taking out his pipe and nursing
it in his palm, 'you and I, Miss Able, represent two aspects
of investigation. Your professional training teaches you that
behaviour is a sort of code or cryptogram disguising the
pathological truth from the uninformed, but revealing it to
the expert. Mine teaches me to regard behaviour as something infinitely variable *after* the fact and often at complete
loggerheads *with* the fact. A policeman watches behaviour, of
course, but his deductions would seem completely superficial
to you.' He opened his hand. 'I see a man turning a dead pipe
about in his hand and I think that, perhaps unconsciously, he's
longing to smoke it. May he?'

'Do,' said Miss Able. 'It's a good illustration. I see a man caressing his pipe and I recognize a very familiar piece of fetishism.'

'Well, don't tell me what it is,' Alleyn said hurriedly.

Miss Able gave a short professional laugh.

'Now, look here,' he said, 'how do you account for these anonymous letters we're all so tired of? What sort of being perpetrated them and why?'

'They probably represent an attempt to make an effect and are done by someone whose normal creative impulses have taken the wrong turning. The desire to be mysterious and omnipotent may be an additional factor. In Patricia's case for instance—'

'Patricia? Oh, I see. That's Panty, of course.'

'We don't use her nickname over here. We don't think it a good idea. We think nicknames can have a very definite effect, particularly when they are of a rather humiliating character.'

'I see. Well, then, in Patricia's case?'

'She formed the habit of perpetrating rather silly jokes on people. This was an attempt to command attention. She used to let her performances remain anonymous. Now she usually brags about them. That, of course, is a good sign.'

'It's an indication, at least, that she's not the author of the more recent practical jokes on her grandfather.'

'I agree.'

'Or the author of the anonymous letters.'

'That, I should have thought,' said Miss Able patiently, 'was perfectly obvious.'

'Who do you think is responsible for the letters?'

'I've told you, I can't make snap decisions or guesses.'

'Couldn't you just unbend far enough to have one little potshot?' he said persuasively. Miss Able opened her mouth, shut it again, looked at him with somewhat diminished composure and finally blushed. 'Come!' he thought, 'she hasn't analysed herself into an iceberg, at least.' And he said aloud: 'Without prejudice, now, who among the grown-ups would you back as the letter-writer?' He leant forward, smiling at her, and thought: 'Troy would grin if she saw this exhibition.' As Miss Able still hesitated, he repeated: 'Come on; who would you back?'

'You're very silly,' Miss Able said, and her manner, if not coy, was at least very much less impersonal.

'Would you say,' Alleyn went on, 'that the person who wrote them is by any chance the practical joker?'

'Quite possible.'

He reached a long arm over the desk and touched the top sheet of the exercises. 'They were written,' he said, 'on this paper.'

Her face was crimson. With a curious and unexpected gesture she covered the paper with her hands. 'I don't believe you,' she said.

'Will you let me look at it?' He drew the sheet out from under her hands and held it to the light. 'Yes,' he said. 'Rather an unusual type with a margin. It's the same watermark.'

'He didn't do it.'

'He?'

'Tom,' she said, and the diminutive cast a new light upon Thomas. 'He's incapable of it.'

'Good,' Alleyn said. 'Then why bring him up?'

'Patricia,' said Miss Able, turning a deeper red, 'must have taken some of this exercise paper over to the other side. Or...' She paused, frowning.

'Yes?'

'Her mother comes over here a great deal. Too often, I sometimes think. She's not very wise with children.'

'Where is the paper kept?'

'In that cupboard. The top one. Out of reach of the children.'

'Do you keep it locked?'

She turned on him quickly. 'You're not going to suggest that I would write anonymous letters? I?'

'But you do keep it locked, don't you?' said Alleyn.

'Certainly. I haven't denied that.'

'And the key?'

'On my ring and in my pocket.'

'Has the cupboard been left open at all? Or the keys left out of your pocket?'

'Never.'

'The paper comes from a village shop, doesn't it?'

'Of course it does. Any one could buy it.'

'So they could,' he agreed cheerfully, 'and we can find out if they have. There's no need, you see, to fly into a huff with me.'

'I do not,' said Miss Able mulishly, 'fly into huffs.'

'Splendid! Now look here. About this medicine your kids had. I want to trace its travels. Not inside the wretched kids, but *en route* to them.'

'I really don't see why—'

'Of course you don't and I'll tell you. A bottle of medicine for Sir Henry came up at the same time and its history is therefore bound up with theirs. Now, as the pudding said to the shop assistant, can you help me, Moddom?'

This laborious pun was not immediately absorbed by Miss Able. She looked at him with wonder but finally produced a tolerably indulgent smile.

'I suppose I can. Miss Orrincourt and Mrs Alleyn...'

Here came the now familiar pause and its inevitable explanation. 'Fancy!' said Miss Able. 'I know,' said Alleyn, 'about the medicine?'

'I was really very annoyed with Miss Orrincourt. It seems that she asked Mrs Alleyn to drive the trap round to the stables and she herself brought in the medicine. Instead of leaving it in the hall, or as you would think she might have done, bringing it in here to me, she simply dumped the whole lot in the flower-room. It seems that Sir Henry had given her some flowers out of the conservatory and she'd left them there. She's abnormally egocentric, of course. I waited and waited, and finally, at about seven o'clock, went over to the other side to ask about it. Mrs Ancred and I hunted everywhere. Finally, it was Fenella who told us where they were.'

'Was Sir Henry's medicine with theirs?'

'Oh, yes. Mrs Ancred sent it up at once.'

'Were the bottles alike?'

'We made no mistake, if that's what you're wondering. They were the same sort of bottles, but ours was much larger and they were both clearly labelled. Ours had the instructions attached. Unnecessarily, as it turned out, because Dr Withers came up himself that evening and he weighed the children again and measured out their doses himself. It was odd, because he'd left it that I should give the medicine and I could have managed perfectly well; but evidently,' said Miss Able with a short laugh, 'he'd decided I was not to be trusted.'

'It's a fault on the right side, I suppose,' Alleyn said vaguely. 'They have to be careful.'

Miss Able looked unconvinced. 'No doubt,' she said. 'But I still can't understand why he wanted to come up to Ancreton, when he was supposed to be so busy. And after all that fuss, we've had to go back to the ointment.'

'By the way,' Alleyn asked, 'did you happen to see the cat Carabbas before it died?'

Instantly she was away on her professional hobby-horse. He listened to an exposition on Panty's fondness for the cat, and the strange deductions which Miss Able drew, with perfect virtuosity, from this not unusual relationship.

'At this stage of her development, it was really a bad disturbance when the link was broken.'

'But,' Alleyn ventured, 'if the cat had ringworm...'

'It wasn't ringworm,' said Miss Able firmly. 'I ought to know. It might have been mange.'

Upon that pronouncement he left her, apparently in two minds about himself. She shook hands with an air of finality, but when he reached the door he thought he heard an indeterminate sound, and turned to find her looking anxiously at him.

'Is there anything else?' he asked.

'It's only that I'm worried about Tom Ancred. They're dragging him in and making him do all their dirty work. He's quite different. He's too good for them. I'm afraid this will upset him.'

And then with a rather strenuous resumption of her professional manner: 'Psychologically, I mean,' said Miss Able.

'I quite understand,' said Alleyn, and left her.

He found Fox waiting for him on the second terrace. Fox was sitting on the steps with his greatcoat drawn closely round him and his spectacles on his nose. He was reading from the manual on poisons which Alleyn had lent him in the train. By his side were two suitcases. One of these Alleyn recognized as Miss Orrincourt's. The other, he presumed, was Isabel's. Near by was a boot-box tied up with string. As Alleyn bent over Fox he noticed an unpleasant smell.

'Carabbas?' he asked, edging the box away with his foot.

Fox nodded. 'I've been asking myself,' he said, and placed a square finger under a line of print. Alleyn read over his shoulder. 'Arsenic. Symptoms. Manifested as progressive cachexia and loss of flesh; falling out of hair...'

Fox glanced up and jerked a thumb at the boot-box.

'Falling out of hair,' he said. 'Wait till you've had a look at Carabbas deceased.'

'You know, Fox,' Alleyn said as they walked back to the village, 'if Thomas Ancred can stand having his lightest cares implacably laid at the door of some infantile impropriety, he and Miss Able will probably get along together very nicely. Obviously, she's in love with him, or should I say that obviously she finds herself adjusted to a condition of rationalized eroticism in relation to poor old Thomas?'

'Courting, do you reckon?'

'I think so. Fox, I think we've had Ancreton for the moment, but I'm going to ask you to stay behind and warn the parson about an exhumation. Return to Katzenjammer Castle in the morning and ask the inmates if they've any objection to having their prints taken. They won't have any if they're not completely dotty. Bailey can come down by the morning train and work round the house for the stuff we want there. Get him to check prints on any relevant surfaces. It'll all be utterly useless no doubt, but it had better be done. I'll go back to the Yard. I want to learn Messrs Mortimer and Loame's recipe for tasteful embalming. As soon as we get the exhumation order through we'll come down and meet you here. There's a train this evening. Let's have a meal at the pub and then I'll catch it. I was going to see Dr Withers again, but I fancy that particular interview had better wait. I want to get the medicine bottle and poor old Carabbas up to London.'

'What's the betting, Mr Alleyn? Arsenic in the medicine or not?'

'I'm betting *not*.'

'Routine job. It'll be a nuisance if they don't find anything, though. Not a hope with the Thermos.'

'No, damn it.'

They walked in silence. Frost tingled in the dusk and hardened the ground under their feet. A pleasant smell of burning wood laced the air and from Ancreton woods came the sound of wings.

'What a job!' Alleyn said suddenly.

'Ours, sir?'

'Yes, ours. Walking down a country lane with a dead cat in a boot-box and working out procedure for disentombing the body of an old man.'

'Somebody's got to do it.'

'Certainly. But the details are unlovely.'

'Not much doubt about it, sir, is there? Homicide?'

'Not much doubt, old thing. No.'

'Well,' said Fox, after a pause, 'as it stands, the evidence all points one way. It's not one of those funny affairs where you have to clear up half a dozen suspects.'

'But *why* kill him? She knew the Will was in her favour. She wanted to be Lady Ancred. She knew he wasn't likely to live much longer. Why incur the appalling risk when all she had to do was marry him and wait?'

'He was always changing his Will. Perhaps she thought he might do it again.'

'She seems to have had him pretty well where she wanted him.'

'Might she be all that keen on the present baronet?'

'Not she,' said Alleyn. 'Not she.'

'Hard to imagine, I must say. Suppose, though, that Miss O. is not the party we'll be after, and suppose we know the old gentleman was done away with. Who's left? Not Sir Cedric, because he knew about the second Will.'

'Unless,' said Alleyn, 'he gambled on marrying the heiress.'

'By gum, yes, there's that, but what a gamble! With that fortune she could have hoped for better, wouldn't you say?'

'She could hardly hope for worse, in my opinion.'

'Well, then,' Fox reasoned, 'suppose we count those two out. Look at the rest of the field.'

'I do so without enthusiasm. They all thought the Will announced at the Birthday Dinner was valid. Desdemona, Millamant, Dr Withers and the servants expected to do moderately well; Thomas's expectations were handsome. The Kentish family, and the Claude Ancreds got damn all. In the haves the only motive is cupidity, in the "have-nots," revenge.'

'Opportunity?' Fox speculated.

'If an analysis of the medicine bottle proves negative, we're left with the Thermos flask, now sterilized, and as far as we can see, Miss O. Unless you entertain a notion of delayed action with Barker inserting arsenic in the crayfish.'

'You will have your joke, Mr Alleyn.'

'You should have heard me trifling with Miss Able,' Alleyn grunted. 'That was pretty ghastly, if you like.'

'And the exhumation's on,' Fox ruminated after another long silence. 'When?'

'As soon as we've got the order and Dr Curtis can manage it. By the way, Ancreton Church is above the village over there. We'll have a look at the churchyard while the light still holds.'

And presently they climbed a gentle lane, now deep in shadow, and pushed open a lych-gate into the churchyard of St Stephen's, Ancreton.

It was pleasant after the dubious grandeurs of the manor house to encircle this church, tranquil, ancient, and steadfastly built. Their feet crunched loudly on the gravelled path, and from the hedges came a faint stir of sleepy birds. The grass was well kept. When they came upon a quiet company of headstones and crosses they found that the mounds and plots before them were also carefully tended. It was possible in the fading light to read inscriptions. 'Susan Gascoigne of this parish. Here rests one who in her life rested not in well-doing.' 'To the Memory of Miles Chitty Bream who for fifty years tended this church-yard and now sleeps with those he faithfully served.' Presently they came upon Ancred graves. 'Henry Gaisbrook Ancreton Ancred, fourth baronet, and Margaret Mirabel, his wife.' 'Percival Gaisbrook Ancred,' and many others, decently and properly bestowed. But such plain harbourage was not for the later generations, and towering over this sober company of stone rose a marble tomb topped by three angels. Here, immortalized in gold inscriptions, rested Sir Henry's predecessor, his wife, his son Henry Irving Ancred, and himself. The tomb, Alleyn read, had been erected by Sir Henry. It had a teak and iron door, emblazoned in the Ancred arms, and with a great keyhole.

'It'll be one of these affairs with shelves,' Fox speculated. 'Not room enough for the doctor, and no light. It'll have to be a canvas enclosure, don't you reckon, Mr Alleyn?'

'Yes.'

The lid of Fox's large silver watch clicked. 'It's five o'clock, sir,' he said. 'Time we moved on if you're to have tea at the pub and catch that train.'

'Come along, then,' said Alleyn quietly, and they retraced their steps to the village.

CHAPTER FIFTEEN

New System

As TROY WAITED FOR Alleyn's return her thoughts moved back through the brief period of their reunion. She examined one event, then another; a phrase, a gesture, an emotion. She was astonished by the simplicity of her happiness; amused to find herself expectant, even a little sleek. She was desired, she was loved, and she loved again. That there were hazards ahead she made no doubt, but for the moment all was well; she could relax and find a perspective.

Yet, like a rough strand in the texture of her happiness, there was an imperfection. Her thoughts, questing fingers, continually and reluctantly sought it out. This was Alleyn's refusal to allow his work a place in their relationship. It was founded, she knew, in her own attitude during their earliest encounters which had taken place against a terrible background; in her shrinking from the part he played at that time and in her expressed horror of capital punishment.

Troy knew very well that Alleyn accepted these reactions as fundamental and implicit in her nature. She knew he did not believe that for her, in love, an ethic unrelated to that love could not impede it. It seemed to him that if his work occasionally brought murderers to execution, then surely, to her, he must at those times be of the same company as the hangman. Only by some miracle of love, he thought, did she overcome her repulsion.

But the bald truth, she told herself helplessly, was that her ideas were remote from her emotions. 'I'm less sensitive than he thinks,' she said. 'What he does is of no importance. I love him.' And although she disliked such generalities, she added: 'I am a woman.'

It seemed to her that while this withdrawal existed they could not be completely happy. 'Perhaps,' she thought, 'this business with the Ancreds will, after all, change everything. Perhaps it's a kind of beastly object lesson. I'm in it. He can't keep me out. I'm in on a homicide case.' And with a sensation of panic she realized that she had been taking it for granted that the old man she had painted was murdered.

As soon as Alleyn came in and stood before her she knew that she had made no mistake. 'Well, Rory,' she said, going to him, 'we're for it, aren't we, darling?'

'It looks a bit like it.' He walked past her, saying quickly: 'I'll see the AC in the morning. He'll let me hand over to someone else. Much better.'

'No,' Troy said, and he turned quickly and looked at her. She was aware, as if she had never before fully appreciated it, of the difference in their heights. She thought: 'That's how he looks when he's taking statements,' and became nervous.

'No?' he said. 'Why not?'

'Because it would be high-falutin, because it would make me feel an ass.'

'I'm sorry.'

'I look upon this case,' Troy said, and wished her voice would sound more normal, 'as a sort of test. Perhaps it's been sent to larn us like acts-of-God; only I must say I always think it's so unfair to call earthquakes and tidal-waves acts-of-God and not bumper harvests and people like Leonardo and Cezanne.'

'What the devil,' Alleyn asked in a mild voice, 'are you talking about?'

'Don't snap at me,' said Troy. He made a quick movement towards her. 'No. Please listen. I want, I really do want you to take this case as long as the AC lets you. I really want you to keep me with you this time. We've got in a muddle about me and your job. When I say I don't mind your job you think I'm not telling the truth, and if I ask you questions about these kinds of cases you think I'm being a brave little woman and biting on the bullet.'

She saw his mouth twist in an involuntary smile.

'Whereas,' she hurried on, 'I'm not. I know I didn't relish having our courtship all muddled up with murder on the premises, and I know I don't think people ought to hang other people. But you do, and you're the policeman, not me. And it doesn't do any good trying to pretend you're dodging out to pinch a petty larcener when I know jolly well what you are up to, and, to be perfectly honest, am often dying to hear about it.'

'That's not quite true, is it—the last bit?'

'I'd infinitely rather talk about it. I'd infinitely rather feel honestly shocked and upset with you, than vaguely worried all by myself.'

He held out a hand and she went to him. 'That's why I said I think this case has been sent to larn you.'

'Troy,' Alleyn said, 'do you know what they say to their best girls in the antipodes?'

'No.'

'You'll do me.'

'Oh!'

'You'll do me, Troy.'

'I thought perhaps you'd prefer me to remain a shrinking violet.'

'The truth is, I've been a bloody fool and never did and never will deserve you.'

'Don't,' said Troy, 'let's talk about deserving.'

'I've only one excuse and logically you'll say it's no excuse. Books about CID men will tell you that running a murderer to earth is just a job to us, as copping a pickpocket is to the ordinary PC. It's not. Because of its termination it's unlike any other job in existence. When I was twenty-two I faced its implications and took it on, but I don't think I fully realized them for another fifteen years and that was when I fell most deeply in love, my love, with you.'

'I've faced its implications, too, and once for all, over this Ancred business. Before you came in I even decided that it would be good for both of us if, by some freak, it turned out that I had a piece of information somewhere in the back of my memory that's of vital importance.'

'You'd got as far as that?'

'Yes. And the queer thing is,' Troy said, driving her fingers through her hair, 'I've got the most extraordinary conviction that somewhere in the back of my memory it is there, waiting to come out.'

❀ ❀ ❀

'I want you,' Alleyn said, 'to tell me again, as fully as you possibly can, about your conversation with Sir Henry after he'd found the writing on the looking-glass and the grease-paint on the cat's whiskers. If you've forgotten how it went at any particular stage, say so. But, for the love of Mike, darling, don't elaborate. Can you remember?'

'I think so. Quite a lot, anyway. He was furious with Panty, of course.'

'He hadn't a suspicion of the egregious Cedric?'

'None. Did Cedric—?'

'He did. He's lisped out an admission.'

'Little devil,' said Troy. 'So it *was* grease-paint on his fingernail.'

'And Sir Henry—?'

'He just went on and on about how much he'd doted on Panty and how she'd grieved him. I tried to persuade him she hadn't done it, but he only made their family noise at me: "T'uh!" you know?'

'Yes, indeed.'

'Then he started to talk about marriages between first cousins and how he disapproved of them, and this got mixed up in no time with a most depressing account of how he was'—Troy swallowed and went on quickly—'was going to be embalmed. We actually mentioned the book. Then I think he sniffed a bit at Cedric as his heir, and said he'd never have children and that poor Thomas wouldn't marry.'

'He was wrong there, I fancy.'

'No! Who?'

'The psychiatrist, or should it be "psychiatriste"?'

'Miss Able?'

'She thinks he's quite satisfactorily sublimated his libido or something.'

'Oh, good! Well, and then as he would keep talking about when he was Gone, I tried to buck him up a bit and had quite a success. He turned mysterious and talked about there being surprises in store for everybody. And upon that Sonia Orrincourt burst in and said they were all plotting against her and she was frightened.'

'And that's all?' Alleyn said after a pause.

'No—no, it isn't. There was something else he said. Rory, I can't remember what it was, but there was something else.'

'That was on Saturday the seventeenth, wasn't it?'

'Let me see. I got there on the sixteenth. Yes. Yes, it was the next day. But I wish,' Troy said slowly, 'I do wish I could remember the other thing he talked about.'

'Don't try. It may come back suddenly.'

'Perhaps Miss Able could screw it out of me,' said Troy with a grin. 'In any case we'll call it a day.'

As they moved away she linked her arm through his. 'First instalment of the new system,' she said. 'It's gone off tolerably quietly, hasn't it?'

'It has, my love. Thank you.'

'One of the things I like about you,' Troy said, 'is your nice manners.'

The next day was a busy one. The Assistant Commissioner after a brisk interview with Alleyn, decided to apply for an exhumation order. 'Sooner the better, I suppose. I was talking to the Home Secretary yesterday and told him we might be on his tracks. You'd better go right ahead.'

'Tomorrow then, sir, if possible,' Alleyn said. 'I'll see Dr Curtis.'

'Do.' And as Alleyn turned away: 'By the way, Rory, if it's at all difficult for Mrs Alleyn—'

'Thank you very much sir, but at the moment she's taking it in her stride.'

'Splendid. Damn' rum go—what?'

'Damn' rum,' Alleyn agreed politely, and went to call on Mr Rattisbon.

Mr Rattisbon's offices in the Strand had survived the pressure of the years, the blitz and the flying bomb. They were, as Alleyn remembered them on the occasion of his first official visit before the war, a discreetly active memorial to the style of Charles Dickens, with the character of Mr Rattisbon himself written across them like an inscription. Here was the same clerk with his trick of slowly raising his head and looking dimly at the inquirer, the same break-neck stairs, the same dark smell of antiquity. And here, at last, shrined in leather, varnish and age was Mr Rattisbon, that elderly legal bird, perched at his desk.

'Ah, yes, Chief Inspector,' Mr Rattisbon gabbled, extending a claw at a modish angle, 'come in, come in, sit down, sit down. Glad to see yer. M-m-maah!' And when Alleyn was seated Mr Rattisbon darted the old glance at him, sharp as the point of a fine nib. 'No trouble, I hope?' he said.

'The truth is,' Alleyn rejoined, 'my visits only arise, I'm afraid, out of some sort of trouble.'

Mr Rattisbon instantly hunched himself, placed his elbows on his desk and joined his finger-tips in front of his chin.

'I've come to ask about certain circumstances that relate to the late Sir Henry Ancred's Will. Or Wills.'

Mr Rattisbon vibrated the tip of his tongue between his lips, rather as if he had scalded it and hoped in this manner to cool it off. He said nothing.

'Without more ado,' Alleyn went on, 'I must tell you that we are going to ask for an exhumation.'

After a considerable pause Mr Rattisbon said: 'This is exceedingly perturbing.'

'May I, before we go any further, say I do think that instead of coming to us with the story I'm about to relate, Sir Henry's successors might have seen fit to consult their solicitor.'

'Thank yer.'

'I don't know, sir, of course, how you would have advised them, but I believe that this visit must sooner or later have taken place. Here is the story.'

Twenty minutes later Mr Rattisbon tipped himself back in his chair and gave a preparatory bay at the ceiling.

'Ma-m-ah!' he said. 'Extraordinary. Disquieting. Very.'

'You will see that all this rigmarole seems to turn about two factors, (*a*) It was common knowledge in his household that Sir Henry Ancred was to be embalmed, (*b*) He repeatedly altered his Will, and on the eve of his death appears to have done so in favour of his intended wife, largely to the exclusion of his family and in direct contradiction to an announcement he made a couple of hours earlier. It's here, I hope, Mr Rattisbon, that you can help us.'

'I am,' said Mr Rattisbon, 'in an unusual, not to say equivocal, position. Um. As you have very properly noted, Chief Inspector, the correct procedure on the part of the family, particularly on the part of Sir Cedric Gaisbrooke Percival Ancred, would have been to consult this office. He has elected not to do so. In the event of a criminal action he will scarcely be able to avoid doing so. It appears that the general intention of the family is to discredit the position of the chief beneficiary and further to suggest that there is a case for a criminal charge against her. I refer, of course, to Miss Gladys Clark.'

'To *whom*?'

'—known professionally as Miss Sonia Orrincourt.'

'"Gladys Clark,"' Alleyn said thoughtfully. 'Well!'

'Now, as the solicitor for the estate, I am concerned in the matter. On consideration, I find no objection to giving you such information as you require. Indeed, I conceive it to be my professional duty to do so.'

'I'm extremely glad,' said Alleyn, who had known perfectly well that Mr Rattisbon, given time, would arrive at precisely this decision. 'Our principal concern at the moment is to discover whether Sir Henry Ancred actually concocted his last Will after he left the party on the eve of his death.'

'Emphatically no. It was drawn up, in this office, on Sir Henry's instruction, on Thursday, the twenty-second of November of this year, together with a second document, which was the one quoted by Sir Henry as his last Will and Testament at his Birthday dinner.'

'This all sounds rather erratic.'

Mr Rattisbon rapidly scratched his nose with the nail of his first finger. 'The procedure,' he said, 'was extraordinary, I ventured to say so at the time. Let me take these events in their order. On Tuesday, the twentieth November, Mrs Henry Irving Ancred telephoned this office to the effect that Sir Henry Ancred wished me to call upon him immediately. It was most inconvenient, but the following day I went down to Ancreton. I found him in a state of considerable agitation and clothed— m-m-m-ah—in a theatrical costume. I understood that he had been posing for his portrait. May I add, in parentheses,' said Mr Rattisbon with a bird-like dip of his head, 'that although your wife was at Ancreton, I had not the pleasure of meeting her on that occasion. I enjoyed this privilege upon my later visit.'

'Troy told me.'

'It was the greatest pleasure. To return. On this first visit of Wednesday the twenty-first of November, Sir Henry Ancred showed me his rough drafts of two Wills. One moment.'

With darting movements, Mr Rattisbon drew from his filing cabinet two sheafs of paper covered in a somewhat flamboyant script. He handed them to Alleyn. A glance showed him their nature. 'Those are the drafts,' said Mr Rattisbon. 'He required me to engross two separate Wills based on these notes. I remarked that this procedure was unusual. He put it to me that he was unable to come to a decision regarding the—ah—the merits of his immediate relatives, and was, at the same time, contemplating a second marriage. His previous Will, in my opinion a reasonable disposition, he had already destroyed. He instructed me to bring these two new documents to Ancreton when I returned for the annual Birthday observances. The first was the Will witnessed and signed before the dinner and quoted by Sir Henry *at* dinner as his last Will and Testament. It was destroyed late that evening. The second is the document upon which we are at present empowered to act. It was signed and witnessed in Sir Henry Ancred's bedroom at twelve-twenty that night—against, may I add, *against* my most earnest representations.'

'Two Wills,' Alleyn said, 'in readiness for a final decision.'

'Precisely. He believed that his health was precarious. Without making any specific accusations he suggested that certain members of his family were acting separately or in collusion against him. I believe, in view of your own exceedingly lucid account,' Mr Rattisbon dipped his head again, 'that he referred, in fact, to these practical jokes. Mrs Alleyn will have described fully the extraordinary incident of the portrait. An admirable likeness, if I may say so. She will have related how Sir Henry left the theatre in anger.'

'Yes.'

'Subsequently the butler came to me with a request from Sir Henry that I should wait upon him in his room. I found him still greatly perturbed. In my presence, and with considerable violence, he tore up the, as I considered, more reasonable of the two drafts, and, in short, threw it on the fire. A Mr and Mrs Candy were shown in and witnessed his signature to the second document. Sir Henry then informed me that he proposed to marry Miss Clark in a week's time and would require my services in the drawing up of a marriage settlement. I persuaded him to postpone this matter until the morning and left him, still agitated and inflamed. That, in effect, is all I can tell you.'

'It's been enormously helpful,' Alleyn said. 'One other point if you don't mind. Sir Henry's two drafts are not dated. He didn't by any chance tell you when he wrote them?'

'No. His behaviour and manner on this point were curious. He stated that he would enjoy no moment's peace until both Wills had been drawn up in my office. But no. Except that the drafts were made before Tuesday, the twentieth, I cannot help you here.'

'I'd be grateful if they might be put away and left untouched.'

'Of course,' said Mr Rattisbon, greatly flustered, 'by all means.'

Alleyn placed the papers between two clean sheets and returned them to their drawer.

That done, he rose, and Mr Rattisbon at once became very lively. He escorted Alleyn to the door, shook hands and uttered a string of valedictory phrases. 'Quite so, quite so,' he gabbled. 'Disquieting. Trust no foundation but nevertheless disquieting. Always depend upon your discretion. Extraordinary. In many ways, I fear, an unpredictable family. No doubt if counsel is required…Well, goodbye. Thank yer. Kindly remember me to Mrs Alleyn. Thank yer.'

But as Alleyn moved, Mr Rattisbon laid a claw on his arm. 'I shall always remember him that night,' he said. 'He stopped me as I reached the door and I turned and saw him, sitting upright in bed with his gown spread about him. He was a fine-looking old fellow. I was quite arrested by his appearance. He made an unaccountable remark, too, I recollect. He said: "I expect to be very well attended, in future, Rattisbon. Opposition to my marriage may not be as strong in some quarters as you anticipate. Goodnight." That was all. It was, of course, the last time I ever saw him.'

The Hon Mrs Claude Ancred had a small house in Chelsea. As a dwelling-place it presented a startling antithesis to Ancreton. Here all was lightness and simplicity. Alleyn was shown into a white drawing-room, modern in treatment, its end wall one huge window overlooking the river. The curtains were pale yellow, powdered with silver stars, and this colour, with accents of clear cerise, appeared throughout the room. There were three pictures—a Matisse, a Christopher Wood, and, to his pleasure, an Agatha Troy. 'So you still stick around, do you?' he said, winking at it, and at that moment Jenetta Ancred came in.

An intelligent looking woman, he thought. She greeted him as if he was a normal visitor, and, with a glance at the painting, said: 'You see that we've got a friend in common,' and began to talk to him about Troy and their meeting at Ancreton.

He noticed that her manner was faintly and recurrently ironic. Nothing, she seemed to say, must be insisted upon or underlined. Nothing really matters very much. Overstatement is stupid and uncomfortable. This impression was conveyed by the crispness of her voice, its avoidance of stresses, and by her eyes and lips, which constantly erected little smiling barriers that half-discredited the frankness of her conversation. She talked intelligently about painting, but always with an air of self-deprecation. He had a notion she was warding off the interview for which he had asked.

At last he said: 'You've guessed, of course, why I wanted you to let me come?'

'Thomas came in last night and told me he'd seen you and that you'd gone down to Ancreton. This is an extremely unpleasant development, isn't it?'

'I'd very much like to hear your views.'

'Mine?' she said, with an air of distaste. 'They can't possibly be of the smallest help, I'm afraid. I'm always a complete onlooker at Ancreton. And please don't tell me the onlooker sees most of the game. In this instance she sees as little as possible.'

'Well,' said Alleyn cheerfully, 'what does she think?'

She waited for a moment, looking past him to the great window. 'I think,' she murmured, 'that it's almost certain to be a tarradiddle. The whole story.'

'Convince us of that,' Alleyn said, 'and we're your slaves for ever in the CID.'

'No, but really. They're so absurd, you know, my in-laws. I'm very attracted to them, but you can't imagine how absurd they can be.' Her voice died away. After a moment's reflection she said: 'But Mrs Alleyn saw them. She must have told you.'

'A little.'

'At one time it was fifth columnists. Pauline suspected such a nice little Austrian doctor who's since taken a very important job at a big clinic. At that time he was helping with the children. She said something told her. And then it was poor Miss Able who was supposed to be undermining her influence with Panty. I wonder if, having left the stage, Pauline's obliged to find some channel for her histrionic instincts. They all do it. Naturally, they resented Miss Orrincourt, and resentment and suspicion are inseparable with the Ancreds.'

'What did you think of Miss Orrincourt?'

'I? She's too lovely, isn't she? In her way, quite flawless.'

'Apart from her beauty?'

'There didn't seem to be anything else. Except a very robust vulgarity.'

'But does she really think as objectively as all that?' Alleyn wondered. 'Her daughter stood to lose a good deal through Sonia Orrincourt. Could she have achieved such complete detachment?' He said: 'You were there, weren't you, when the book on embalming appeared in the cheese-dish?'

She made a slight grimace. 'Oh, yes.'

'Have you any idea who could have put it there?'

'I'm afraid I rather suspected Cedric. Though why...For no reason except that I can't believe any of the others would do it. It was quite horrible.'

'And the anonymous letters?'

'I feel it must have been the same person. I can't imagine how any of the Ancreds—after all they're not—However.'

She had a trick of letting her voice fade out as if she had lost faith in the virtue of her sentences. Alleyn felt that she pushed the suggestion of murder away from her, with both hands, not so much for its dreadfulness as for its offence against taste.

'You think, then,' he said, 'that their suspicion of Miss Orrincourt is unfounded and that Sir Henry died naturally?'

'That's it. I'm quite sure it's all a make-up. They think it's true. They've just got one of their "things" about it.'

'That explanation doesn't quite cover the discovery of a tin of rat-bane in her suitcase, does it?'

'Then there must be some other explanation.'

'The only one that occurs to me,' Alleyn said, 'is that the tin was deliberately planted, and if you accept that you accept something equally serious: an attempt to place suspicion of murder upon an innocent person. That in itself constitutes—'

'No, no,' she cried out. 'No, you don't understand the Ancreds. They plunge into fantasies of their own making, without thinking of the consequences. This wretched tin must have been put in the suitcase by a maid or have got there by some other freakish accident. It may have been in the attic for years. None of their alarms ever means anything. Mr Alleyn, may I implore you to dismiss the whole thing as nonsense? Dangerous and idiotic nonsense, but, believe me, utter nonsense.'

She had leant forward, and her hands were pressed together. There was a vehemence and an intensity in her manner that had not appeared before.

'If it's nonsense,' he said, 'it's malevolent nonsense.'

'Stupid,' she insisted, 'spiteful, too, perhaps, but only childishly so.'

'I shall be very glad if it turns out to be no more.'

'Yes, but you don't think it will.'

'I'm wide open to conviction,' he said lightly.

'If I could convince you!'

'You can at least help by filling in some of the gaps. For instance, can you tell me anything about the party in the drawing-room when you all returned from the little theatre? What happened?'

Instead of answering him directly she said, with a return to her earlier manner, 'Please forgive me for being so insistent. It's silly to try and ram one's convictions down other people's throats. They merely feel that one protests too much. But, you see, I know my Ancreds.'

'And I'm learning mine. About the aftermath of the Birthday Party?'

'Well, two of our visitors, the rector and a local squire, said goodnight in the hall. Very thankfully, poor darlings, I'm sure. Miss Orrincourt had already gone up. Mrs Alleyn had stayed behind in the theatre with Paul and Fenella. The rest of us went into the drawing-room and there the usual family arguments started, this time on the subject of that abominable disfigurement of the portrait. Paul and Fenella came in and told us that no damage had been done. Naturally, they were very angry. I may tell you that my daughter, who has not quite grown out of the hero-worship state-of-affairs, admires your wife enormously. These two children planned what they fondly imagined to be a piece of detective work. Did Mrs Alleyn tell you?'

Troy had told Alleyn, but he listened again to the tale of the paintbrush and finger-prints. She dwelt at some length on this, inviting his laughter, making, he thought, a little too much of a slight incident. When he asked her for further details of the discussion in the drawing-room she became vague. They had talked about Sir Henry's fury, about his indiscretions at dinner.

Mr Rattisbon had been sent for by Sir Henry. 'It was just one more of the interminable emotional parties,' she said. 'Everyone, except Cedric and Milly, terrifically hurt and grand because of the Will he told us about at dinner.'

'Every one? Your daughter and Mr Paul Ancred too?'

She said much too lightly: 'My poor Fen does go in a little for the Ancred temperament, but not, I'm glad to say, to excess. Paul, thank goodness, seems to have escaped it, which is such a very good thing, as it appears he's to be my son-in-law.'

'Would you say that during this discussion any of them displayed singular vindictiveness against Miss Orrincourt?'

'They were all perfectly livid about her. Except Cedric. But they're lividly angry with somebody or another a dozen times a month. It means nothing.'

'Mrs Ancred,' Alleyn said, 'if you've been suddenly done out of a very pretty fortune your anger isn't altogether meaningless. You yourself must surely have resented a little your daughter's position.'

'No,' she said quickly. 'I knew, as soon as she told me of her engagement to Paul, that her grandfather would disapprove. Marriage between cousins was one of his bugbears. I knew he'd take it out of them both. He was a vindictive old man. And Fen hadn't bothered to hide her dislike of Miss Orrincourt. She'd said...' She stopped short. He saw her hands move convulsively.

'Yes?'

'She was perfectly frank. The association offended her taste. That was all.'

'What are her views of all this business—the letters and so on?'

'She agrees with me.'

'That the whole story is simply a flight of fancy on the part of the more imaginative members of the family?'

'Yes.'

'I should like to see her if I may?'

The silence that fell between them was momentary, a brief check in the even flow of their voices, but he found it illuminating. It was as if she winced from an expected hurt, and poised herself to counter it. She leant forward, and with an air of great frankness made a direct appeal.

'Mr Alleyn,' she said, 'I'm going to ask a favour. Please let Fenella off. She's highly strung and sensitive. Really sensitive. It's not the rather bogus Ancred sensibility. All the unhappy wrangling over her engagement and the shock of her grandfather's death and then—this horrid and really dreadful business: it's fussed her rather badly. She overheard me speaking to you when you rang up for this talk and even that upset her. I've sent them both out. Please, will you be very understanding and let her off?'

He hesitated, wondering how to frame his refusal, and if her anxiety was based on some much graver reason than the one she gave him.

'Believe me,' she said, 'Fenella can be of no help to you.'

Before he could reply Fenella herself walked in, followed by Paul. 'I'm sorry, Mummy,' she said rapidly and in a high voice. 'I know you didn't want me to come. I had to. There's something Mr Alleyn doesn't know, and I've got to tell him.'

CHAPTER SIXTEEN

Positively the Last Appearance of Sir Henry Ancred

AFTERWARDS, WHEN HE told Troy about Fenella's entrance, Alleyn said the thing that struck him most at the time was Jenetta Ancred's command of *savoir-faire*. Obviously this was a development she had not foreseen and one which filled her with dismay. Yet her quiet assurance never wavered, nor did she neglect the tinge of irony that was implicit in her good manners.

She said: 'Darling, how dramatic and alarming. This is my girl, Fenella, Mr Alleyn. And this is my nephew, Paul Ancred.'

'I'm sorry to burst in,' said Fenella. 'How do you do? Please may we talk to you?' She held out her hand.

'*Not* just at this moment,' said her mother. 'Mr Alleyn and I really are rather busy. Do you mind, darling?'

Fenella's grip on his hand had been urgent and nervous. She had whispered: 'Please.' Alleyn said: 'May we just hear what this is about, Mrs Ancred?'

'Mummy, it's important. Really.'

'Paul,' said her mother, 'can't you manage this firebrand of yours?'

'I think it's important too, Aunt Jen.'

'My dearest children, I honestly don't think you know—'

'But Aunt Jen, we do. We've talked it over quite cold-bloodedly. We know that what we've got to say may bring a lot of publicity and scandal on the family,' said Paul with something very like relish. 'We don't enjoy the prospect, but we think any other course would be dishonest.'

'We accept the protection of the law,' said Fenella rather loudly. 'It'd be illogical and dishonest to try and circumvent justice to save the family face. We know we're up against something pretty horrible. We accept the responsibility, don't we, Paul?'

'Yes,' said Paul. 'We don't like it, but we do it.'

'Oh,' Jenetta cried out vehemently, 'for pity's sake don't be so heroic! Ancreds, Ancreds, both of you!'

'Mummy, we're *not*. You don't even know what we're going to say. This isn't a matter of theatre; it's a matter of principle, and, if you like, of sacrifice.'

'And you both see yourselves being sacrificial and high-principled. Mr Alleyn,' Jenetta said, and it was as if she added: 'After all, we speak the same language, you and I. I do most earnestly beg you to take whatever these ridiculous children have to say with a colossal pinch of salt.'

'Mummy, it's important.'

'Then,' said Alleyn, 'let's have it.'

She gave in, as he had expected, lightly and with grace. 'Well, then, if we must be instructed...Do at least sit down, both of you, and let poor Mr Alleyn sit down too.'

Fenella obeyed, with the charm of movement that was characteristic of all the female Ancreds. She was, as Troy had told him, a vivid girl. Her mother's spareness was joined in Fenella with the spectacular Ancred beauty and lent it delicacy. 'Nevertheless,' Alleyn thought, 'she can make an entrance with the best of them.'

'Paul and I,' she began at once, speaking very rapidly, 'have talked and talked about it. Ever since those letters came. We said at first that we wouldn't have anything to do with it. We thought people who wrote that kind of letter were beyond everything, and it made us feel perfectly beastly to think there was any one in the house who could do such a thing. We were absolutely certain that what the letter said was an odious, malicious lie.'

'Which is precisely,' her mother said without emphasis, 'what I have been telling Mr Alleyn. I really do think, darling—'

'Yes, but that's not all,' Fenella interrupted vehemently. 'You can't just shrug your shoulders and say it's horrid. If you don't mind my saying so, Mummy dear, that's your generation all over. It's muddled thinking. In its way it's the kind of attitude that leads to wars. That's what Paul and I think anyway. Don't we, Paul?'

Paul, with a red determined face, said: 'What Fen means, I think, Aunt Jenetta, is that one can't just say "Jolly bad form and all ballyhoo," and let it go at that. Because of the implications. If Sonia Orrincourt didn't poison Grandfather, there's somebody in the house who's trying to get her hanged for something she didn't do, and that's as much as to say there's somebody in the house who's as good as a murderer.' He turned to Alleyn: 'Isn't that right, sir?'

'Not necessarily right,' Alleyn said. 'A false accusation may be made in good faith.'

'Not,' Fenella objected, 'by the kind of person who writes anonymous letters. And anyway, even if it was in good faith, we know it's a false accusation, and the realistic thing to do is to say so and, and...' She stumbled, shook her head angrily and ended with childish lameness, 'and jolly well make them admit it and pay the penalty.'

'Let's take things in their order?' Alleyn suggested. 'You say you know the suggestion made in the letters is untrue. How do you know this?'

Fenella glanced at Paul with an air of achievement and then turned to Alleyn and eagerly poured out her story.

'It was that evening when she and Mrs Alleyn drove down to the chemist's and brought back the children's medicine. Cedric and Paul and Aunt Pauline were dining out, I'd got a cold and cried off. I'd been doing the drawing-room flowers for Aunt Milly and I was tidying up in a sink-room where the vases are kept. It's down some steps off the passage from the hall to the library. Grandfather had had some orchids sent for Sonia and she came to get them. I must say she looked lovely. Sort of sparkling, with furs pulled up round her face. She swept in and asked in that ghastly voice for what she called her bokay, and when she saw it was a spray of absolutely heavenly orchids she said: "Quite small, isn't it? Not reely much like flowers, are they?" Everything she'd done and everything she meant at Ancreton seemed to sort of ooze out of her and everything I felt about her suddenly boiled over in me. I'd got a cold and was feeling pretty ghastly, anyway. I absolutely blazed. I said some pretty frightful things about even a common little gold-digger having the decency to be grateful. I said I thought her presence in the house was an insult to all of us, and I supposed that when she'd bamboozled Grandfather into marrying her she'd amuse herself with her frightful boy-friends until he was obliging enough to die and leave her his money. Yes, Mummy, I know it was awful, but it just *steamed* out of me and I couldn't stop it.'

'Oh, my poor Fen!' Jenetta Ancred murmured.

'It's the way she took it that's important,' Fenella continued, still gazing at Alleyn. 'I must admit she took it pretty well. She said, quite calmly, that it was all very fine for me to talk, but I didn't know what it was like to be on my beam-ends with no chance of getting anywhere in my job. She said she knew she wasn't any good for the stage except as a showgirl, and that didn't last long. I can remember the actual words she used. Fifth-rate theatrical slang. She said: "I know what you all think. You think I'm playing Noddy up for

what I can get out of him. You think that when we're married
I'll begin to work in some of the funny business. Look, I've
had all that, and I reckon I'll be as good a judge as anybody
of what's due to my position." And then she said she'd always
thought she was the Cinderella type. She said she didn't
expect me to understand what a kick she'd get out of being
Lady Ancred. She was extraordinarily frank and completely
childish about it. She told me she used to lie in bed imagining
how she'd give her name and address to people in shops, and
what it would sound like when they called her m'lady. "Gee,"
she said, "will that sound good! Boy, oh boy!" I really think
she'd almost forgotten I was there, and the queer thing is that
I didn't feel angry with her any longer. She asked me all sorts
of questions about precedence; about whether at a dinner-
party she'd go in before Lady Baumstein. Benny Baumstein is
the frightful little man who owns the Sunshine Circuit shows.
She was in one of his No. 3 companies. When I said she
would, she said "Yip-ee" like a cow-girl. It was frightful, of
course, but it was so completely real that in a way I respected
it. She actually said she knew what she called her "accent"
wasn't so hot, but she was going to ask "Noddy" to teach her to
speak more refined.' Fenella looked from her mother to Paul
and shook her head helplessly. 'It was no good,' she said, 'I just
succumbed. It was awful, and it was funny, and most of all it
was somehow genuinely pathetic.' She turned back to Alleyn:
'I don't know if you can believe that,' she said.

'Very easily,' Alleyn returned. 'She was on the defensive and angry when I saw her, but I noticed something of
the same quality myself. Toughness, naivety, and candour all
rolled into one. Always very disarming. One meets it occasionally in pickpockets.'

'But in a funny sort of way,' Fenella said, 'I felt that she
was honest and had got standards. And much as I loathed
the thought of her marriage to Grandfather, I felt sure that
according to her lights she'd play fair. And most important
of all, I felt that the title meant much more to her than the

money. She was grateful and affectionate because he was going to give her the title, and never would she have done anything to prevent him doing so. While I was still gaping at her she took my arm, and believe it or not, we went upstairs together like a couple of schoolgirls. She asked me into her frightful rooms, and I actually sat on the bed while she drenched herself in pre-war scent, repainted her face and dressed for dinner. Then she came along to my room and sat on my bed while I changed. She never left off talking, and I suffered it all in a trance. It really was most peculiar. Down we went, together still, and there was Aunt Milly, howling for the kids' and Grandfather's medicine. We'd left it, of course, in the flower-room, and the queerest thing of all,' Fenella slowly wound up, 'was that, although I still took the gloomiest possible view of her relationship with Grandfather, I simply could not continue to loathe her guts. And, Mr Alleyn, I swear she never did anything to harm him. Do you believe me? Is all this as important as Paul and I think it is?'

Alleyn, who had been watching Jenetta Ancred's hands relax and the colour return to her face, roused himself and said: 'It may be of enormous importance. I think you may have tidied up a very messy corner.'

'A messy corner,' she repeated. 'Do you mean—?'

'Is there anything else?'

'The next part really belongs to Paul. Go on, Paul.'

'Darling,' said Jenetta Ancred, and the two syllables, in her deepish voice, sounded like a reiterated warning. 'Don't you think you've made your point? Must we?'

'Yes, Mummy, we must. Now then, Paul.'

Paul began rather stiffly and with a deprecatory air: 'I'm afraid, sir, that all this is going to sound extremely obvious and perhaps a bit high-falutin, but Fen and I have talked it over pretty thoroughly and we've come to a definite conclusion. Of course it was obvious from the beginning that the letters meant Sonia Orrincourt. She was the only person who didn't get one, and she's the one who benefited most by

Grandfather's death. But those letters were written before they found the rat-bane in her suitcase, and, in fact, before there was a shred of evidence against her. So that if she's innocent, and I agree with Fenella that she is, it means one of two things. Either the letter-writer knew something that he or she genuinely thought suspicious, and none of us did know anything of the sort; or, the letter was written out of pure spite, and not to mince matters, with the intention of getting her hanged. If that's so, it seems to me that the tin of rat-bane was deliberately planted. And it seems to me—to Fen and me—that the same person put that book on embalming in the cheese-dish because he was afraid nobody would ever remember it, and was shoving it under our noses in the most startling form he could think of.'

He paused and glanced nervously at Alleyn, who said: 'That sounds like perfectly sound reasoning to me.'

'Well, then, sir,' said Paul quickly, 'I think you'll agree that the next point is important. It's about this same damn' silly business with the book in the cheese-dish, and I may as well say at the outset it casts a pretty murky light on my cousin Cedric. In fact, if we're right, we've got to face the responsibility of practically accusing Cedric of attempted murder.'

'*Paul!*'

'I'm sorry, Aunt Jen, but we've decided.'

'If you're right, and I'm sure you're wrong, have you thought of the sequel? The newspapers. The beastliness. Have you thought of poor Milly, who dotes on the little wretch?'

'We're sorry,' Paul repeated stubbornly.

'You're inhuman,' cried his aunt and threw up her hands.

'Well,' said Alleyn peaceably, 'let's tackle this luncheon-party while we're at it. What was everybody doing before the book on embalming made its appearance?'

This seemed to nonplus them. Fenella said impatiently: 'Just sitting. Waiting for someone to break it up. Aunt Milly does hostess at Ancreton, but Aunt Pauline (Paul's mother) rather feels she ought to when in residence. She—you don't mind my mentioning it Paul, darling?—she huffs and puffs about it a bit, and makes a point of waiting for Aunt Milly to give the imperceptible signal to rise. I rather fancied Aunt Milly kept us sitting for pure devilment. Anyway, there we stuck.'

'Sonia fidgeted,' said Paul, 'and sort of groaned.'

'Aunt Dessy said she thought it would be nice if we could escape having luncheon dishes that looked like the village pond when the floods had subsided. That was maddening for Aunt Milly. She said with a short laugh that Dessy wasn't obliged to stay on at Ancreton.'

'And Dessy,' Paul continued, 'said that to her certain knowledge Milly and Pauline were holding back some tins of whitebait.'

'Everybody began talking at once, and Sonia said: "Pardon me, but how does the chorus go?" Cedric tittered and got up and wandered to the sideboard.'

'And this is our point, sir,' Paul cut in with determination. 'The cheese was found by my cousin Cedric. He went to the sideboard and came back with a book, and dropped it over my mother's shoulder on to her plate. It gave her a shock as you can imagine.'

'She gave a screech and fainted, actually,' Fenella added.

'My Mama,' said Paul unhappily, 'was a bit wrought up by the funeral and so on. She really fainted, Aunt Jen.'

'My dear boy, I'm sure she did.'

'It gave her a fright.'

'Naturally,' Alleyn murmured, 'books on embalming don't fall out of cheese-dishes every day in the week.'

'We'd all,' Paul went on, 'just about *had* Cedric. Nobody paid any attention to the book itself. We merely suggested that it wasn't amazingly funny to frighten people, and that anyway he stank.'

'I was watching Cedric, then,' Fenella said. 'There was something queer about him. He never took his eyes off Sonia. And then, just as we were all herding Aunt Pauline out of the room, he gave one of his yelps and said he'd remembered something in the book. He ran to the door and began reading out of it about arsenic.'

'And then somebody remembered that Sonia had been seen looking at the book.'

'And I'll swear,' Fenella cut in, 'she didn't know what he was driving at. I don't believe she ever really understood. Aunt Dessy did her stuff and wailed and said: "No, no, don't go on! I can't bear it!" and Cedric purred: "But, Dessy, my sweet, what have I said? Why shouldn't darling Sonia read about her fiancé's coming embalmment?" and Sonia burst into tears and said we were all plotting against her and rushed out of the room.'

'The point is, sir, if Cedric hadn't behaved as he did, nobody would have thought of connecting the book with the suggestion in the letters. You see?'

Alleyn said: 'It's a point.'

'There's something else,' Paul added, again with that tinge of satisfaction in his voice. '*Why* did Cedric look in the cheese-dish?'

'Presumably because he wanted some cheese?'

'No!' Paul said triumphantly. 'That's just where we've got him, sir. He never touches cheese. He detests it.'

'So you see,' said Fenella.

When Alleyn left, Paul showed him into the hall, and, after some hesitation, asked if he might walk with him a little way. They went together, head-down against a blustering wind, along Cheyne Walk. Ragged clouds scurried across the sky, and the sounds of river traffic were blown intermittently against their chilled ears. Paul, using his stick, limped along at a round pace, and for some minutes in silence.

At last he said: 'I suppose it's true that you can't escape your heredity.' And as Alleyn turned his head to look at him, he went on slowly: 'I meant to tell you that story quite differently. Without any build-up. Fen did, too. But somehow when we got going something happened to us. Perhaps it was Aunt Jen's opposition. Or perhaps when there's anything like a crisis we can't escape a sense of audience. I heard myself doing the same sort of thing over there.' He jerked his head vaguely towards the east. 'The gay young officer rallying his men. It went down quite well with them, too, but it makes me feel pretty hot under the collar when I think about it now. And about the way we strutted our stuff back there at Aunt Jen's.'

'You made your points very neatly,' said Alleyn.

'A damn' sight too neatly,' Paul rejoined, grimly. 'That's why I did think I'd like to try and say without any flourishes that we do honestly believe that all this stuff about poison has simply been concocted by Cedric to try and upset the Will. And we think it would be a pretty poor show to let him get away with it. On all counts.'

Alleyn didn't reply immediately, and Paul said, nervously: 'I suppose it'd be quite out of order for me to ask whether you think we're right.'

'Ethically,' said Alleyn, 'yes. But I don't think you realized the implications. Your aunt did.'

'I know, Aunt Jen's very fastidious. It's the dirty linen in public that she hates.'

'And with reason,' said Alleyn.

'Well, we'll all have to lump it. But what I meant really was, were we right in our deductions?'

'I ought to return an official and ambiguous answer to that,' Alleyn said. 'But I won't. I may be wrong, but on the evidence that we've got up to date I should say your deductions were ingenious and almost entirely wrong.'

A sharp gust carried away the sound of his voice.

'What?' said Paul, distantly and without emphasis. 'I didn't quite hear—'

'Wrong,' Alleyn repeated, strongly. 'As far as I can judge, you know, quite wrong.'

Paul stopped short, and, dipping his head to meet the wind, stared at Alleyn with an expression not of dismay, but of doubt, as if he still thought he must have misunderstood.

'But I don't see...we thought...it all hangs together—'

'As an isolated group of facts, perhaps it does.'

They resumed their walk, and Alleyn heard him say fretfully: 'I wish you'd explain.' And after another pause he peered rather anxiously at Alleyn. 'Perhaps it wouldn't do, though,' he added.

Alleyn thought for a moment, and then, taking Paul by the elbow, steered him into the shelter of a side street. 'We can't go on bawling at each other in a gale,' he said, 'but I don't see that it can do any harm to explain this much. It's quite possible that if all this dust had not been raised after your grandfather's death, Miss Orrincourt might still have become Lady Ancred.'

Paul's jaw dropped. 'I don't get that.'

'You don't?'

'Good God,' Paul roared out suddenly, 'you can't mean Cedric?'

'Sir Cedric,' said Alleyn, dryly, 'is my authority. He tells me he has seriously considered marrying her.'

After a long silence Paul said slowly: 'They're as thick as thieves, of course. But I never guessed...No, it'd be too much...I'm sorry, sir, but you're sure—?'

'Unless he invented the story.'

'To cover up his tracks,' said Paul instantly.

'Extremely elaborate and she could deny it. As a matter of fact her manner suggested some sort of understanding between them.'

Paul raised his clasped hands to his mouth and thoughtfully blew into them. 'Suppose,' he said, 'he suspected her, and wanted to make sure?'

'That would be an entirely different story.'

'Is that your theory, sir?'

'Theory?' Alleyn repeated vaguely. 'I haven't got a theory. I haven't sorted things out. Mustn't keep you standing here in the cold.' He held out his hand. Paul's was like ice. 'Goodbye,' said Alleyn.

'One minute, sir. Will you tell me this? I give you my word it'll go no further. Was my Grandfather murdered?'

'Oh, yes,' said Alleyn. 'Yes. I'm afraid we may be sure of that. He was murdered.' He walked down the street, leaving Paul, still blowing on his frozen knuckles, to stare after him.

The canvas walls were faintly luminous. They were laced to their poles with ropes and glowed in the darkness. Blobs of light from hurricane lanterns suspended within formed a globular pattern across the surface. One of these lanterns must have been touching the wall, for the village constable on duty outside could clearly make out shadows of wire and the precise source of light.

He glanced uneasily at the motionless figure of his companion, a police officer from London, wearing a short cape. 'Bitter cold,' he said.

'That's right.'

'Be long, d'yew reckon?'

'Can't say.'

The constable would have enjoyed a walk. He was a moralist and a philosopher, well known in Ancreton for his pronouncements upon the conduct of politicians and for his independent views in the matter of religion. But his companion's taciturnity, and the uncomfortable knowledge that anything he said would be audible on the other side of the canvas, put a damper on conversation. He stamped once or twice, finding reassurance in the crunch of gravel under his feet. There were noises within the enclosure: voices, soft thumps. At the far end and high above them, as if suspended in the night, and lit theatrically from below, knelt three angels. 'Through the long night watches,' the constable said to himself, 'may Thine angels spread their white wings above me, watching round my head.'

Within the enclosure, but, close beside him, the voice of the Chief Inspector from the Yard said: 'Are we ready, Curtis?' His shadowy figure suddenly loomed up inside the canvas wall. 'Quite ready,' somebody else said. 'Then if I may have the key, Mr Ancred?' 'Oh—oh—er—yes.' That was poor Mr Thomas Ancred.

The constable listened, yet desired not to listen, to the next too-lucid train of sounds. He had heard them before, on the day of the funeral, when he came down early to have a look while his cousin, the sexton, got things fixed up. Very heavy lock. They'd had to give it a drop of oil. Seldom used. His flesh leapt on his bones as a screech rent the cold air. 'Them ruddy hinges,' he thought. The blobs of light were withdrawn and the voices with them. He could still hear them, however, though now they sounded hollow. Beyond the hedge a match flared up in the dark. That would be the driver of the long black car, of course, waiting in the lane. The constable wouldn't have minded a pipe himself.

The Chief Inspector's voice, reflected from stone walls, said distinctly: 'Get those acetylene lamps going, Bailey.' 'Yes, sir,' someone answered, so close to the constable that he jumped again. With a hissing noise, a new brilliance sprang up behind the canvas. Strange distorted shadows leapt among the trees about the cemetery.

Now came sounds to which he had looked forward with squeamish relish. A drag of wood on stone followed by the uneven scuffles of boots and heavy breathing. He cleared his throat and glanced stealthily at his companion.

The enclosure was again full of invisible men. 'Straight down on the trestles. Right.' The squeak of wood and then silence.

The constable drove his hands deep into his pockets and looked up at the three angels and at the shape of St Stephen's spire against the stars. 'Bats in that belfry,' he thought. 'Funny how a chap'll say it, not thinking.' An owl hooted up in Ancreton woods.

Beyond the canvas there was movement. A light voice said jerkily: 'I think, if it doesn't make any difference, I'd like to wait outside. I won't go away. You can call me, you know.'

'Yes, of course.'

A canvas flap was pulled aside, letting out a triangle of light on the grass. A man came out. He wore a heavy overcoat and muffler and his hat was pulled over his face, but the constable had recognized his voice and shifted uneasily.

'Oh, it's you, Bream,' said Thomas Ancred.

'Yes, Mr Thomas.'

'Cold, isn't it?'

'Hard frost before dawn, sir.'

Above them the church clock gave a preparatory whirr and with a sweet voice told two in the morning.

'I don't like this much, Bream.'

'Very upsetting, sir, I'm sure.'

'Terribly upsetting, yes.'

'And yet, sir,' said Bream with a didactic air, 'I been thinking: this here poor remains beant a matter to scare a chap, if rightly considered. It beant your respected father hisself as you might put it, sir. He's well away receiving his reward by now, and what you are called to look upon is a harmless enough affair. No more, if you'll excuse me, than a left-off garment. As has been preached at us souls regular in this very church.'

'I dare say,' said Thomas. 'Nevertheless...Well, thank you.'

He moved away down the gravel path. The London officer turned to watch him. Thomas did not move quite out of range of the veiled light. He stood, with his head bent, near the dim shape of a gravestone and seemed to be rubbing his hands together.

'Cold and nervous, poor chap,' Bream said to himself.

'Before we go any further' (that was Chief Inspector Alleyn again), 'will you make a formal examination, Mr Mortimer? We'd like your identification of the name-plate and your assurance that everything is as it was at the time of the funeral.'

A clearing of the throat, a pause and then a muffled voice. 'Perfectly in order. Our own workmanship, Mr Alleyn. Casket and plate.'

'Thank you. All right, Thompson.'

The click of metal and the faint grind of disengaging screws. This seemed to Bream to continue an unconscionable time. Nobody spoke. From his mouth and nostrils and those of the London constable, little jets of breath drifted out and condensed on the frozen air. The London man switched on his flash-lamp. Its beam illuminated Thomas Ancred, who looked up and blinked.

'I'm just waiting,' he said. 'I won't go away.'

'Quite all right, sir.'

'Now,' ordered the voice in the enclosure, 'everything free? Right!'

'Just ease a little, it's a precision fit. That's right. Slide.'

'Oh, cripes!' Bream said to himself.

Wood whispered along wood. This sound was followed by complete silence. Thomas Ancred turned away from grass to gravel path and walked aimlessly to and fro.

'Curtis? Will you and Dr Withers—?'

'Yes. Thanks. Move that light a little this way, Thompson. Will you come here, Dr Withers?'

'The—ah—the process is quite satisfactory, don't you consider, Doctor? Only a short time, of course, but I can assure you there would be no deterioration.'

'Indeed? Remarkable.'

'One is gratified.'

'I think we'll have that bandage taken away, if you please. Fox, will you tell Mr Ancred we're ready for him?'

Bream watched the thick-set Inspector Fox emerge and walk over towards Thomas. Before he had gone more than a few paces there was a sudden and violent ejaculation inside the enclosure. 'Good God, look at that!' Inspector Fox paused. The Chief Inspector's voice said, very sharply, 'Quiet, Dr Withers, please,' and there followed a rapid whispering.

Inspector Fox moved away and joined Thomas Ancred. 'If you'll come this way, Mr Ancred.' 'Oh! yes, of course. Very good. Right ho!' said Thomas in a high voice, and followed him back to the enclosure. 'If I moved a bit,' Bream thought, 'when they opened the flaps I'd see in.' But he did not move. The London constable held the doorway open, glancing impassively into the tent before he let the canvas fall. The voices began again.

'Now, this is not going to be a very big ordeal, Mr Ancred.'

'Oh, isn't it? Oh, good.'

'Will you—?'

Bream heard Thomas move. 'There, you see. Quite peaceful.'

'I—yes—I identify him.'

'That's all right, then. Thank you.'

'No,' said Thomas, and his voice rose hysterically, 'it's not all right. There's something all wrong, in fact. Papa had a fine head of hair. Hadn't he, Dr Withers? He was very proud of it, wasn't he? And his moustache. This is bald. *What have they done with his hair?*'

'Steady! Put your head down. You'll be all right. Give me that brandy, Fox, will you? Damn, he's fainted.'

'Well, Curtis,' Alleyn said as the car slid between rows of sleeping houses, 'I hope you'll be able to give us something definite.'

'Hope so,' said Dr Curtis, stifling a heavy yawn.

'I'd like to ask you, Doctor,' said Fox, 'whether you'd expect one fatal dose of arsenic to have that effect.'

'What effect? Oh, the hair. No. I wouldn't. It's more often a symptom of chronic poisoning.'

'In for one of those messes, are we?' Fox grumbled. 'That will be nice. Fields of suspects opened up wide, with the possibility of Miss O. being framed.'

'There are objections to chronic poisoning, Br'er Fox,' Alleyn said. 'He might die when he'd concocted a Will unfavourable to the poisoner. And moreover, you'd expect a progressive loss of hair, not a sudden post-mortem moult. Is that right, Curtis?'

'Certainly.'

'Well, then,' Fox persisted heavily, 'how about the embalming process? Would that account for it?'

'Emphatically not,' Mr Mortimer interjected. 'I've given the Chief Inspector our own formula. An unusual step, but in the circumstances desirable. No doubt, Doctor, he has made you conversant—'

'Oh, yes,' sighed Dr Curtis. 'Formalin. Glycerine. Boric acid. Menthol. Potassium nitrate. Sodium citrate. Oil of cloves. Water.'

'Precisely.'

'Hey!' said Fox. 'No arsenic?'

'You're two days late with the news, Br'er Fox. Things have moved while you were at Ancreton. Arsenic went out some time ago, didn't it, Mr Mortimer?'

'Formalin,' Mr Mortimer agreed with hauteur, 'is infinitely superior.'

'There now,' Fox rumbled with great satisfaction. 'That does clear things up a bit, doesn't it, Mr Alleyn? If arsenic's found it's got no business to be there. That's something definite. And what's more, any individual who banked on its being used by the embalmer made the mistake of his or her life. Nothing for counsel to muddle the jury with, either. Mr Mortimer's evidence would settle that. Well.'

Alleyn said: 'Mr Mortimer, had Sir Henry any notion of the method used?'

In a voice so drowsy that it reminded Alleyn of the dormouse's, Mr Mortimer said: 'It's very curious, Chief

Inspector, that you should ask that question. Oh, very curious. Because, between you and I, the deceased gentleman showed quite an unusual interest. He sent for me and discussed the arrangements for the interment. Two years ago, that was.'

'Good Lord!'

'That is not so unusual in itself. Gentlemen of his position do occasionally give detailed instructions. But the deceased was so very particular. He—well, really,' Mr Mortimer said, coughing slightly, 'he quite read me a little lecture on embalming. He had a little book. Yes,' said Mr Mortimer, swallowing a yawn, 'rather a quaint little book. Very old. It seemed an ancestor of his had been embalmed by the method, *quate* outdated, I may say, outlined in this tainy tome. Sir Henry wished to ascertain if our method was similar. When I ventured to suggest the book was somewhat demode, he became—well, *so* annoyed that it was rather awkward. Very awkward, in fact. He was insistent that we should use the same process on— ah—for—ah—himself. He quate *ordered* me to do it.'

'But you didn't consent?'

'I must confess, Chief Inspector, I—I—the situation was most awkward. I feared he would upset himself seriously. I must confess that I compromaysed. In point of fact, I—'

'You consented?'

'I would have gladly refused the commission altogether but he would take no refusal. He forced me to take the book away with me. I returned it with compliments, and without comment through the registered post. He replied that when the time came I was to understand my instructions. The— ah—the time came and—and—'

'You followed your own method, and said nothing to anybody?'

'It seemed the only thing to do. Anything else was impossible from the point of view of technique. Ridiculous, in fact. Such preposterous ingredients! You can't imagine.'

'Well,' said Fox, 'as long as you can testify there was no arsenic. Eh, Mr Alleyn?'

'I must say,' said Mr Mortimer, 'I don't at all care for the idea of giving evidence in an affair of this sort. Ours is a delicate, and you might say exclusive, profession, Chief Inspector. Publicity of this kind is most undesirable.'

'You may not be subpoenaed, after all,' said Alleyn.

'Not? But I understood Inspector Fox to say—'

'You never know. Cheer up, Mr Mortimer.'

Mr Mortimer muttered to himself disconsolately and fell into a doze.

'What about the cat?' Fox asked. 'And the bottle of medicine?'

'No report yet.'

'We've been busy,' Dr Curtis complained. 'You and your cats! The report should be in some time today. What's all this about a cat anyway?'

'Never you mind,' Alleyn grunted, 'you do your Marsh-Berzelius tests with a nice open mind. And your Fresenius process later on, I shouldn't wonder.'

Dr Curtis paused in the act of lighting his pipe. 'Fresenius process?' he said.

'Yes, and your ammonium chloride and your potassium iodide and your Bunsen flame and your platinum wire. And look for the pretty green line, blast you!'

After a long silence Dr Curtis said: 'It's like that, is it?' and glanced at Mr Mortimer.

'It may be like that.'

'Having regard to the general lay-out?'

'That's the burden of our song.'

Fox said suddenly: 'Was he bald when they laid him out?'

'Not he. Mrs Henry Ancred and Mrs Kentish were both present. They'd have noticed. Besides, the hair was there, Fox. We collected it while you were ministering to Thomas.'

'Oh!' Fox ruminated for a time and then said loudly: 'Mr Mortimer! Mr Mortimer!'

'Wha—?'

'Did you notice Sir Henry's hair when you were working on him?'

'Eh? Oh, yes,' said Mr Mortimer, hurriedly, but in a voice slurred with sleep. 'Yes, indeed. We all remarked on it. A magnificent head of hair.' He yawned hideously. 'A magnificent head of hair,' he repeated.

Alleyn looked at Dr Curtis. 'Consistent?' he asked.

'With your green line? Yes.'

'Pardon?' said Mr Mortimer anxiously.

'All right, Mr Mortimer. Nothing. We're in London. You'll be in bed by daybreak.'

CHAPTER SEVENTEEN

Escape of Miss O.

AT BREAKFAST ALLEYN SAID: 'This case of ours is doing the usual snowball business, Troy.'

'Gathering up complications as it goes?'

'A mass of murky stuff in this instance. Grubby stuff, and a lot of it waste matter. Do you want an interim report?'

'Only if you feel like making one. And is there enough time?'

'Actually there's not. I can answer a crisp question or two, though, if you care to rap them out at me.'

'You know, I expect, what they'll be.'

'Was Ancred murdered? I think so. Did Sonia Orrincourt do it? I don't know. I shall know, I believe, when the analyst sends in his report.'

'If he finds the arsenic?'

'If he finds it in one place, then I'm afraid it's Sonia Orrincourt. If he finds it in three places, it's Sonia Orrincourt or one other. If he doesn't find it at all, then I *think* it's that other. I'm not positive.'

'And—the one other?'

'I suppose it's no more unpleasant for you to speculate about one than about several.'

'I'd rather know, if it's all right to tell me.'

'Very well,' Alleyn said, and told her.

After a long silence she said: 'But it seems completely unreal. I can't possibly believe it.'

'Didn't everything they did at Ancreton seem a bit unreal?'

'Yes, of course. But to imagine that underneath all the showings-off and temperaments *this* could be happening...I can't. Of all of them...that one!'

'Remember, I may be wrong.'

'You've a habit of not being wrong, though, haven't you?'

'The Yard,' said Alleyn, 'is littered with my blunders. Ask Fox. Troy, is this very beastly for you?'

'No,' said Troy, 'it's mostly bewildering. I didn't form any attachments at Ancreton. I can't give it a personal application.'

'Thank God for that,' he said and went to the Yard.

Here he found Fox in waiting with the tin of rat-bane. 'I haven't had a chance to hear your further adventures at Ancreton, Foxkin. The presence of Mr Mortimer rather cramped our style last night. How did you get on?'

'Quite nicely, sir. No trouble really about getting the prints. Well, when I say no trouble, there was quite a bit of high-striking in some quarters as was to be expected in that family. Miss O. made trouble, and, for a while, stuck out she wouldn't have it, but I talked her round. Nobody else actually objected, though you'd have thought Mrs Kentish and Miss Desdemona Ancred were being asked to walk into the condemned cell, the way they carried on. Bailey got down by the early train in the morning and worked through the prints you asked for. We found a good enough impression in paint on the wall of Mrs Alleyn's tower. Miss O. all right. *And* her prints are in the book. Lots of others too, of course. Prints all over the cover, from when they looked at it after it turned up in the cheese-dish, no doubt. I've checked up on the letters, but there's nothing in it. They handed them round and there you are. Same thing in the flower-room. Regular mess of prints and some odds and ends where they'd missed sweeping. Coloured tape off florist's boxes, leaves and stalks, scraps of sealing-wax, fancy paper and so on. I've kept all of it in case there was anything. I took a chance to slip into Miss O.'s room. Nothing beyond some skittish literature and a few letters from men written before Sir Henry's day. One, more recent, from a young lady. I memorized it. "Dear S. Good for you, kid, stick to it, and don't forget your old pals when you're Lady A. Think the boy friend'd do anything for me in the business? God knows, I'm not so hot on this Shakespeare, but he must know other managements. Does he wear bed-socks? Regards Clarrie."'

'No mention of the egregious Cedric?'

'Not a word. We looked at Miss Able's cupboard—Only her own prints. I called in at Mr Juniper's. He says the last lot of that paper was taken up with some stuff for the rest of the house a fortnight ago. Two sets of prints on the bell-push from Sir Henry's room—his own and old Barker's. Looks as if Sir Henry had grabbed at it, tried to use it and dragged it off.'

'As we thought.'

'Mr Juniper got in a great way when I started asking questions. I went very easy with him, but he made me a regular speech about how careful he is and showed me his books. He reckons he always double-checks everything he makes up. He's particularly careful, he says, because of Dr Withers being uncommonly fussy. It seems they had a bit of a row. The doctor reckoned the kids' medicine wasn't right, and Juniper took it for an insult. He says the doctor must have made the mistake himself and tried to save his face by turning round on him. He let on the doctor's a bit of a lad and a great betting man, and he thinks he'd been losing pretty solidly and was worried, and made a mistake weighing the kids or something. But that wouldn't apply to Sir Henry's medicine, because it was the mixture as before. And I found out that at the time he made it up he was out of arsenic and hasn't got any yet.'

'Good for Mr Juniper,' said Alleyn dryly.

'Which brings us,' Fox continued, 'to this tin.' He laid his great hand beside it on the desk. 'Bailey's gone over it for dabs. And here we have got something, Mr Alleyn, and about time too, you'll be thinking. Now this tin has got the usual set of prints. Some of the search party's, in fact. Latent, but Bailey brought them up and got some good photographs. There's Mrs Kentish's. She must have just touched it. Miss Desdemona Ancred seems to have picked it up by the edge. Mr Thomas Ancred grasped it more solidly round the sides and handled it again when he took it out of his bag. Mrs Henry Ancred held it firmly towards the bottom. Sir Cedric's prints are all over it, and there, you'll notice, are the marks round the lid where he had a shot at opening it.'

'Not a very determined shot.'

'No. Probably scared of getting rat-bane on his mani-cure,' said Fox. 'But the point is, you see—'

'No Orrincourt?'

'Not a sign of her. Not a sign of glove-marks either. It was a dusty affair, and the dust, except for the prints we got, wasn't disturbed.'

'It's a point. Well, Fox, now Bailey's finished with it we can open it.'

The lid was firm and it took a penny and considerable force to prise it up. An accretion of the contents had sealed it. The tin was three-parts full, and the greyish paste bore traces of the implement that had been used to scoop it out.

'We'll have a photo-micrograph of this,' Alleyn said.

'If Orrincourt's our bird, sir, it looks as if we'll have to hand the tin over to the defence, doesn't it?'

'We'll have to get an expert's opinion, Fox. Curtis's boys can speak up when they've finished the job in hand. Pray continue, as the Immortal used to say, with your most inter-esting narrative.'

'There's not much more. I took a little peep at the young baronet's room, too. Dunning letters, lawyer's letters, letters from his stockbroker. I should say he was in deep. I've made a note of the principal creditors.'

'For an officer without a search warrant you seem to have got on very comfortably.'

'Isabel helped. She's taken quite a fancy for investigation. She kept a lookout in the passage.'

'With parlour-maids,' Alleyn said, 'you're out on your own. A masterly technique.'

'I called on Dr Withers yesterday afternoon and told him you'd decided on the exhumation.'

'How did he take it?'

'He didn't say much but he went a queer colour. Well, naturally. They never like it. Reflection on their professional standing and so on. He thought a bit and then said he'd prefer to be present. I said we'd expect that, anyway. I was just going when he called me back. "Here!" he said, kind of hurriedly and as if he wasn't sure he might not be making a fool of himself, "you don't want to pay too much attention to anything that idiot Juniper may have told you. The man's an ass." As soon as I was out of the house,' said Fox, 'I made a note of that to be sure the words were correct. The maid was showing me out at the time.'

'Curtis asked him last night, after we'd tidied up in the cemetery, if he'd like to come up and watch the analysis. He agreed. He's sticking to it that the embalmers must have used something that caused the hair to fall out. Mr Mortimer was touched to the professional quick, of course.'

'It's a line defending counsel may fancy,' said Fox gloomily. The telephone rang and Fox answered it.

'It's Mr Mortimer,' he said.

'Oh, Lord! You take it, Fox.'

'He's engaged at the moment, Mr Mortimer. Can I help you?'

The telephone cackled lengthily and Fox looked at Alleyn with bland astonishment. 'Just a moment.' He laid down the receiver. 'I don't follow this. Mr Alleyn hasn't got a secretary.'

'What's all this?' said Alleyn sharply.

Fox clapped his hand over the receiver. 'He says your secretary rang up their office half an hour ago and asked them to repeat the formula for embalming. His partner, Mr Loame, answered. He wants to know if it was all right.'

'Did Loame give the formula?'

'Yes.'

'Bloody fool,' Alleyn said violently. 'Tell him it's all wrong and ring off.'

'I'll let Mr Alleyn know,' said Fox, and hung up the receiver. Alleyn reached for it and pulled the telephone towards him.

'Ancreton, 2A,' he said. 'Priority. Quick as you can.' And while he waited: 'We may want a car at once, Fox. Ring down, will you? We'll take Thompson with us. And we'll need a search warrant.' Fox went into the next room and telephoned. When he returned Alleyn was speaking. 'Hallo. May I speak to Miss Orrincourt?...Out?...When will she be in?...I see. Get me Miss Able, Barker, will you?...It's Scotland Yard here.' He looked round at Fox. 'We'll be going,' he said. 'She came up to London last night and is expected back for lunch. Damn! Why the hell doesn't the Home Office come to light with that report? We need it now, and badly. What's the time?'

'Ten to twelve, sir.'

'Her train gets in at twelve. We haven't an earthly... Hallo! Hallo! Is that you, Miss Able?...Alleyn here. Don't answer anything but yes or no, please. I want you to do something that is urgent and important. Miss Orrincourt is returning by the train that arrives at midday. Please find out if any one has left to meet her. If not, make some excuse for going yourself in the pony-cart. If it's too late for that, meet it when it arrives at the house. Take Miss Orrincourt into your part of the house and keep her there. Tell her I said so and take no refusal. It's urgent. She's not to go into the other part of the house. Got that?...Sure?...Right. Splendid. Goodbye.'

He rang off, and found Fox waiting with his overcoat and hat. 'Wait a bit,' he said. 'That's not good enough.' And turned back to the telephone. 'Get me Camber Cross Police Station. They're the nearest to Ancreton, aren't they, Fox?'

'Three miles. The local PC lives in Ancreton parish, though. On duty last night.'

'That's the chap, Bream...Hallo!...Chief Inspector Alleyn, Scotland Yard. Is your chap Bream in the station?... Can you find him?...Good! The Ancreton pub. I'd be much obliged if you'd ring through. Tell him to go at once to Ancreton Halt. A Miss Orrincourt will get off the midday train. She'll be met from the Manor House. He's to let the trap go away without her, take her to the pub, and wait there for me. Right! Thanks.'

'Will he make it?' Fox asked.

'He has his dinner at the pub and he's got a bike. It's no more than a mile and a half. Here we go, Fox. If, in the ripeness of time, Mr Loame is embalmed by his own firm, I hope they make a mess of him. What precisely did this bogus secretary say?'

'Just that you'd told him to get a confirmation of the formula. It was a toll-call, but, of course, Loame thought you were back at Ancreton.'

'And so he tells poor old Ancred's killer that there was no arsenic used in the embalming and blows our smoke-screen to hell. As Miss O. would say, what a pal! Where's my bag? Come on.'

But as they reached the door the telephone rang again.

'I'll go,' Alleyn said. 'With any luck it's Curtis.'

It was Dr Curtis. 'I don't know whether you'll like this,' he said. 'It's the Home Office report on the cat, the medicine and the deceased. First analysis completed. No arsenic anywhere.'

'Good!' said Alleyn. 'Now tell them to try for thallium acetate, and ring me at Ancreton when they've found it.'

❧ ❧ ❧

They were to encounter yet another interruption. As they went out to the waiting car, they found Thomas, very white and pinched, on the bottom step.

'Oh, hallo,' he said. 'I was coming to see you. I want to see you awfully.'

'Important?' Alleyn said.

'To me,' Thomas rejoined with the air of innocence, 'it's as important as anything. You see, I came in by the morning train on purpose. I felt I had to. I'm going back this evening.'

'We're on our way to Ancreton now.'

'Really? Then I suppose you wouldn't...? Or shouldn't one suggest it?'

'We can take you with us. Certainly,' said Alleyn after a fractional pause.

'Isn't that lucky?' said Thomas wistfully and got into the back seat with them. Detective-Sergeant Thompson was already seated by the driver. They drove away in a silence lasting so long that Alleyn began to wonder if Thomas, after all, had nothing to say. At last, however, he plunged into conversation with an abruptness that startled his hearers.

'First of all,' said Thomas loudly, 'I want to apologize for my behaviour last night. Fainting! Well! I thought I left that kind of thing to Pauline. Everybody was so nice, too. The doctors and you,' he said, smiling wanly at Fox, 'driving me home and everything. I couldn't be more sorry.'

'Very understandable, I'm sure,' said Fox comfortably. 'You'd had a nasty shock.'

'Well, I had. Frightful, really. And the worst of it is, you know, I can't shake it off. When I *did* go to sleep it was so beastly. The dreams. And this morning with the family asking questions.'

'You said nothing, of course,' said Alleyn.

'You'd asked me not to, so I didn't, but they took it awfully badly. Cedric was quite furious, and Pauline said I was siding against the family. The point is, Alleyn, I honestly don't think I can stand any more. It's unlike me,' said Thomas. 'I must have a temperament after all. Fancy!'

'What exactly do you want to see us about?'

'I want to know. It's the uncertainty. I want to know why Papa's hair had fallen out. I want to know if he was poisoned and if you think Sonia did it. I'm quite discreet, really, and if you tell me I'll give you my solemn word of honour not to say anything. Not even to Caroline Able, though I dare say she could explain why I feel so peculiar. I want to know.'

'Everything from the beginning?'

'Yes, if you don't mind. Everything.'

'That's a tall order. We don't know everything. We're trying, very laboriously, to piece things together, and we've got, I think, almost the whole pattern. We believe your father was poisoned.'

Thomas rubbed the palms of his hands across the back of the driver's seat. 'Are you certain? That's horrible.'

'The bell-push in his room had been manipulated in such a way that it wouldn't ring. One of the wires had been released. The bell-push hung by the other wire and when he grasped it the wooden end came away in his hand. We started from there.'

'That seems a simple little thing.'

'There are lots of more complicated things. Your father made two Wills, and signed neither of them until the day of his Birthday party. The first he signed, as I think he told you, before the dinner. The second and valid one he signed late that night. We believe that Miss Orrincourt and your nephew Cedric were the only two people, apart from his solicitor, who knew of this action. She benefited greatly by the valid Will. He lost heavily.'

'Then why bring him into the picture?' Thomas asked instantly.

'He won't stay out. He hovers. For one thing, he and Miss Orrincourt planned all the practical jokes.'

'Goodness! But Papa's death wasn't a practical joke. Or was it?'

'Indirectly, it's just possible that it was caused by one. The final practical joke, the flying cow on the picture, probably caused Sir Henry to fix on the second draft.'

'I don't know anything about all that,' Thomas said dismally. 'I don't understand. I hoped you'd just tell me if Sonia did it.'

'We're still waiting for one bit of the pattern. Without it we can't be positive. It would be against one of our most stringent rules for me to name a suspect to an interested person when the case is still incomplete.'

'Well, couldn't you behave like they do in books? Give me a pointer or two?'

Alleyn raised an eyebrow and glanced at Fox. 'I'm afraid,' he said, 'that without a full knowledge of the information our pointers wouldn't mean very much.'

'Oh, dear! Still, I may as well hear them. Anything's better than this awful blank worrying. I'm not quite such a fool,' Thomas added, 'as I dare say I seem. I'm a good producer of plays. I'm used to analysing character and I've got a great eye for a situation. When I read the script of a murder play I always know who did it.'

'Well,' Alleyn said dubiously, 'here, for what they're worth, are some relative bits of fact. The bell-push. The children's ringworm. The fact that the anonymous letters were written on the children's school paper. The fact that only Sir Cedric and Miss Orrincourt knew your father signed the second Will. The book on embalming. The nature of arsenical poisoning, and the fact that none has been found in his body, his medicine, or in the body of his cat.'

'Carabbas? Does he come in? That *is* surprising. Go on.'

'His fur fell out, he was suspected of ringworm and destroyed. He had not got ringworm. The children had. They were dosed with a medicine that acts as a depilatory and their fur did *not* fall out. The cat was in your father's room on the night of his death.'

'And Papa gave him some hot milk as usual. I see.'

'The milk was cleared away and the Thermos scalded out and used afterwards. No chemical analysis was possible. Now, for the tin of rat-bane. It was sealed with an accretion of its content and had not been opened for a very long time.'

'So Sonia didn't put arsenic in the Thermos?'

'Not out of the tin, at any rate.'

'Not at all, if it wasn't—if—'

'Not at all, it seems.'

'And you think that somehow or another he took the Dr Withers ringworm poison.'

'If he did, analysis will show it. We've yet to find out if it does.'

'But,' said Thomas. 'Sonia brought it back from the chemist's. I remember hearing something about that.'

'She brought it, yes, together with Sir Henry's medicine. She put the bottles in the flower-room. Miss Fenella Ancred was there and left the room with her.'

'And Dr Withers,' Thomas went on, rather in the manner of a child continuing a narrative, 'came up that night and gave the children the medicine. Caroline was rather annoyed because he'd said she could do it. She felt,' Thomas said thoughtfully, 'that it rather reflected on her capability. But he quite insisted and wouldn't let her touch it. And then, you know, it didn't work. They should have been as bald as eggs, but they were not. As bald as eggs,' Thomas repeated with a shudder. 'Oh, yes, I see. Papa *was*, of course.'

He remained sitting very upright, with his hands on his knees, for some twenty minutes. The car had left London behind and slipped through a frozen landscape. Alleyn, with a deliberate effort, retraced the history of the case: Troy's long and detailed account, the turgid statements of the Ancreds, the visit to Dr Withers, the scene in the churchyard. What could it have been that Troy knew she had forgotten and believed to be important?

Thomas, with that disconcerting air of switching himself on, broke the long silence.

'Then I suppose,' he said very abruptly and in a high voice, 'that you think either Sonia gave him the children's medicine or one of us did. But we are not at all murderous people. But I suppose you'll say that lots of murderers have been otherwise quite nice quiet people, like the Dusseldorf Monster. But what about motive? You say Cedric knew Papa had signed the Will that cut him out of almost everything, so Cedric wouldn't. On the other hand, Milly didn't know he'd signed a second Will, and she was quite pleased about the first one, really, so *she* wouldn't. And that goes for Dessy too. She wasn't best pleased, but she wasn't much surprised or worried. And I hope you don't think…However,' Thomas hurried on, 'we come to Pauline. Pauline might have been very hurt about Paul and Panty and herself, but it was quite true what Papa said. Her husband left her very nicely off and she's not at all revengeful. It's not as if Dessy and Milly or I *wanted* money desperately, and it's not as if Pauline or Panty or Fenella (I'd forgotten Fenella and Jen) are vindictive slayers. They just aren't. And Cedric thought he was all right. And *honestly*,' Thomas ended, 'you can't suspect Barker and the maids.'

'No,' said Alleyn, 'we don't.'

'So it seems you must suspect a person who wanted money very badly and was left some in the first Will. And, of course, didn't much care for Papa. And Cedric, who's the only one who fits, won't do.'

He turned, after making this profound understatement, to fix upon Alleyn a most troubled and searching gaze.

'I think that's a pretty accurate summing up,' Alleyn said.

'Who could it be!' Thomas mused distractedly and added with a sidelong glance: 'But, then, you've picked up all sorts of information which you haven't mentioned.'

'Which I haven't time to mention,' Alleyn rejoined. 'There are Ancreton woods above that hill. We'll stop at the pub.'

PC Bream was standing outside the pub and stepped forward to open the door of the car. He was scarlet in the face.

'Well, Bream,' Alleyn said, 'carried out your job?'

'In a manner of speaking, sir,' said Bream, 'no. Good afternoon, Mr Thomas.'

Alleyn stopped short in the act of getting out. 'What? Isn't she there?'

'Circumstances,' Bream said indistinctly, 'over which I 'ad no control, intervened, sir.' He waved an arm at a bicycle leaning against the pub. The front tyre hung in a deflated festoon about the axle. 'Rubber being not of the best—'

'Where is she?'

'On my arrival, having run one mile and a quarter—'

'Where is she?'

'Hup,' said Bream miserably, 'at the 'ouse.'

'Get in here and tell us on the way.'

Bream wedged himself into one of the tip-up seats and the driver turned the car. 'Quick as you can,' Alleyn said. 'Now, Bream.'

'Having received instructions, sir, by telephone, from the Super at Camber Cross, me having my dinner at the pub, I proceeded upon my bicycle in the direction of Ancreton 'Alt at eleven-fifty a.m.'

'All right, all right,' said Fox. 'And your tyre blew out.'

'At eleven-fifty-one, sir, she blew on me. I inspected the damage, and formed the opinion it was impossible to proceed on my bicycle. Accordingly I ran.'

'You didn't run fast enough, seemingly. Don't you know you're supposed to keep yourself fit in the force?' said Fox severely.

'I ran, sir,' Bream rejoined with dignity, 'at the rate of one mile in ten minutes and arrived at the 'Alt at twelve-four, the train 'aving departed at twelve-one, and the ladies in the pony-carriage being still in view on the road to the Manor.'

'The ladies?' said Alleyn.

'There was two of them. I attempted to attract their attention by raising my voice, but without success. I then returned to the pub, picking up that there cantankerous bike ong rowt.'

Fox muttered to himself.

'I reported by phone to the Super. He give me a blast, and said he would ring the Manor and request the lady in question to return. She 'as not done so.'

'No,' Alleyn said. 'I imagine she'd see him damned first.'

The car turned in at the great entrance and climbed through the woods. Half-way up the drive they met what appeared to be the entire school, marching and singing under the leadership of Miss Caroline Able's assistant. They stood aside to let the car pass. Alleyn could not see Panty among them.

'Not their usual time for a walk,' said Thomas.

The car drew up at last into the shadow of the enormous house.

'If nothing else has gone cock-eyed,' Alleyn said, 'she'll be in the school.'

Thomas cried out in alarm: 'Are you talking about Caroline Able?'

'No. See here, Ancred. We're going into the school. There's a separate entrance back there, and we'll use it. Will you go into this part of the house and please say nothing about our arrival?'

'Well, all right,' said Thomas, 'though I must say I don't quite see—'

'It's all very confusing. Away you go.'

They watched Thomas walk slowly up the steps, push open the great door, and pause for a second in the shadowy lobby. Then he turned and the door closed between them.

'Now, Fox,' Alleyn said, 'you and I will go into the school. I think the best thing we can do is to ask her to come back with us to London and make a statement. Awkward if she refuses, but if she does we'll have to take the next step. Drive back to the end of the building there.'

The car was turned, and stopped again at a smaller door in the west wing. 'Thompson, you and Bream wait back there in the car. If we want you, we'll get you. Come on, Fox.'

They got out. The car moved away. They had turned to the doorway when Alleyn heard his name called. Thomas was coming down the steps from the main entrance. He ran towards them, his coat flapping, and waved his arm.

'Alleyn! *Alleyn!* Stop!'

'Now what?' Alleyn said.

Thomas was breathless when he reached them. He laid his hands on the lapels of Alleyn's coat. His face was colourless and his lips shook. 'You've got to come,' he said. 'It's frightful. Something frightful's happened. Sonia's in there, horribly ill. Withers says she's been poisoned. He says she's going to die.'

CHAPTER EIGHTEEN

The Last Appearance of Miss O.

THEY HAD CARRIED HER into a small bedroom in the school.

When Alleyn and Fox, accompanied as far as the door by Thomas, walked unheralded into the room, they found Dr Withers in the act of turning Pauline and Desdemona out of it. Pauline appeared to be in an advanced state of hysteria.

'*Out*, both of you. At once, please. Mrs Ancred and I can do all that is necessary. And Miss Able.'

'A curse. That's what I feel. There's a curse upon this house. That's what it is, Dessy.'

'Out, I say. Miss Ancred, take this note. I've written it clearly. Ring up my surgery and tell them to send the things up immediately the car arrives. Can your brother drive my car? Very well.'

'There's a man and a car outside,' Alleyn said. 'Fox, take the note, will you?'

Pauline and Desdemona, who had backed before the doctor to the door, turned at the sound of Alleyn's voice, uttered incoherent cries, and darted past him into the passage. Fox, having secured the note, followed them.

'What the hell are you doing here!' Dr Withers demanded. 'Get out!' He glared at Alleyn and turned back to the bed. Millamant Ancred and Caroline Able were stooped above it, working, it seemed with difficulty, over something that struggled and made harsh inhuman noises. A heavy stench hung in the air.

'Get the clothes away, but put that other thing on her. Keep her covered as far as possible. That's right. Take my coat, Mrs Ancred, please; I can't do with it. Now, we'll try the emetic again. Careful! Don't let me break the glass.'

Miss Able moved away with an armful of clothes. Millamant stood back a little, holding the doctor's jacket, her hands working nervously.

There, on a child's bed with a gay counterpane, Sonia Orrincourt strained and agonized, the grace of her body distorted by revolt and the beauty of her face obliterated in pain. As Alleyn looked at her, she arched herself and seemed to stare at him. Her eyes were bloodshot; one lid drooped and fluttered and winked. One arm, like that of a mechanical toy, repeatedly jerked up its hand to her forehead in a reiterated salaam.

He waited, at the end of the room, and watched. Dr Withers seemed to have forgotten him. The two women after a startled glance turned again to their task. The harsh cries, the straining and agonizing, rose in an intolerable crescendo.

'I'm going to give a second injection. Keep the arm still, if you can. Very well, then, get that thing out of the way. Now.'

The door opened a fraction. Alleyn moved to it, saw Fox and slipped through.

'Our chap ought to be back any minute with the doctor's gear,' Fox muttered.

'Have you rung for Dr Curtis and Co.?'

'They're on the way.'

'Thompson and Bream still on the premises?'

'Yes, sir.'

'Bring them in. Keep the servants in their own quarters. Shut up any rooms she's been in since she got here. Herd the family together and keep them together.'

'That's all been fixed, Mr Alleyn. They're in the drawing-room.'

'Good. I don't want to leave her yet.'

Fox jerked his thumb. 'Any chance of a statement?'

'None at the moment, far as I can see. Have you got anything, Fox?'

Fox moved closer to him, and in a toneless bass began to mutter rapidly: 'She and the doctor and Miss Able had tea together in Miss Able's room. He'd come up to see the kids. She sent the little Kentish girl through to order it. Didn't fancy schoolroom tea. Tea set out for the rest of the family in the dining-room. Second tray brought from the pantry by Barker with tea for one. Second pot brewed by Mrs Kentish in the dining-room. Miss Desdemona put some biscuits on the tray. It was handed over to Miss Panty by Mrs Ancred. Miss Panty brought it back here. Miss O. was taken bad straight away before the other two had touched anything. The little girl was there and noticed everything.'

'Got the tea things?'

'Thompson's got them. Mrs Ancred kept her head and said they ought to be locked up, but in the fluster of getting the patient out, the tray was knocked over. She left Mrs Kentish to carry on, but Mrs Kentish took hysterics and Isabel swept it up in the finish. Tea and hot water and broken china all over the shop. We ought to get a trace, though, somewhere, if there's anything. That little girl's sharp, by gum she is.'

Alleyn laid his hand swiftly on Fox's arm. In the room the broken sounds changed into a loud and rapid babbling— 'Ba-ba-ba-ba'—and stopped abruptly. At the same moment the uniformed driver appeared at the far end of the passage carrying a small case. Alleyn met him, took the case, and, motioning to Fox to come after, reentered the room.

'Here's your case, Dr Withers.'

'All right. Put it down. When you go out, tell those women to get in touch with her people if she's got any. If they want to see her, they'll have to be quick.'

'Fox, will you—?'

Fox slipped away.

'I said: When you go out,' Dr Withers repeated angrily.

'I'm afraid I must stay. This is a police matter, Dr Withers.'

'I'm perfectly well aware of what's happened. My duty is to my patient, and I insist on the room being cleared.'

'If she should become conscious...' Alleyn began, looking at the terrible face with its half-open eyes and mouth.

'If she regains consciousness, which she won't, I'll inform you.' Dr Withers opened the case, glanced up at Alleyn and said fiercely: 'If you don't clear out I'll take the matter up with the Chief Constable.'

Alleyn said briskly: 'That won't do at all, you know. We're both on duty here and here we both stay. Your patient's been given thallium acetate. I suggest that you carry on with the treatment, Dr Withers.'

There was a violent ejaculation from Caroline Able. Millamant said: 'That's the ringworm stuff! What nonsense!'

'How the hell...' Dr Withers began, and then: 'Very well. Very well. Sorry. I'm worried. Now, Mrs Ancred, I'll want your help here. Lay the patient—'

Forty minutes later, without regaining consciousness, Sonia Orrincourt died.

'The room,' Alleyn said, 'will be left exactly as it is. The police surgeon is on his way and will take charge. In the meantime, you'll all please join the others in the drawing-room. Mrs Ancred, will you and Miss Able go ahead with Inspector Fox?'

'At least, Alleyn,' said Dr Withers, struggling into his jacket, 'you'll allow us to wash up.'

'Certainly. I'll come with you.'

Millamant and Caroline Able, after exchanging glances, raised a subdued outcry. 'You must see...' Dr Withers protested.

'If you'll come out, I'll explain.'

He led the way and they followed in silence. Fox came out last and nodded severely to Bream, who was in the passage. Bream moved forward and stationed himself before the door.

Alleyn said: 'It's perfectly clear, I'm sure, to all of you that this is a police matter. She was poisoned, and we've no reason to suppose she poisoned herself. I may be obliged to make a search of the house (here is the warrant), and I must have a search of the persons in it. Until this has been done none of you may be alone. There is a wardress coming by car from London, and you may, of course, wait for her if you wish.'

He looked at the three faces, all of them marked by the same signs of exhaustion, all turned resentfully towards him. There was a long silence.

'Well,' Millamant said at last, with an echo of her old short laugh, 'you *can* search me. The thing I want to do most is sit down. I'm tired.'

'I must say,' Caroline Able began, 'I don't quite—'

'Here!' Dr Withers cut in. 'Will this suit you? I'm these ladies' medical man. Search me and then let them search each other in my presence. Any good?'

'That will do admirably. This room here is vacant, I see. Fox, will you take Dr Withers in?' Without further ado, Dr Withers turned on his heel and made for the open door. Fox followed him in and shut it.

Alleyn turned to the two women. 'We shan't keep you long,' he said, 'but if, in the meantime, you would like to join the others, I can take you to them.'

'Where are they?' Millamant demanded.

'In the drawing-room.'

'Personally,' she said, 'I'm beyond minding who searches me and who looks on.' Bream gave a self-conscious cough. 'If you and Miss Able like to take me into the children's play-room, which I believe is vacant, I shall be glad to get it over.'

'Well, really,' said Miss Able, 'well, of course, that is an extremely sane point of view, Mrs Ancred. Well, if *you* don't object.'

'Good,' Alleyn said. 'Shall we go?'

There was a screen, with Italian primitives pasted over it, in the play-room. The two women, at Alleyn's suggestion, retired behind it. First Millamant's extremely sensible garments were thrown out one by one, examined by Alleyn, collected again by Miss Able, and then, after an interval, the process was reversed. Nothing was discovered, and Alleyn, walking between them, escorted the two ladies to the bathroom, and finally through the green baize door and across the hall to the drawing-room.

Here they found Desdemona, Pauline, Panty, Thomas and Cedric, assembled under the eye of Detective-Sergeant Thompson. Pauline and Desdemona were in tears. Pauline's tears were real and ugly. They had left little traces, like those of a snail, down her carefully restrained make-up. Her eyes were red and swollen and she looked frightened. Desdemona, however, was misty, tragic and still beautiful. Thomas sat with his eyebrows raised to their limit and his hair ruffled, gazing in alarm at nothing in particular. Cedric, white and startled, seemed to be checked, by Alleyn's arrival, in a restless prowl round the room. A paperknife fell from his hands and clattered on the glass top of the curio cabinet.

Panty said: 'Hallo! Is Sonia dead? Why?'

'Ssh, darling! Darling, ssh!' Pauline moaned, and attempted vainly to clasp her daughter in her arms. Panty advanced into the centre of the room and faced Alleyn squarely. 'Cedric,' she said loudly, 'says Sonia's been murdered. Has she? Has she, Miss Able?'

'Goodness,' said Caroline Able in an uneven voice, 'I call that rather a stupid thing to say, Patricia, don't you?'

Thomas suddenly walked up to her and put his arm about her shoulders.

'Has she, Mr Alleyn?' Panty insisted.

'You cut off and don't worry about it,' Alleyn said. 'Are you at all hungry?'

'You bet.'

'Well, ask Barker from me to give you something rather special, and then put your coat on and see if you can meet the others coming home. Is that all right, Mrs Kentish?'

Pauline waved her hands and he turned to Caroline Able.

'An excellent idea,' she said more firmly. Thomas's hand still rested on her shoulder.

Alleyn led Panty to the door. 'I won't go,' she announced, 'unless you tell me if Sonia's dead.'

'All right, old girl, she is.' A multiple ejaculation sounded behind him.

'Like Carabbas?'

'No!' said her Aunt Millamant strongly, and added: 'Pauline, must your child behave like this?'

'They've both gone away,' Alleyn said. 'Now cut along and don't worry about it.'

'I'm not worrying,' Panty said, 'particularly. I dare say they're in Heaven, and Mummy says I can have a kitten. But a person likes to know.' She went out.

Alleyn turned and found himself face to face with Thomas.

Behind Thomas he saw Caroline Able stooping over Millamant, who sat fetching her breath in dry sobs, while Cedric bit his nails and looked on. 'I'm sorry,' Millamant stammered: 'it's just reaction, I suppose. Thank you, Miss Able.'

'You've been perfectly splendid, Mrs Ancred.'

'Oh, Milly, Milly!' wailed Pauline. 'Even you! Even your iron reserve. Oh, Milly!'

'Oh, *God!*' Cedric muttered savagely. 'I'm so *sick* of all this.'

'You,' Desdemona said, and laughed with professional bitterness. 'In less tragic circumstances, Cedric, that would be funny.'

'Please, all of you *stop*.'

Thomas's voice rang out with authority, and the dolorous buzz of reproach and impatience was instantly hushed.

'I dare say you're all upset,' he said. 'So are other people. Caroline is, and I am. Who wouldn't be? But you can't go on flinging temperaments right and left. It's very trying for other people and it gets us nowhere. So I'm afraid I'm going to ask you all to shut up, because I've got something to say to Alleyn, and if I'm right, and he says I'm right, you can all have hysterics and get on with the big scene. But I've got to know.'

He paused, still facing Alleyn squarely, and in his voice and his manner Alleyn heard an echo of Panty. 'A person likes to know,' Panty had said.

'Caroline's just told me,' Thomas said, 'that you think somebody gave Sonia the medicine Dr Withers prescribed for those kids. She says Sonia had tea with her. Well, it seems to me that means somebody's got to look after Caroline, and I'm the person to do it, because I'm going to marry her. I dare say that's a surprise to all of you, but I am, so that's that, and nobody need bother to say anything, please.'

With his back still turned to his dumbfounded family, Thomas, looking at once astonished and determined, grasped himself by the lapels of his coat and continued. 'You've told me you think Papa was poisoned with this stuff and I suppose you think the same person killed Sonia. Well, there's one person who ordered the stuff for the kids and wouldn't let Caroline touch it, and who ordered the medicine for Papa, and who is pretty well known to be in debt, and who was left quite a lot of money by Papa, and who had tea with Sonia. He's not in the room, now,' said Thomas, 'and I want to know where he is, and whether he's a murderer. That's all.'

Before Alleyn could answer, there was a tap on the door and Thompson came in. 'A call from London, for you, sir,' he said. 'Will you take it out here?'

Alleyn went out, leaving Thompson on guard, and the Ancreds still gaping. He found the small telephone-room across the hall, and, expecting a voice from the Yard, was astonished to hear Troy's.

'I wouldn't have done this if it mightn't be important,' said Troy's voice, twenty miles away. 'I telephoned the Yard and they told me you were at Ancreton.'

'Nothing wrong?'

'Not here. It's just that I've remembered what Sir Henry said that morning. When he'd found the writing on his looking-glass.'

'Bless you. What was it?'

'He said he was particularly angry because Panty, he insisted it was Panty, had disturbed two important documents that were on his dressing-table. He said that if she'd been able to understand them she would have realized they concerned her very closely. That's all. Is it anything?'

'It's almost everything.'

'I'm sorry I didn't remember before, Rory.'

'It wouldn't have fitted before. I'll be home tonight. I love you very much.'

'Goodbye.'

'Goodbye.'

When Alleyn came out into the hall, Fox was there waiting for him.

'I've been having a bit of a time with the doctor,' Fox said. 'Bream and our chap are with him now. I thought I'd better let you know, Mr Alleyn.'

'What happened?'

'When I searched him I found this in his left-hand side pocket.' Fox laid his handkerchief on the hall table and opened it out, disclosing a very small bottle with a screw top. It was almost empty. A little colourless fluid lay at the bottom.

'He swears,' said Fox, 'that he's never seen it before, but it was on him all right.'

Alleyn stood looking at the little phial for a long moment. Then he said: 'I think this settles it, Fox. I think we'll have to take a risk.'

'Ask a certain party to come up to the Yard?'

'Yes. And hold a certain party while this stuff is analysed. But there's no doubt in my mind about it, Fox. It'll be thallium acetate.'

'I'll be glad to make this arrest,' said Fox heavily, 'and that's a fact.'

Alleyn did not answer, and after another pause Fox jerked his head at the drawing-room door. 'Shall I—?'

'Yes.'

Fox went away and Alleyn waited alone in the hall. Behind the great expanse of stained-glass windows there was sunlight. A patchwork of primary colours lay across the wall where Henry Ancred's portrait was to have hung. The staircase mounted into shadows, and out of sight, on the landing, a clock ticked. Above the enormous fireplace, the fifth baronet pointed his sword complacently at a perpetual cloudburst. A smouldering log settled with a whisper on the hearth, and somewhere, away in the servants' quarters, a voice was raised and placidly answered.

The drawing-room door opened, and with a firm step, and a faint meaningless smile on her lips, Millamant Ancred came out and crossed the hall to Alleyn.

'I believe you wanted me,' she said.

CHAPTER NINETEEN

Final Curtain

'It WAS THE MASS of detail,' Troy said slowly, 'that muddled me at first. I kept trying to fit the practical jokes into the pattern and they wouldn't go.'

'They fit,' Alleyn rejoined, 'but only because she used them after the event.'

'I'd be glad if you'd sort out the essentials, Rory.'

'I'll try. It's a case of maternal obsession. A cold, hard woman, with a son for whom she has a morbid adoration. Miss Able would tell you all about that. The son is heavily in debt, loves luxury, and is intensely unpopular with his relations. She hates them for that. One day, in the ordinary course of her duties, she goes up to her father-in-law's room. The drafts of two Wills are lying on the dressing-table. One of them leaves her son, who is his heir, more than generous means to support his title and property. The other cuts him down to the bare bones of the entailed estate. Across the looking-glass someone has scrawled "Grandfather is a bloody old fool." As she stands there, and before she can rearrange the papers, her father-in-law walks in. He immediately supposes, and you may be sure she shares and encourages the belief that his small grand-daughter, with a reputation for practical jokes, is responsible for the insulting legend. Millamant is a familiar figure in his room, and he has no cause to suspect her of such an idiotic prank. Still less does he suspect the real perpetrator, her son Cedric Ancred, who has since admitted that this was one of a series of stunts designed by himself and Sonia Orrincourt to set the old man against Panty, hitherto his favourite.

'Millamant Ancred leaves the room with the memory of those two drafts rankling in her extremely tortuous mind. She knows the old man changes his Will as often as he loses his temper. Already Cedric is unpopular. Some time during the next few days, perhaps gradually, perhaps in an abrupt access of resentment, an idea is born to Millamant. The Will is to be made public at the Birthday dinner. Suppose the one that is favourable to Cedric is read, how fortunate if Sir Henry should die before he changes his mind! And if the dinner is rich, and he, as is most probable, eats and drinks unwisely, what more likely than he should have one of his attacks and die that very night? If, for instance, there was tinned cray-fish? She orders tinned crayfish.'

'Just—hoping?'

'Perhaps no more than that. What do you think, Fox?'

Fox, who was sitting by the fire with his hands on his knees, said: 'Isabel reckons she ordered it on the previous Sunday when they talked over the dinner.'

'The day after the looking-glass incident. And on the following Monday evening, the Monday before the Birthday when Cedric and Paul and his mother were all out, Millamant Ancred went into the flower-room and found a large bottle of medicine marked "Poison" for the school children, and another smaller bottle for Sir Henry. The bottles had been left on the bench by Sonia Orrincourt, who had joined

Fenella Ancred there and had gone upstairs with her and had
never been alone in the flower-room.'

'And I,' Troy said, 'was putting the trap away and coming
in by the east wing door. If...Suppose I'd let Sonia do that and
taken the medicine into the school—'

'If you'll excuse my interrupting you, Mrs Alleyn,' Fox
said, 'it's our experience that, when a woman makes up her
mind to turn poisoner, nothing will stop her.'

'He's right, Troy.'

'Well,' said Troy, 'go on.'

'She had to chip away the chemist's sealing-wax before
she got the corks out, and Fox found bits of it on the floor
and some burnt matches. She had to find another bottle for
her purpose. She emptied Sir Henry's bottle, filled it up with
thallium, and in case of failure, poured the remainder into
her own small phial. Then she filled the children's bottle with
water and re-corked and re-sealed both Mr Juniper's bottles.
When Miss Able came in for the children's medicine she and
Millamant hunted everywhere for it. It was not found until
Fenella came downstairs, and who was more astonished than
Millamant to learn that Sonia had so carelessly left the medicine in the flower-room?'

'But suppose,' Troy said, 'he'd wanted the medicine
before she knew about the Will?'

'There was the old bottle with a dose still in it. I fancy
she removed that one some time during the Birthday. If a
Will unfavourable to Cedric had been made public, that
bottle would have been replaced and the other kept for a
more propitious occasion. As it was, she saw to it that she was
never alone from dinner until the next morning. Barker beat
on the door of the room she shared with Desdemona. She had
talked to Desdemona, you remember, until three o'clock—
well after the time of Sir Henry's death. She built herself up
a sort of emergency alibi with the same elaborate attention
which she gives to that aimless embroidery of hers. In a way
this led to her downfall. If she'd risked a solitary trip along

those passages that night to Cedric's room she would have heard, no doubt, that Sir Henry had signed the second Will, and she would have made a desperate attempt to stop him taking his medicine.'

'Then she didn't mean at that time to throw suspicion on Sonia?'

'No, indeed. His death would appear to be the natural result of rash eating and pure temper. It was only when the terms of his last Will were made known that she got her second idea.'

'An atrocious idea.'

'It was all of that. It was also completely in character— tortuous and elaborate. Sonia had come between Cedric and the money. Very well, Sonia must go and the second Will be set aside. She remembered that she had found Sonia reading it. She remembered the rat-bane with its printed antidote to arsenical poisoning. So, the anonymous letters printed on the kids' paper she herself fetched from the village, appeared on the breakfast table. A little later, as nobody seemed to have caught on the right idea, the book on embalming appeared on the cheese-dish, and finally the tin of rat-bane appeared in Sonia's suitcase. At about this time she got a horrible jolt.'

'The cat,' said Fox.

'Carabbas!' Troy ejaculated.

'Carabbas had been in Sir Henry's room. Sir Henry had poured out milk for him. But the bottle of medicine had over-turned into the saucer and presently Carabbas began to lose his fur. No wonder. He'd lapped up thallium acetate, poor chap. Millamant couldn't stand the sight of him about the house. He was one too much for her iron nerve. Accusing him of ringworm, and with the hearty consent of every one but Panty, she had him destroyed.

'She sat back awaiting events and unobtrusively jogging them along. She put the tin of arsenical rat-bane in Sonia Orrincourt's suitcase and joined in the search for it. She declared that it had been a full tin, but the servants disagreed.

She forgot, however, to ease the lid, which was cemented in with the accretion of years.'

'But to risk everything and plan everything on the chance that arsenic was used by the embalmers!' Troy exclaimed.

'It didn't seem like a chance. Sir Henry had ordered Mortimer and Loame to use it, and Mr Mortimer had let him suppose they would do so. Her nerve went a bit, though, after the exhumation. She rang up the embalmers, using, no doubt, the deepest notes of her masculine voice, and said she was my secretary. Loame, the unspeakable ass, gave her their formula. That must have been a bitter moment for Millamant. Cedric's only means of avoiding financial ruin was by marrying the woman she loathed and against whom she had plotted; and now she knew that the frame-up against Sonia Orrincourt was no go. She didn't know, however, that we considered thallium acetate a possible agent and would look for it. She'd kept the surplus over from the amount she could not get into Sir Henry's bottle and she waited her chance. Sonia could still be disposed of; Cedric could still get the money.'

'She must be mad.'

'They're like that, Mrs Alleyn,' Fox said. 'Female poisoners behave like that. Always come at it a second time, and a third and fourth, too, if they get the chance.'

'Her last idea,' Alleyn said, 'was to throw suspicion on Dr Withers, who's a considerable beneficiary in both Wills. She put thallium in the milk when the tea-tray was sent in to Miss Able, knowing Withers and Sonia Orrincourt were there and knowing Sonia was the only one who took milk. A little later she slipped the bottle into Withers's jacket. With Sonia dead, she thought, the money would revert after all to Cedric.'

'Very nasty, you know,' Fox said mildly. 'Very nasty case indeed, wouldn't you say?'

'Horrible,' Troy said under her breath.

'And yet, you know,' Fox went on, 'it's a guinea to a gooseberry she only gets a lifer. What do you reckon, sir?'

'Oh, yes,' Alleyn said, looking at Troy. 'It'll be that if it's not an acquittal.'

'But surely——' Troy began.

'We haven't got an eye-witness, Mrs Alleyn, to a single action that would clinch the case. Not one.' Fox got up slowly. 'Well, if you'll excuse me. It's been a long day.'

Alleyn saw him out. When he returned, Troy was in her accustomed place on the hearthrug. He sat down and after a moment she leant towards him, resting her arm across his knees.

'Nothing is clear-cut,' she said, 'when it comes to one's views. Nothing.' He waited. 'But we're together,' she said. 'Quite together now. Aren't we?'

'Quite together,' Alleyn said.

Gilbert Kyem Jnr
Big City

Theatre includes: *Hamlet, Oresteia* (Broadway/Almeida Theatre); *Never Not Once* (Park Theatre).

Television includes: *Rivals* (Disney/Happy Prince).

Film includes: *Prizefighter* (Amazon).

Carol Moses
Tanty

Theatre includes: *Unseen Unheard* (Theatre Peckham); *Hoxton St* (Hoxton Hall); *Forty* (Hackney Empire); *Clockwork* (National Theatre).

Television includes: *The Ballad of Renegade Nell* (Disney+); *Holby City, A Class Apart, Call the Midwife* (BBC); *The Bill, Perrin* (ITV).

Film includes: *Mama, The Change, In Da Mix, Side Hustle*.

Carol Moses trained at Rose Bruford College.

Aimee Powell
Christina

Theatre includes: *Family Tree, Crongton Knights* (UK tour); *Nothello* (Belgrade Theatre); *Freeman* (international tour); *Feed The Beast* (Birmingham REP).

Television includes: *Doctors* (BBC), *SeaView* (Prime Video).

Film includes: *Sent to Cov* (Sky Arts).

Romario Simpson
Galahad

Theatre includes: *Syndrome* (Tristan Bates Theatre); *Coming Home* (ALRA); *Sket* (Park Theatre); *Think* (Edinburgh Fringe); *And Then There Was War* (Stratford Circus Theatre);

Reflection, Scratch Me If You Can (Southbank Vaults); *Love Clots* (Mountview); *Our Country's Good* (WKC Theatre).

Television includes: *Granite Harbour S1/S2* (BBC Scotland); *Riches* (ITV); *Django* (Sky Atlantic); *Andor* (Disney+); *Small Axe: Lover's Rock* (BBC); *Noughts + Crosses* (BBC); *Timewasters S2* (ITV); *Dixi* (CBBC).

Sam Selvon
Writer

Born in Trinidad in 1923, Selvon migrated to London in 1950. One of the most distinctive voices in twentieth century Caribbean and British writing, his first novel, *A Brighter Sun*, appeared in 1952. Several major works followed: the London books – *The Lonely Londoners* (1956), *The Housing Lark* (1965), *Moses Ascending* (1975), *Moses Migrating* (1983); a collection of short stories, *Ways of Sunlight* (1958), set in Trinidad and London (many first published in the Evening Standard); and his Trinidad novels, including *An Island is a World* (1955), *Turn Again Tiger* (1958) and *Those Who Eat the Cascadura* (1972). Though best known for his fiction, Selvon was a ventriloquist and wrote in several genres. Poet and essayist, he scripted two collections of plays, originally broadcast on BBC radio: *El Dorado: West One* (1988) and *Highway in the Sun* (1991); and co-wrote the screenplay for *Pressure* (1975), Britain's first black feature film. Frequently heralded as father of black writing in Britain, Selvon is celebrated for his imaginative invention of London as a black city of words and his intimate chronicling of the experiences of ordinary black immigrants during the period of Windrush. Selvon left Britain to live in Canada in 1978. He died in 1994 on a trip home to Trinidad.

Roy Williams
Adaptor

Theatre includes: *The Fellowship* (Hampstead Theatre); *Go, Girl* (Lyric Hammersmith); *Death of England, Death of England: Delroy, Death of England: Closing Time* (co-written with Clint Dyer, National Theatre); *Sucker Punch, Fallout, Clubland, Lift Off* (Royal Court Theatre); *Days of Significance* (RSC); *Sing Yer Heart Out for the Lads* (National Theatre); *NW Trilogy* (Kiln Theatre).

Television includes: *Death of England: Face to Face* (co-written with Clint Dyer for Sabel Productions/National Theatre/Sky Arts); *Soon Gone: A Windrush Chronicle* (Douglas Road Productions/BBC4); *Fallout* (Company Pictures/Channel 4); *Offside*, *Babyfather* (BBC).

Film includes: *Fast Girls* (DJ Films).

Radio includes: *A Choice of Straws*, *To Sir With Love*, *The Midwich Cuckoos*, *Tell Tale*, *Homeboys*, *Interrogation*, *Faith, Hope and Glory*.

Roy Williams began writing plays in 1990 and is now arguably one of the country's leading dramatists. In 2000, he was the joint-winner of the George Devine Award and in 2001 he was awarded the Evening Standard Award for Most Promising Playwright. He was awarded an OBE for Services to Drama in the 2008 Birthday Honours List and was made a fellow of The Royal Society of Literature in 2018.

Ebenezer Bamgboye
Director

Previously for Jermyn Street Theatre: *The Anarchist*, *Two Horsemen*.

Theatre includes: *Under the Kunde Tree* (Southwark Playhouse); *The Cherry Orchard* (RADA); *Boys Cry* (Riverside Studios); *Six Artists in Search of a Play* (Almeida Theatre).

Ebenezer Bamgboye was previously Carne Deputy Director at Jermyn Street Theatre.

Laura Ann Price
Designer

Design includes: *Our Town* (Silk Street Theatre, Barbican); *In This Smoking Chaos*, *The Rising Sun* (Queen's Theatre Hornchurch); *The Snow Queen* (Polka Theatre); *Children's Day: Reimagined* (Fevered Sleep/Leeds2023); *Hello and Goodbye* (York Theatre Royal); *Talking Heads* (Leeds

Playhouse); *Economy of Ecology* (New Diorama Theatre/ HOME Manchester).

Laura Ann Price is a designer whose research and practice is concerned with the material and sensorial potential of performance. Laura represented the UK at the International Design Festival Prague Quadrennial with her design for *Talking Heads* at Leeds Playhouse. Subsequently, the design was exhibited in the V&A Museum and the National Centre for Craft and Design.

Anett Black
Costume Designer

For Jermyn Street Theatre: *Yours Unfaithfully, Love All, Something in the Air, The Tempest, A Christmas Carol, All's Well That Ends Well* (also Guildford Shakespeare Company).

Theatre includes: *She Stoops to Conquer* (Orange Tree Theatre); *Pandora's Box* (Royal Academy of Music/London Youth Opera); *Christmas Wish* (National Trust – Polesden Lacey); *Hamlet, Macbeth, King Arthur, Much Ado About Nothing, Romeo and Juliet, Julius Caesar, King Lear, Othello* (Guildford Shakespeare Company); *The Trials of Oscar Wilde* (Theatre Royal Windsor); *Jekyll and Hyde, Pygmalion, The Picture of Dorian Gray* (EuropeanArts/Trafalgar Studios/ Italian Tour); *Christmas Carol* (UK Tour); *The Bacchae* (National Trust); *Pippin, 9 to 5, The Fix, Blood Wedding, Our Country's Good* (Bellairs); *Bittergirls* (King's Head Theatre); *The Promise* (Elizabeth Hall London); *For Ever Young, The Price* (Hammersmith); *Antigone* (Spruce Wood).

Elliot Griggs
Lighting Designer

Theatre includes: *Blue Mist, all of it, Purple Snowflakes and Titty Wanks, A Fight Against, On Bear Ridge, Yen* (Royal Court Theatre); *The Big Life, Beautiful Thing* (Theatre Royal Stratford East); *Jitney* (Old Vic/Leeds Playhouse/Headlong); *Amélie the Musical* (Criterion Theatre/The Other Palace/

Watermill Theatre/UK tour); *The Wild Duck* (Almeida Theatre); *The Lover/The Collection* (Harold Pinter Theatre); *Fleabag* (Wyndham's Theatre/New York/Soho Theatre/Edinburgh Festival/tour); *No Pay? No Way!*, *Queens of the Coal Age*, *The Night Watch* (Royal Exchange Theatre); *Feeling Afraid As If Something Terrible Is Going To Happen...*, *Sleepova*, *The P Word*, *Hir* (Bush Theatre); *An Octoroon*, *Pomona* (National Theatre/Orange Tree Theatre); *Ivan and the Dogs* (Young Vic); *Richard III* (Headlong); *Disco Pigs* (Trafalgar Studios/Irish Rep, NY); *The Swell*, *The Misfortune of the English*, *Last Easter*, *The Sugar Syndrome*, *Low Level Panic*, *Sheppey*, *buckets* (Orange Tree Theatre); *The Oracles* (Punchdrunk).

Elliot Griggs trained at RADA. He received an Off West End Award for Best Lighting Designer for *Pomona*.

Tony Gayle
Sound Designer

Theatre includes: *My Neighbour Totoro* (RSC/Barbican Theatre); *Two Strangers (Carry a Cake Across New York)* (Kiln Theatre); *High Times and Dirty Monsters* (Liverpool Playhouse); *Next to Normal* (Donmar Warehouse); *Pygmalion*, *Sylvia*, *The 47th* (Old Vic Theatre); *Beneatha's Place* (Young Vic); *School Girls; or, The African Mean Girls Play* (Lyric Hammersmith); *Greatest Days*, *Beautiful – The Carole King Musical*, *Salad Days*, *American Idiot* (UK tour); Disney's *AIDA* (Holland); *Newsies* (Troubadour Theatre); *Kinky Boots* (New Wolsey Theatre); *Running With Lions* (Talawa/Lyric Hammersmith); *Spring Awakening*, *And Breathe...* (Almeida Theatre); *The Wiz* (Hope Mill Theatre); *Get Up, Stand Up! The Bob Marley Musical* (Lyric Theatre); *A Place for We* (Talawa/Park Theatre); *Blue/Orange* (Theatre Royal Bath); *Gin Craze!* (Royal & Derngate); *The Living Newspaper*, *Shoe Lady* (Royal Court Theatre); *Poet in da Corner* (Royal Court/UK tour); *Lazarus* (King's Cross Theatre).

Tony Gayle recently received an Olivier Award and Whatsonstage Award for Best Sound Design for the RSC's

My Neighbour Totoro, was awarded the Black British Theatre Awards (BBTA) Light and Sound Recognition Award – 2019 and 2021 – and is a Wise Children Trustee, Stage Sight Co-Director.

Paloma Sierra
Assistant Director

Theatre as Assistant Director includes: *The Taming of the Shrew* (Santa Cruz Shakespeare).

Theatre as Writer includes: *BuT yOuR eNgLiSh Is So GoOd!* (Poetic Theatre Productions); *Close But Not Too Close!* (Project Y Theater); *Cola'o: A Bilingual Trova* (Theatre Now New York); *Rosa: The Day of the Dead* (White Snake Projects).

Theatre as Dramaturg includes: *Spanglish Sh!t* (Berkeley Rep); *The Revolution of Evelyn Serrano* (New Hazlett Theater/Edinburgh Fringe); *Reset New Work Series* (Conch Shell Productions).

Film as Director includes: *I Am Soil Breaking Off*.

Paloma Sierra trained at LAMDA and Carnegie Mellon. Her website is: *www.pasierra.com*.

Nevena Stojkov
Movement Director

Theatre as Movement Director includes: *Weeverfish* (RCSSD); *Coram Boy* (Tower Theatre/Minack Theatre); *The Boy Who Fell in a Book*, *Lizard Evidilleh Marmarok*, *The Little Prince* (Tower Theatre); *On the Line* (Camden People's Theatre); *You're So F***ing Croydon* (Croydonites Festival).

Theatre as Choreographer includes: *In the Solitude of the Cotton Fields* (RCSSD).

Nevena Stojkov is currently training at The Royal Central School of Speech and Drama on the MFA in Movement: Directing and Teaching.

Abby Galvin
Casting Director

Previously for Jermyn Street Theatre: *Yours Unfaithfully*.

Theatre as Casting Director includes: *The Book Thief* (Curve Theatre, Leicester/Belgrade Theatre); *A Sherlock Carol* (Marylebone Theatre); *Time and Tide* (Norwich Theatre/UK tour); *Anything Is Possible If You Think About It Hard Enough* (Southwark Playhouse).

Theatre as Casting Associate for Jessica Ronane Casting includes: *Stranger Things: The First Shadow* (Sonia Friedman Productions); *Ulster American* (Riverside Studios); *A Mirror* (Second Half Productions/Almeida Theatre); *The Lehman Trilogy, 2.22: A Ghost Story* (West End); *The Glass Menagerie* (Second Half Productions/West End); *Girl from the North Country* (The Old Vic/West End/UK tour); *A Number, Camp Siegfried, 4000 Miles, Present Laughter, Sylvia, A Monster Calls, Mood Music, Fanny and Alexander, Woyzeck, Rosencrantz and Guildenstern Are Dead, King Lear, The Caretaker, The Master Builder, The Hairy Ape, Future Conditional* (The Old Vic); *The Divide* (The Old Vic/EIF).

Television includes: *True Detective: Night Country* (HBO); *The Amazing Mr Blunden* (Sky).

Film includes: *Good Grief* (Netflix); *Mickey 17* (Warner Brothers); *Rumpelstilzchen* (Ballet Boyz).

Aundrea Fudge
Voice and Dialect Coach

Theatre includes: *Clyde's* (Donmar Warehouse); *Choir Boy* (Bristol Old Vic); *A View from the Bridge* (UK tour/Headlong); *Meetings, Yellowman* (Orange Tree Theatre); *Start Swimming!* (Young Vic); *Once on this Island* (Regent's Park Open Air); *Blackout Songs* (Hampstead Theatre); *Bootycandy* (Gate Theatre); *Refilwe* (Bernie Grant Arts Centre); *Cinderella* (Brixton House); *On the Ropes* (Park Theatre); *Driving Miss Daisy* (Barn Theatre); *Bring it on! The Musical* (Southbank Centre).

Film includes: *Bernard & The Genie, Locked In-Film, Wheel of Time*.

TV includes: *Andor* (Season 2).

Aundrea Fudge is a voice and dialect coach with an MFA in Voice Studies from RCSSD.

Summer Keeling
Stage Manager

For Jermyn Street Theatre: *The Pursuit of Joy, Infamous, Thrill Me: The Leopold and Loeb Story*.

Theatre includes: *Never Look Back* (Crucible Theatre); *Manic Street Creature, Sugar Coat, Instructions for a Teenage Armageddon* (Southwark Playhouse); *The Boys Are Kissing, Til Death Do Us Part* (Theatre503); *The Haunting of Susan A* (King's Head Theatre); *21 Round for Christmas, Ghosts of the Titanic* (Park Theatre); *The Grotto* (Drayton Arms Theatre); *The Light Trail, The Moors, Hand of God, 21 Round for Christmas, Darling, Fever Pitch* (The Hope Theatre); *Mario! A Super Musical* (The Cockpit).

The West End's Studio Theatre at 30

Jermyn Street Theatre is a unique seventy seat theatre in Piccadilly Circus. World-class, household-name playwrights, directors and theatrical legends like Siân Phillips and Trevor Nunn work here alongside those taking their first steps in professional theatre. It is a crucible for multigenerational talent.

We stage world premieres, rare revivals, and reimagined classics and collaborate with theatres across the world. Our productions have transferred across the UK, to Broadway and beyond.

30 years ago in 1994, Howard Jameson and Penny Horner (who continue to serve as Chair of the Board and Executive Director today) created the theatre out of what had been the staff changing room for the restaurant upstairs with no core funding. Since then, the theatre has flourished thanks to a mixture of earned income from box office sales and the generosity of individual patrons and trusts and foundations. In 2017, the theatre became a full-time producing house. We won the Stage Award for Fringe Theatre of the Year in both 2012 and 2021.

Caroline Quentin in *Infamous*.
Photography by Steve Gregson.

Archie Backhouse, Forbes Masson and Daniel Boyd in *Farm Hall*. Photography by Alex Brenner.

Support Us at 30

Wondering what to get us for our big birthday? Your Friendship makes the best present of all!

Over the last 30 years, we've made a name for ourselves as the West End's Studio theatre. With just 70 seats, **our small scale is our greatest strength**: a unique place where artists can afford to take risks and audiences can afford to see the work.

But even with every seat filled, **ticket sales only generate 60%** of what we need to build our productions, fund our small team, and champion the next generation of artists. We rely on the generosity of donors like you for the remaining 40%. **Your support ensures we can build on the legacy of the last three decades** and make the next 30 years the most exciting yet.

Lifeboat Friends

(From £4.50 a month)

Our **Lifeboat Friends** are the heart of Jermyn Street Theatre. Benefits include:
- Dedicated Priority Booking period.
- Invitation to a Friends Night for each production, with a chance to meet the cast.

The Ariel Club

(From £12.50 a month)

Ariel Club members receive all the benefits of Lifeboat Friends, plus:
- Chances to attend Press Nights.
- Complimentary signed programme or playtext for each production.
- Acknowledgement in programmes, playtexts, and on our website.

The Miranda Club

(From £45 a month)

Members of **The Miranda Club** enjoy all the benefits of the Ariel club, plus:
- Acknowledgment in our Front of House.
- Annual Friends Lunch with our Artistic Director.
- Invitation to one Press Night/Gala Night per year.
- Behind-the-scenes access and a closer relationship with our team.

The Director's Circle

(From £250 a month)

The **Director's Circle** is an inner circle of our most generous donors. They are invited to every Press Night and enjoy regular informal contact with our Artistic Director and team. The first to hear our plans they often act as a valuable sounding board.

To join us, visit, www.jermynstreettheatre.co.uk/friends/
Jermyn Street Theatre is a Registered Charity No. 1186940

Our Friends

The Ariel Club

Richard Alexander
David Barnard
Derek Baum
Martin Bishop
Dmitry Bosky
Katie Bradford
Nigel Britten
Christopher Brown
Donald Campbell
James Carroll
Ted Craig
Jeanette Culver
Shomit Dutta
Jill & Paul Dymock
Bernard Fleckney
Lucy Fleming
Anthony Gabriel
Carol Gallagher
Roger Gaynham
Paul Guinery
Debbie Guthrie
Diana Halfnight
Julie Harries
Eleanor Harvey
Andrew Hughes
Jennifer Jacobs
Mark Jones
Margaret Karliner
David Lanch
Caroline Latham
Isabelle Laurent
Christine MacCallum
Keith Macdonald
Vivien Macmillan-Smith
Nicky Oliver
Sally Padovan
Kate & John Peck
Lydia Petty
Adrian Platt

Alexander Powell
Oliver Prenn
Mart Ralph
Martin Sanderson
Carolyn Shapiro
Nigel Silby
Philip Somervail
Robert Swift
Gary Trimby
George Warren
Lavinia Webb
Ann White
Ian Williams
John Wise

The Miranda Club

Anonymous
Anthony Ashplant
Gyles & Michèle Brandreth
Marcia Brocklebank
Sylvia de Bertodano
Robyn Durie
Richard Edgecliffe-Johnson
Maureen Elton
Nora Franglen
Mary Godwin
Louise Greenberg
Ros & Alan Haigh
Phyllis Huvos
Pauline Kelly
Marta Kinally
Yvonne Koenig
Hilary Lemaire
Jane Mennie
Dr Tiziana Morosetti
Charles Paine
John & Terry Pearson
Iain Reid
Ros Shelley
Martin Shenfield

Carol Shephard-Blandy
Jenny Sheridan
Sir Bernard Silverman
Brian Smith
Frank Southern
Mark Tantam
Paul Taylor
Geraldine Terry
Brian & Esme Tyers

Director's Circle

Anonymous
Philip Carne MBE &
Christine Carne
Jocelyn Abbey & Tom
Carney
Colin Clark RIP
Lynette & Robert Craig
Gary Fethke
Flora Fraser
Robert & Pirjo Gardiner
Charles Glanville & James
Hogan
Crawford & Mary Harris
Ros & Duncan McMillan
Leslie & Peter MacLeod-
Miller
James L. Simon
Peter Soros & Electra Toub
Fiona Stone
Melanie Vere Nicoll
Robert Westlake & Marit
Mohn

The Lonely Londoners

Cast

Moses
Galahad
Lewis
Big City
Tanty
Agnes
Christina

Setting

London, 1956

Location

Moses' *room*

Lewis'*s room*

The Streets of London

Factory floor

Act One

Bayswater

Lights on **Moses**, **Big City** *and* **Lewis** *in* **Moses**' *bedsit. A single bed, a table, a chair, a broken cupboard which passes for a wardrobe, a few kitchen utensils.*

Moses *is in mid conversation with an unseen young West Indian man.*

Moses   I know you are desperate. I can see that you are desperate. You think I weren't desperate when I first come here? You should have been here in fifty-two. London was so cold. It get so bad here, when you try and speak, the words freeze as they come out of your mouth, and you have to melt it to hear the talk. If I lie, I die. But fellars, good fellars I should say, helped me when I was lonely. That is the only reason I'm going to help you. But what was it that you just said to me? (*Listens.*) You know what you just said, come on. What did you say? The streets of London are paved with gold? I did hear you correctly, that is what you said? Is that what you said to me? Yes or no? Well, let me tell you something. If you are thinking to carry on with that kind of foolishness then I cannot help you, I have better things to do than help you! You had better mind yourself! Or this London city will eat you alive, it will swallow you up whole, believe that. Tell me something else, why the hell you come to me in the first place? Who tell you my name and address? Address man, who tell you? Jackson? Jackson? That wurtless son of a bitch! He know I am seeing hell myself. But he's right. Cos only I know which of London where dem slam doors in your face, and which ones will you let us in. Like here. No, there's no room here. (*Listens.*) Hold on man, that is not what I said, that is not what I meant. But there are too many spades in the water as it is man. Now listen to me very carefully, Try *Clapham*. Not *Clapdam*! Or *Clapfarm*, or *Claphand*, it is *CLAP. HAM*! As in what you eat. There is a bus stop right outside, it'll show you which bus you take. It's *Clap-ham Junction* station you want. As soon as you get there, ask for a fellar name *Samson*, he works in luggage, he will help you with a job. Do you have all of that? Would you like me to repeat? Alright then. Well. Go! And hey, good luck.

The man leaves.

Big City   Well, there goes another one.

Moses   And another one soon come. Where's my blasted coat?

Big City   What's the hurry, Moses? You have wife waiting for you at station or summin?

Moses   Not that it is any of your business, City, but I have another favour for a friend back home, another fellar I have to meet, show him around, although why they call for me, I do not know.

Lewis   Ca yer Moses.

Moses   And what does that even mean, Lewis? (*Mimics.*) Ca yer Moses?

Lewis   I don't know, it's just summin you say.

Moses   And City?

Big City   Yeah, man?

Moses   Why are you even here, it's not Sunday?

Big City   Cigarette.

Lewis   You come all across the river for a cigarette?

Big City   Nuttin else to do. What you have man?

Moses *teases him with the cigarette. Pulling it away whenever* **Big City** *tries to take it.*

Big City   Hey Moses, man, what the hell, come on.

Moses   Tell me what brought you over the river, true talk now.

Big City   Well, if you must know. I was buying some things.

Moses   Buying some things?

Big City   From a test. Some white guy. He meet me on *Chefski Bridge*.

Moses   *Chelsea Bridge*.

Big City   That's what mi say.

Moses   So, what did you buy from this white test?

Big City *reveals a bunch of flyers and a wad of printed tickets.*

Moses   Oh City, man, not another one of your schemes.

Big City   Hear me out.

Lewis (*reads from one of the flyers*)   Another dance? Come on, City.

Big City   Hear me out nuh.

Lewis   We heard you out last time.

Moses   When you planned that other dance down Kilburn way.

Lewis   When no one come.

Big City   That hall was small.

Lewis   Every hall you find is small, City.

Moses   And there is never anyone there but us.

Big City   It's a bigger hall this time.

Moses   Listen to yourself, man.

Big City   It is up by *St Pancreek*.

Moses   What?

Big City   *ST. PAN. CREEK.*

Moses (*corrects*)   *ST. PAN. CRAS!*

Big City   That's what mi say. A hall with a stage to be precise. I spoke to a very nice man who works at the council, and they have very kindly given me use of the hall for two whole nights. So, I thought it would be nice to have all of our people round to come together, . . .

Moses (*knows what's coming*)   to meet, talk . . .

Lewis   . . . Get to know each other.

Big City   Don't laugh at me.

Moses   How much will it cost you this time?

Big City   One shilling a head. I kick back half a shilling to the council. And this time, it won't just be a record player, I will have speakers out in the hall as well. It will be a terrific atmosphere. This time I know it. Them Irish know how to throw a party as well as drink a bar dry. If it works for them, why can't it work for us?

Lewis   Them Irish are white.

Moses   They want your ideas, City, but they don't want you.

Big City   See, that is the trouble with you, Moses, you think white people are all bad.

Moses   I never said they were bad.

Big City   You just have to think like them, on their terms, it takes time.

Moses   What terms?

Big City   You see me?

Moses   Yes, I see someone who looks black, talks white.

Lewis   But sees money.

Big City   You have a problem with money, Lewis? Is that why you never have any?

Lewis I have money. Plenty of money.

Big City And this time I have a steel band to play music. A bar for people to drink. I'm going to fill that place up! And proper people to come this time. No riff raff.

Lewis Proper people? You mean proper white people, right?

Big City Did I say that?

Lewis You don't need to.

Moses So, what do you need me for?

Big City To help me sell tickets of course. You know people. And everyone know you. I'll pay you a half crown.

Moses One.

Big City Done! A pleasure doing business with you as always, Moses.

Lewis I tell you, City, the only thing missing from you right now is a bowler, umbrella and a briefcase.

Big City Nothing wrong with wanting to better myself, Lewis. It's me one who have nuttin but a cold floor on my landlady's kitchen, and she still charge me like she give me a room.

Lewis So move out.

Moses If you get fed up of sleeping on the floor, you can share my bed with me.

Big City See, that is exactly what I am talking about. First night I spend in London, I share a little something of a bed with three other men. Three! I'm tired of that. Look me in the eye, both of you and tell you're not? Eh?

Moses City, shut up and have your smoke.

Big City I find me a new room anyhow.

Moses Where?

Big City   Nearby. Lickle place, just off *Shepherd's Hill*.

Moses   *Shepherd's Bush!*

Big City   That's what I say.

Big City *is having trouble lighting his cigarette because of the cold air.*

Big City   Backside!

Moses   Cup it.

Big City   What?

Moses   Your hands, cup your hands like you are on the top deck on a ship and the wind is blowing in your face.

Moses *shows him.* **Big City** *does as instructed, he is able to light the cigarette and takes a long-awaited draw which he relishes.*

Big City   Dam, Moses, you don't have a heater or summin in this room?

Moses   Yes, City, I do. I just decided to turn it off and keep it off even though it is minus seven outside!

Big City   Alright, man!

Lewis   Alright him say!

Big City   You know, I hope your wife coming here don't cramp your style, Lewis.

Lewis   I'll be alright.

Big City   A lie you a tell. Nobody love them white women in the park, more than you.

Lewis   Hey, what Agnes don't know, she can't feel. Besides, what do I need a white gal for when I have my wife now? You carry on with them in the park, man.

Big City   I go see you in the park.

Lewis   No you won't. Not anymore.

Big City   You one can't keep away, admit it.

Moses   Of course he can't.

Lewis   Well, let me show you this.

Lewis *takes out a picture of* **Agnes** *and shows it to him.*

Big City   Oh my Lawd!

Lewis   Yes, you were saying, City?

Big City   This is Agnes?

Lewis   My wife, yes!

Big City   This is the woman you left behind? Back home, I wouldn't let she out of my sight. You must be mad, Lewis.

Lewis   Agnes would never stray. She's is a church girl.

Moses   He means you must be mad to bring her here.

Lewis   She, my wife.

Moses   I wish I was like all you Jamaicans, all you could live on two, three pound a week, and save up money in a suitcase under the bed, then when you have enough you sending for the family. I can't save a cent out of mi pay.

Lewis   What I do is my business.

Moses   Alright boy, so it goes.

Big City   So, Agnes can cook?

Lewis   Yes, she can cook, my Agnes can do anything she can set her mind to.

Moses   Like living here.

Lewis   She'll adapt. But I know she will want a bigger room for the pickne when deh come. You know about any?

Big City   Tolroy told me yesterday about a house with big rooms down by *Ladbreek Grave*.

Moses   What?

Big City   *Ladbreek Grave.*

Moses (*corrects*)   *Ladbroke Grove*!

Big City   That's what mi say. Stop fucking me up. Go ask he?

Lewis   Right, I will.

Big City   So, Your wife, Agnes, she good?

Lewis   Yes, she's good.

Big City   Very good?

Lewis   What do you mean?

Big City   I mean, is she *very* good?

Moses   City, behave man.

Big City   It's only a joke.

Lewis   Hey City, I don't have time for your nastiness. You had better mind that I don't box you down!

Moses   Alright you two.

Big City   Oh yes!

Lewis   Come if mi lie!

Big City   You tell her, you lost your job yet?

Lewis   That's none of your business.

Moses   Enough now!

Moses *gets between the two men.*

Moses   Come on, you're sorry, he's sorry. Shake hands now.

The two shake hands.

Big City   No hard feelings, man.

Lewis (*through gritted teeth*)   Come near my wife and I go kill you.

Moses   Lewis?

Lewis   Only a joke.

Moses   Good.

Lewis   A lickle one.

Moses   Come on you two, let's just hit the road.

A knock on the door.

What the hell did I tell that boy, I say Clapham!

Moses *opens the door,* **Galahad** *enters.*

Moses   Something I can help you with, boy?

Galahad   Moses? You are Moses? Yes?

Moses   Yes.

Galahad   Pleased to meet you.

Moses   Right?

Galahad   May I come in?

Moses   And you are?

Galahad   Oliver! My name is Oliver!

Moses   You *Oliver*, *Henry Oliver*! Frank's friend?

Galahad   Friends call me *Henry*.

Moses   Pleased to meet, you, *Henry Oliver.* Come in, man. I am confused however, did Frank not say I would come to meet you at *Waterloo* station?

Galahad   No need.

Moses   Evidently.

Galahad   I got an earlier train from Portsmouth Harbour, I decided to take a walk.

Big City   Take a walk?

Lewis   In this cold?

Moses   How did you find your way here?

Galahad   Quite simple, actually.

Moses   Oh, is that right?

Galahad   I asked for directions.

Big City   From *Waterfarm*?

Moses (*corrects*)   *Waterloo*!

Galahad   Some people, a couple of policeman?

Big City   You talk to the police?

Galahad   Yes.

Big City   Without them licking you down?

Galahad   Why would they lick me down?

Big City   Why? Look in the mirror, boy.

Galahad   I am no boy.

Moses   It's alright, don't mind him. City, you have had your smoke, why don't you two boys run along now, eh?

Big City   Long walk back to the water.

Moses *gives him some change.*

Moses   Take a bus then.

Big City   You have another cigarette?

Moses *hands* **Big City** *another cigarette.*

Big City   Long ride on the bus.

Moses *hands him a few more.*

Moses   Anything else? Filling outta my teeth, while yer at it?

Big City   No, this will do.

Lewis   I'll walk you out, City. Agnes must reach the station by now.

Big City   Say hello to her for me?

Lewis   I go say something else to you, how about that?

Big City   Quiet horse!

They leave.

Galahad   Frank said you'll help; I am much obliged for that.

Moses   Where's your coat?

Galahad   I'm alright.

Moses   You don't feel cold, *Oliver*? You had better buy yourself a coat.

Galahad   It not so bad. In fact, I feel a little warm.

Moses   Warm?

Galahad   It's what me say.

Moses   You feel warm, right now?

Galahad   Feel my hands?

Moses   Are you sick?

Galahad   Me, you making joke?

Moses   Tonight you stay with me, but tomorrow, if the landlord don't agree to you staying here, we will find you somewhere to live.

Galahad   Fair enough.

Moses   Good. Where's your luggage?

Galahad   I don't have any.

Moses   What?

Galahad   I figure is no sense to load myself with a set of things, when I start work, I will buy things. Make sense, right?

Moses   Hold on a minute, are you telling me, you come all the way from *Trinidad* with nothing?

Galahad   Well, the old toothbrush always in my pocket. And a pair of pyjamas that I have on already.

Moses   Well, no wonder you feel warm.

Galahad   Don't worry, I will get fix up as soon as I find work. I don't suppose you have another?

Moses   Another what?

Galahad   A smoke. I finish my last packet on the train. Please?

Moses   You mean to say you come off the ship with no cigarettes?

Galahad   Well?

Moses   Well what?

Galahad   Yes, I did.

Moses   You don't know they does allow you to land with 200? And that it have fellars who manage to come with five, six hundred? You don't know how cigarettes are expensive like hell in this country? Nobody tell you anything at all about *London*? Frank didn't give you tips before you left *Trinidad*?

Galahad   He tell me a lot of things, but you know, how them fellars always like to exaggerate. I only listen halfway to what him say.

Moses   You drink?

Galahad   Yes.

Moses   But you bring no rum?

Galahad   Do you see any on me?

Moses   You mean to say you come off the ship with no rum? You don't know they does allow you to land with two bottles and some of the boys does manage to come ashore with four or five, getting other people who aint have none to bring it for them? You know how much a bottle of rum cost in *London*?

Galahad   How much?

Moses   Thirty-seven and six.

Galahad   Whew!

Moses   You bring any money?

Galahad   I have three pound.

Moses   It's five pounds you can land with, you know.

Galahad   Man, why don't you give it a rest with the questions! Do I have this? Did I come with that? I have had a very long journey, and I am tired.

Moses   Just tell me what happen with the two?

Galahad   I get in on a *wappe* game on board with some of the fellars and lose two.

Moses   Alright Oliver, Henry . . .

Galahad   It's *Henry Oliver*!

Moses   No mind.

Galahad   I mind.

Moses   You *Sir Galahad* for truth.

Galahad   Galahad?

Moses   From *King Arthur*, son of *Lancelot*, the most noble and assured of all of the knights of the round table.

Galahad   *Galahad*? I like that.

Moses   *London* will do for you for now.

Galahad   And I will do for *London*.

Moses   What do you think of the place?

Galahad   It's nice.

Moses   A lie you a tell.

Galahad   No, I mean it.

Moses   Tell me something, have you ever see a room like this back home?

Galahad   Alright then, it's nasty. It's bad!

Moses   That's better.

Galahad   So, what part of *London* is this?

Moses   *Bayswater.*

Galahad   Why do they call it *Bayswater*? It have a bay, it have water?

Moses   Just take it easy, you can't learn everything in the first day you land.

You are going to meet a lot of fellars from London who don't even want talk to you, because they have their own matters.

Galahad   Right.

Moses   It's important to them!

Galahad   OK!

Moses   Sooner you get settled the better. This is *London*, yes?

Galahad   Yes, Moses.

Moses   Not *Port of Spain*.

Galahad   I got it, thank you.

Moses *succeeds in lighting the fire.*

Moses   Yes, at last! You saved me a long walk to the station, Galahad. I suppose I should be thanking you. So, thank you . . . Right now, bed time. Top or tail?

Galahad   Tail, please.

Moses   You don't fidget?

Galahad   No.

Moses   Good. Can't stand ones who fidget.

Moses *prepares himself for bed, as does* **Galahad**, *removing his clothes to reveal the pyjamas he is already wearing.* **Moses** *laughs as he strips down to his vest and underpants and climbs into bed.*

Galahad   That it?

Moses   You want me to read you a bed time story?

Galahad   Good night, Moses.

Moses   Good night.

Galahad   Oh, and Moses?

Moses   What?

Galahad   Thank you.

Moses   Don't thank me.

Galahad *goes to sleep.* **Moses** *gets out of bed; he goes to his desk and begins writing a letter.*

Moses (*recites*)   It was the grimmest of all the winter evenings my dearest William. The fog would be sleeping restlessly over the city and the lights showing the blur as if it is not London at all but some strange place on another planet, but there was I, William, ready to meet a fellar who was coming from Trinidad on the boat train. And his name was Henry Oliver. I tell you William, I don't know how I am always getting in position like this, helping people out. Often, I would sigh as the buses crawl their way through the fog, and the evening so melancholy that I wish I was back in bed.

Lights on **Christina** (*black, 20s*) *singing quite softly 'Be Thou My Vision' as she lays prayer sheets on the chairs in her father's church.* **Moses** *watches her from afar with great affection. As far as* **Moses** *is concerned, it is Trinidad, 1949. As* **Christina** *finishes singing, she turns around to see* **Moses** *watching her, smiling. She looks frightened.*

Moses   I love your voice.

Christina   I know who you are.

Moses   Oh yes, who am I?

Christina   You're a heathen.

Moses   Is that right, Christina.

Christina   How do you know my name?

Moses   I've seen you around town, you are hard to miss.

Christina   How can a man like you, with a name like yours, be so . . .

Moses   Charming?

Christina   Contemptible!

Moses   And how do you know my name?

Christina   A man who walks down the street gets shouted Moses Aloetta is bound to get attention.

Moses   You've been watching me?

Christina   It's thirty degrees outside.

Moses   What of it?

Christina   You have not come in here to get warm. This is a church. There is nothing of worth here.

Moses   Look, just pretend you didn't see me, yes?

Christina   I will scream. (*Waits, then screams.*) Father!

Moses   Hey!

Christina   Father?

Moses   Why are you screaming? I was only looking for money.

Christina   I knew it!

Moses   I wasn't not going to hurt you . . .

Christina   Father, quick! One of those worthless good for nothing from across the road has come into our church!

Christina *runs off.*

Moses   Who are you calling . . .

Galahad *begins stirring in his sleep.*

Galahad (*half asleep*)   Hey, what's the noise, man?

Moses   Nothing, go back to sleep.

Galahad *goes back to sleep.*

Moses   Come on, Moses man, don't do this, don't do it.

Moses *goes to the bathroom.*

Waterloo

Tanty *talking to an unseen news reporter.*

Tanty   Mister, you best had better mind what you are doing, yes. If you touch me with that thing, I call a policeman for you. (*Listens.*) A what? A microphone. Oh, I see, now I understand you wish to speak to me? Very well. (*Listens.*) Lewis, why are you so prejudiced? The gentleman asked me a perfectly good question, why should I answer? We have to show that we have good manners. Sorry about that. Yes, this is my first trip to England. (*Listens.*) Why? Well, I am glad that you asked. It's the same ting I say, I tell all of them who coming. Why all you leaving the country to go to England? Over there it so cold, only white people do live there and dem rude. No offence. But they say they have more work in

England and better pay. When I hear my son Lewis getting five pound a week, him over there with the scowling face, I had to agree. So, here I am. I come mind my family, of course. Who else go cook, wash clothes and clean the big house Lewis say he got for us? Well, precisely. I knew you would understand. (*Listens.*) Oh, why yes of course. Come you two, him want tek photo. Agnes, Lewis, come! (*Listens.*) I'm sorry? Well, you can't take me alone. You have to take the whole family. Agnes, you stand right there. Lewis, pick up yer face nuh boy and stand over here. Right here. Come on.

The family bustle together to pose.

Tanty   Hold on a minute.

Tanty *searches her bag. She takes out a straw hat and puts it on her head.*

Tanty   I am ready now.

Tanty *poses. The reporter takes the picture.*

Bayswater

It is now the next morning. **Moses** *comes out of the bathroom with his face washed and toothbrush inside his mouth.*

Moses   Get up, man, what you think this is, a holiday camp? Time to look for work. Galahad?

Galahad   What?

Moses   Up! Why are you shivering like that?

Galahad   I never thought my first morning in London would be like this?

Moses   What you thought, you wake up in the *Savoy*? (*Chuckles.*) You want me to come wid you, find work?

Galahad   No, no thank you.

Moses   Are you sure?

Galahad   I can take care of myself.

Moses   Work not so easy to get as you think. Suppose you get one far from the water, it won't make no sense to find a room round here. You will have to try and get one near work.

Galahad   Thank you, but I got this.

Moses   *You got this?*

Galahad   No offence, Moses, but you are as nosey as Frank.

Moses   I know a whole heap of fellars like you know. Bart. Tolroy, Big City, Cap. Five Past Midnight.

Galahad   Are any of those names supposed to mean something?

Moses   Try to fool people that you know everything, then when you get lash, you come home bawling.

Galahad   Alright, *Mister London*? What would you advise me as a newcomer to do?

Moses   Hustle yourself a home back to *Trinidad*. But I know you would never want to do that.

Galahad   Correct.

Moses   So what I would tell you is this. Take it easy. This is not a race. Give yourself time to get to know *London*, give *London* a chance to know you.

Galahad   London? To *know* me? Come on.

Moses   Laugh all you want, Galahad, but this city is funny, this city has eyes, and it watches every move you make. You don't believe me, do you?

Galahad   I didn't say that.

Moses   You'll find out.

Galahad   We are British subjects.

Galahad *goes into the bathroom.*

Moses   That don't mean shit.

Galahad (*from the bathroom*)   It does to me.

Moses   Listen, I will give you the name of a place in London. It's called *Barnet*. There it have a restaurant run by a Polish man called *The Rendezvous Restaurant*. Go there and see if they will serve you. Go there and see all their tables taken by white people eating their food. And you know the worst part of this? That Polish man have no more right to be here than me. In fact, as you say, we are British subjects, he is the foreigner, we have more right to live and work than he, because it is we who bleed to make this country good.

Galahad *comes back out.*

Galahad   That is all very interesting, Moses, and as much as I enjoy hearing you, I had better go and look for work, don't you think? I'm not as green as I may look, you know. Where do you have to go?

Moses   The employment exchange by Edgware Road.

Galahad   I hear some fellars say on the train about how you could go on the dole, if you aint working, said they intend to find out about it before they start to hustle.

Moses   It have fellars like that, you want to be something like that?

Galahad   I am a born hustler, Moses.

Moses   Oh, is that so?

Galahad   I won't start taking money off the state unless I have to. Tell me something, why is one of your friends called Five Past Midnight?

Moses   Because he is so dark-skinned when a person looks at him, he or she says, 'Boy, you black like midnight,' before adding, 'No, you more like Five Past Twelve.'

Galahad I'm almost sorry I asked.

Moses Mind yourself, Galahad.

Galahad I will.

Moses A lot of parasites muddy the water for the boys, and these days when one spade do something wrong, they crying down on the lot.

Galahad Why don't you let me find all of this out for myself, Moses, yes? Are you not working today?

Moses I work when the construction people have work to give me.

Galahad So employment exchange? Where again?

Moses Go down the road, until you come to *Westbourne Park Grove*, and there is any bus going up towards *Paddington*. Five stops. Edgware Road.

Galahad Tell me something, what are the white women like?

Moses Like their country, cold.

Galahad Thank you. Wish me luck?

Moses Luck.

Galahad *smiles as he leaves. From the floor below,* **Moses** *can hear the muted voice of a couple arguing.*

Lights on **Lewis** *and* **Agnes** *in the flat below, fighting.* **Tanty** *looks on.*

Agnes You told me, in your letters, you have a house.

Lewis This is a house, Agnes, our house!

Agnes A big glorious house, Lewis.

Lewis I know what I said, but it is big at least from the outside.

Tanty All of us in this little summin of a room, Lewis?

Lewis   Mama please, don't shout about our business.

Tanty   I was not shouting.

Lewis   Well, you are not quiet. These walls are paper thin, you want the landlord to find another excuse to throw us out?

Tanty   What do yo mean, throw us out? We just arrived.

Agnes   Why would he want to do that?

Lewis   He is not doing that.

Agnes   But why, Lewis?

Tanty   Yes boy, why?

Lewis   On the account I may be temporarily unemployed.

Tanty   Oh Jesus!

Lewis   It's only for short while.

Tanty   I know all about your short whiles, boy.

Lewis   Will you please stop calling me that? It will be alright, Mama, I'm telling you. I will get another job, I will find a bigger place for us all, and for the pickne when they come. Our life here will be grand I am telling you both. Believe that. Believe me.

Lewis *goes to leave.*

Agnes   Where are you going now?

Lewis   To find work of course. Come on my sweet, smile for me? It's going to be alright, I'm telling you. (*Kisses her.*) Welcome to England!

Agnes *and* **Tanty** *inspect the room. They both wipe dust off everything with their fingers.*

Agnes   Disgusting, Tanty. Absolutely, disgusting.

Tanty   Come, child.

Tanty *rolls up her sleeves.* **Agnes** *does the same.* **Tanty** *finds some cleaning materials including a couple of cloths under the sink. She throws one to* **Agnes** *and they both begins furiously giving everything in the room a wipe.*

Agnes (*recites*)   Peter Piper picked a peck of pickled peppers. A peck of pickled peppers Peter Piper picked.

Tanty (*curious*)   What is that?

Agnes   If Peter Piper picked a peck of pickled peppers, where's the peck of pickled peppers Peter Piper picked? Two toads, totally tired, trying to trot to Tewkesbury.

Tanty *goes to leave.*

Agnes   Tanty?

Tanty   Back in a minute, child.

Moses *shines his shoes when suddenly* **Tanty** *comes through the door.*

Tanty   You Moses?

Moses   I am.

Tanty   You have cloth we can borrow?

Moses   For what?

Tanty   To clean, of course.

Moses *hands* **Tanty** *some cloths from the kitchen.*

Moses   You must be Lewis's mother. I heard you all arrive late last night.

Tanty   You friend with my son Lewis, yes?

Moses   You could say that.

Tanty   Well, let me ask you summin?

Moses   I wish you would.

Tanty   What the hell is wrong wid him?

Moses   As far as I know, not a thing.

Tanty   I know he is not pleased to see us, and yet he is carrying on like everything will be fine and he has not a care in the world.

Moses   Yes, I can hear you all from up here. These walls are thin you know.

Tanty   So, is there anything going on that I should know about?

Moses   As a matter of fact. Yes.

Tanty   What?

Moses   That none of you should have come here.

Tanty   What a boy, rude!

Tanty *leaves.*

Soho

Lights on **Big City**, *giving out flyers.*

Big City   Yes my friends, a soirée to end all soirées! One big arse hall. I tell you! What, you don't believe me? Well, allow me to tell you *Wings Crust Road*, if I lie, mi die! (*Listens.*) What? What you say? Yes, that's what I said, *King's Cross Road*, don't fuck me up, excuse me, madam, pardon my language. You want ticket or not? All the drink you can drink, food you can eat. Nice fine looking ladies if you are hot to trot. So what do you say? Come nuh? Oh, don't be like that! Anyone else? Anyone want ticket? Come on, did you not hear me say, it is the soirées to end all soirées! Last Friday of the month! Come on now? Will I see you there? What about you, madam, would you like to come to a soirée? Everyone is welcome. You know, in Jamaica, we have a saying, out of many, we are one people . . .

Big City *is suddenly spat at. He slowly wipes the spit from his face.*

Big City   Yes, and a good day to you, madam. Take care now.

Bayswater

Later that morning. **Galahad** *is back in* **Moses'** *room. Looking rather agitated.*

Moses   So, how far did you get?

Galahad   End of the street, outside some place called *Whitneys?*

Moses (*corrects*)   *Whiteleys.* What happened?

Galahad   It is hard to describe.

Moses   Try.

Galahad   It was like I lost myself. I lost all composure.

Moses   Go on.

Galahad   I never knew the sky could be so grey and the people, the way they all huddled against the cold, all hustle and bustle as they go by me. I did see a red bus though, with my own eyes. And a red telephone box, the black cabs with their bright yellow lights, all just as I had seen in the pictures back home.

Moses   But?

Galahad   I realized I didn't know where I was, OK? My mouth was so dry I goes to ask a woman for direction she side steps me and carries on her way. Some little white girl with her mother, is pointing at me, screaming 'Look Mummy, there is a black man' for the whole street to hear. The traffic is rushing by so fast on these streets, the bus conductors are yelling 'Getting on or getting off'. Everybody doing something or going somewhere. Even this little dog I see, look busier than me. It's as if it's all spinning out of control for me.

Moses   So what did you do?

Galahad   I came back here of course.

Moses (*laughs*)   You mean you ran. You ran away, boy.

Galahad   Alright, you have had your fun.

Moses   Told you. You'll learn.

Galahad   Yes. So now what?

Moses   You tell me.

Galahad   I thought you was my teacher.

Moses   Tell me what you want to learn, then I will teach.

Galahad   Does it ever get warm in London?

Moses   That is what you want to learn?

Galahad   No.

Moses   Why are you so stubborn?

Galahad   I was lost.

Moses   I know.

Galahad   I am cold.

Moses   Welcome to London. So?

Galahad   Will you help me please, with the employment exchange?

Moses   Two conditions.

Galahad   Name them.

Moses   You are done with all this big man talk. You do what I tell you. When I tell you.

Galahad   OK. So what do I do now?

Moses   Sit.

Galahad *sits.*

Moses   Tell me, what did you do before you come here?

Galahad   Is this really necessary?

Moses   Are you going to do as I say or not?

Galahad I worked on the oilfields. Pointe-a-Pierre.

Moses Where did you used to live?

Galahad Down south. San Fernando, in Urcapo Street.

Moses That is not far from where I lived.

Galahad I know that.

Moses What's this I hear about them building over the market?

Galahad They are no longer building, they are done. Market gone.

Moses Gone?

Galahad Yes.

Moses I love that market. You know if I shut my eyes I can hear them selling fruit on the Saturday, Mama picking mango, the freshest kind, she would check its firmness by squeezing like so with her own hand. She fill up the bag and I have to carry it all the way home. So what there now, Galahad, over the market, what they build, not a blasted subway or summin like that?

Galahad A street.

Moses A street?

Galahad To make way for the subway they nuh build yet. Besides, why do you care so much? You here, it is there, move on. It's not your home anymore.

Moses (*sighs*) No, it isn't. Right, now listen good. Don't worry about the bus this time. Come out the house. Turn left, keep walking until you reach Paddington station. You can't miss it. Take a right, you will soon find Edgware Road. Don't mind anybody else, just carry on with your own business. No need to look at anyone in the eye. They don't want to talk to you, so don't talk to them. The employment exchange will be the fifth block on your left. There. The people there will have cards with your details. Name, age, address, it also has JA stamped on it, so people know you're from Jamaica.

Galahad   But I'm not.

Moses   Jamaica, Trinidad, they think we all come from the same place. It just means you're coloured and very useful to potential employers. What work did you used to do in the oilfields?

Galahad   I was an electrician.

Moses   You should tell them that, or else they will want to throw some hard work at you. Lift iron or something, heavy box. Or worse yet, pack your arse up to join the army. Do whatever you must to avoid that, Galahad.

Galahad   I will.

Moses   Right then. You had best get going.

Galahad   You're not coming with me?

Moses   You'll be alright now. Remember what I tell you.

Galahad   Yes but . . .

Moses   You know where I am. You know who I am. Everyone knows. I'm Moses.

Moses *throws him his overcoat.*

Galahad *leaves.*

Bayswater

Later that day. **Lewis's** *flat.* **Tanty** *and* **Agnes** *enter, carrying bags.*

Tanty   Two, toads . . .

Agnes   No Tanty, two toads.

Tanty   Two toads.

Agnes   Trying?

Tanty   Trying to trot, to . . . where again?

Agnes (*giggles*)   Tewkesbury.

Tanty   Where dat?

Agnes   Never mind where, come on, try again.

Tanty   Two . . .

Agnes   Toads . . .

Tanty   Two toads, trying trot to Tewkesbury! See, me do it!

Agnes   You left some out.

Tanty   Oh lawd.

Agnes   It is . . . Two toads, totally tired, trying to trot to Tewkesbury. Try this one. Peter Piper picked a peck of pickled peppers . . .

Tanty   No.

Agnes   Yes. Come on.

Tanty   Child, I give up.

Agnes   Don't you worry, you will get there.

Lewis   Will the two of you hush up, please?

Agnes   But it was our first day of shopping in England,
Lewis

Tanty   Don't budda just sit there, be a gentleman and help us with the bags, please?

Lewis   You went out and about by yourself?

Agnes   I was not out there all by myself. I went with Tanty.

Lewis   From now on, you don't go out without me. I want no one taking advantage of you.

Agnes   What on earth are you talking about?

Lewis   This country will have no time for your hoity-toity ways, Agnes.

Agnes   *Hoity-toity?*

Lewis   You understand?

Tanty   I understand you want a good cuff round your head.

Lewis   Mama please, you don't interfere in business between a husband and him wife, you one told me that.

Tanty   Even so!

Lewis   Mama, back off.

Tanty   What you say to me, boy?

Lewis   I told you to stop calling me that.

Tanty   Don't blame the two a' we because you can't be bothered to find work.

Lewis   *Can't be bothered?*

Tanty   You hear what I said.

Lewis   One day here and you think you know.

Tanty   Well, come on then, tell me, bwoi.

Lewis   Mama?

Agnes   Tanty, it's alright. Lewis, I am sorry.

Tanty   It seems I come here in time.

Lewis   For what?

Tanty   To knock some foolishness out of your head!

Lewis   I told you both that I will find work, and I shall.

Lewis *leaves in a huff.*

Agnes   Lewis?

Tanty   Oh just leave him, Agnes.

Chiswick

A few days later. **Galahad** *is hard at work on the floor. A young white woman* (**Daisy**) *enters with her tea trolley. Two white colleagues pass by in the opposite direction. They deliberately knock the boxes out of his arms, laughing as they leave.* **Galahad** *gets down on his knees to collect all the parts and put them back in the boxes.* **Daisy** *kneels down to help him.*

Galahad   I do not want your help, madam, I can manage, thank you.

I just don't like being made fun of, alright? So, you saw what happened? Why are you saying sorry, you didn't say it. Is that what you think? You think I should not be here too? Well, I am very pleased to hear that. A pleasure to meet you at last, Daisy. Well, I have seen you aroun. You know, around, and I know you have seen me. May I ask, am I the first? The first coloured man you've seen? You have? And do either of them look like me? Is that so? Forgive me, but you do not know what is it that I want. Except to know your name. My apologies I do not mean to cause offence. I am just been friendly. Sorry? Women? In the park? I do not know what you mean. I can assure you, my lady, I do not. All I want is the pleasure of knowing your name. Daisy. Like the flower. Pleased to make your acquaintance, Daisy, I am Henry, but you may call me Galahad. (*Repeats.*) *Galahad.* It's from *King Arthur.* Why? I do not know why. Moses says it is because I am noble. (*Repeats.*) Moses. He is my friend. Another one that you think shouldn't be here. Then what are you saying, Daisy? I know you don't. To the likes of me, you do not have to say or do anything. Well, thank you. Yes, I will do as I like. You tell your friends they had better watch themselves. There is only so much a man can take. (*Listens.*) Who? Victor Mature? Me? You like *Victor Mature*? Because I love Victor Mature. I just the love the scene where he fights all of them Roman soldiers with his sword in *Samson and Delilah*! Yes, he did I saw it. He was fighting the *Philistines.* Or was it *Demetrius and the Gladiators*, yes, that is the one. You know, Daisy, there's a double bill showing at the Coronet tomorrow night, two *Victor Mature* films. Perhaps I might, you know, see you there?

No funny stuff, you have my word. Good. Tomorrow night then. I shall be looking forward to it. Daisy.

Galahad *smiles.* **Daisy** *leaves with her trolley.*

Streets of London

Three days have passed.

Lights on **Big City**, *facing a row of white councillors.*

Big City   . . . But I have sold fifty tickets already, the money is right here in my hand! Are you saying you don't want it? Who the hell are you giving the hall to now? (*Listen*s.) The Irish? But you say the hall is mine. No, I can fill it up as easily as the Irish men den, I know I can, I sell fifty tickets. These people will come, more people will come, I tell you! I have as steel band, I have drink. Please? You want to see a grown man beg, please? It works for the Irish, let it work for me. But it's the idea you want but not me, right? Not a whole room full of *no good coloureds*, am I right? Come on, just say it. If I had sold a thousand tickets today, you'll still say no, right? Just say it? Say it man, say it! You'll be sorry. All of you, I swear to God, you will be sorry.

Bayswater

Lights only on **Lewis** *who is by* **Moses'** *window stalking a pigeon.*

Lewis   It was when I arrived here in fifty-four. For six days I could not find a room, anywhere. Them fucking English people with their no Black, no Irish, no dog shit. I meet up with Bart, Harris and a few other fellars who find bench to sleep on in the park. Lord, it was cold, If I lie, mi die. I spent most of the night *shooing* away the blasted pigeons, who decide they want to shit all over us during the night. One cold morning, I was so hungry, I wake up to find this pigeon just sitting on me. Still as anything. Not doing anything, except just sit. It reminded me of this chicken my grandaddy had on his farm back home, in Jamaica. It would lay the nicest biggest eggs you see. But one time, Grandaddy was as hungry as me, and had to kill his favourite chicken to eat. So, then I thought about this pigeon sitting on me. And then it had occurred to me. It may be a pigeon, but bird is bird, right? Chicken, pigeon, they all bird. And people eat bird. So why not, I thought? Why the hell not? The pigeon laying on me was ever so still. Like it had done this before. I ready my hand like so, ever slowly, getting closer and close to its neck then I pounce, pinch the neck and twist, and it's done. Harris then told me about his friend Moses who not only has a room but it has an oven, so we can cook. That is how Moses and I first met. I was good, I am still good. Ask anyone and they will say 'Lewis, single-handedly has reduced the pigeon population in the whole of London.'

Lewis *manages to grab the bird. He snaps the pigeon's neck.*

Lights come up on the fellars cheering and applauding him.

Big City   Yes, Lewis! Nice and plump, like my women.

Moses   Do you want to eat it or marry it, City? Pass it me, Lewis.

Galahad   I'm sorry but what is it that are you doing?

Moses   Why don't you tell me what you think it looks like he is doing?

Lewis   Pigeon meat is sweet.

Galahad   Pigeon meat? (*Dawns on him.*) You mean to say, you are going to eat that?

Oh my God!

Moses   Don't pull your face like that. That stew you ate on your second day here, what did you think that was?

Galahad   Chicken?

Moses *shakes his head.*

Galahad   Pork? Beef?

Big City   Give it up, boy, it's pigeon you eat.

Galahad   No! Oh my God, no!

Lewis   Pick up your face, man.

Moses   Oh, just relax, boy. Hey, City, tell Galahad the story about when you . . .

Big City   Oh, here we go again!

Moses   Come on, man.

Big City   No!

Moses   If you don't, I will. Sorry, man.

Big City   You are not sorry, Moses, don't. Come on, man. Why is it always me?

Lewis   Because it's funny.

Big City   Fuck off, man.

Galahad   Tell me.

Moses   We need to help take his mind off from eating pigeon.

Big City   Well, go on then, see if I care.

Moses   Me and City, used to coast *Bayswater Road* from the *Arch* to the *Grove*, almost every night. Well, it had one woman used to be hustling there, dress up nice, wearing fur coat and every time when the boys pass she saying, 'Bon soir' in this hoarse voice of hers. And we would politely answer, 'Bon soir' and walk on. But on this night in particular, things was scarce on the patrol, and City's thirst bad, so I tell him why don't he broach that big woman who always telling us, 'Bon soir'. City broach and he take the woman by *Gloucester Road* and he was so hurry he couldn't wait but had to begin as soon as she turns the lights off in the room. Couple of nights later, Cap and I are talking with a couple of gal in the pub, when one of dem turn to City and say, 'It was you slept with that man the other night'. (*Roars with laughter.*) Turns out this 'Bon soir' woman was really a test who used to dress up like a woman and patrol the area? I laugh so hard, I piss myself.

Big City   Oh, have you finished now? Have you all had a good old laugh at my expense.

Moses   Oh City, you know you love us.

Galahad   Good one, man.

Big City   What you say?

Galahad   Sorry?

Big City   Good one, man?

Galahad   Well, yes.

Big City   You think you know me well enough to say that?

Galahad   Take it easy, man.

Big City   Deh you go again with this, *man?*

Moses   Come on, City, relax.

Galahad   I'm just responding to the story.

Big City   You don't even know if it was true or not.

Galahad   Well, is it or isn't it?

Big City   That is not the point.

Galahad   Alright, easy.

Big City   Easy?

Galahad   Just back off a little, OK.

Big City   What him say?

Moses   Big City, don't.

Big City   Don't what.

Moses   He is only a boy.

Galahad   You're not much older than me, City

Moses   Galahad, shut up.

Galahad   I am just saying.

Big City   You saying poop.

Galahad   I just don't like people getting in my face like that, that is all.

Big City *gets right into* **Galahad***'s face.*

Big City   What, like this?

Galahad   Don't.

Big City   Moses, where you find him?

Moses   No mind him.

Galahad   No, do mind me. Getting in my face like he wants summin.

Big City   You know this bwoi won't last.

Galahad   I can last longer than you.

Moses   Come on, fellars, enough of this foolishness now.

Lewis (*gazes out of the window*)   Yes, any minute now, the park will be filled with some fine ladies of the night, we go have a good time or what?

Moses   Why are you in such in hurry for trim, Lewis?

Big City   Agnes nuh treat you right?

Lewis   How many more times, keep yer mind and your eyes off my wife.

Big City   You nuh give her some *satisfaction,* Lewis? You forget to know how?

Lewis   You one lie down with man.

Big City   Carry on wid yer mout, I go lie you down.

Moses   Stop. Lewis?

Lewis   I am fine, don't worry yourself about me.

Lewis *leaves.*

Moses   Alright, then. Come, City, pickings are slim tonight. What you waiting for, Galahad, a letter from your mother?

Galahad   No thank you.

Big City   You tink him a poof, Moses?

Galahad   Say what?

Big City   I ask if you are a nasty dirty poof, Galahad?

Galahad   Watch it.

Big City   I don't mind if you are, more white gal for me.

Galahad   You might mind a thump in your face.

Big City   Try me, boy.

Moses   .

Big City   You're lucky you have Moses sticking up for you.

Galahad   I don't need Moses.

Moses   Alright, what the hell is wrong with all of you fellars today? It is a Sunday, enough. He is just finding his feet, City. Galahad, it's alright for you to have the itch you know. How long has it been?

Galahad   None of yer damn business, Moses, no offence.

Moses   That long?

Galahad   That is not what I said.

Moses   And I said drop the big man act. It's not going to help you here. Now, do you have the itch or not?

Galahad   Of course I have the itch. I wouldn't be a man without the itch.

Moses   Well, take it from me here are plenty of ladies in the park that can help you scratch it, now tek look from the window, take a good look, man. Which one do you like? Come on, which one?

Galahad   Well, that red head looks nice.

Moses   Mandy! You choose well. Yeah, she is nice but she is also popular, you best run an get her before some other fellar.

Galahad (*now eager*)   Alright then!

Galahad *dashes to the door.*

Galahad   You not coming?

Moses   Right behind you.

Moses *and* **Big City** *laugh.*

Big City   Oh yes, he have more than one itch! And it's Mandy you send him to? Boy will be lucky if he can walk when she done.

Moses   I best go and keep an eye on him.

Big City   Hold on a second, Moses. I want to talk to you.

Moses   About what?

Big City   Business.

Moses   Look, if this is about the dance, I haven't started selling tickets yet, but I . . .

Big City   Forget about the dance hall, just forget it.

Moses   But your deal with the council?

Big City   They make money when I make money, and I don't make no money.

Moses   They blow you out?

Big City   If you like.

Moses   I'm sorry, City.

Big City   Do not worry yourself about it, I'm alright.

Moses   I'm sorry all the same.

Big City   I'm alright, Moses, did you not hear me say?

Moses   I heard. So what now, City, what other business?

Big City *reveals the small handgun.* **Moses** *is aghast.*

Moses   What the hell? Where the hell did you get it?

Big City   From a white guy I meet 'pon *Musket Hill.*

Moses   *Muswell Hill.*

Big City   It's what mi say.

Moses   And if you had any sense left in your head, you would go and give it back to yer white guy.

Big City   Mi nuh done wid it.

Moses   Big City, what the hell are you going to do?

Big City   I go shoot that man who work in the post office if he gives me shit.

Moses   Post office? And what has this man in the post office ever done to you?

Big City   Him nuh do nuttin to me.

Moses   So, why do you want to hurt him?

Big City   It's not me, least not just me.

Moses   I thought you said you were alright.

Big City   I am, only thing is now I have my eyes wide open.

Moses   What does that even mean?

Big City   I go tell you if you shut up. A couple of boys I drink with in this bar in Soho. Tell me about this job. One a dem boys drop out so, they need a man to watch by the door.

Moses   What?

Big City   We rob the post office!

Moses   These wouldn't be a couple of white boys by any chance, City?

Big City   I don't see how that matters.

Moses   No self-respecting criminal is going to be seen dead with one of us. No offence.

Big City   None taken.

Moses   Sounds more like a couple of fools with too much shrapnel in their brains who are too lazy to get up from their backsides and find work.

Big City   It's a good plan.

Moses   Have you lost your head?

Big City   They need another man.

Moses   For what?

Big City   Someone who can drive the getaway.

Moses   City, you are a fool.

Big City   There could be over 200 pound in that post office. Think what you can do with that kind of money, Moses.

Moses   What post office, where is it?

Big City   Lickle one just off *Nottingham Gate*.

Moses   *Notting Hill Gate*.

Big City   That's what I said.

Moses   No it's not.

Big City   Stop fucking me up. You think I don't know London? When them English people tell strangers they don't know where so and so is, I always know. From *Pentonvilla* right up to *Hensington High Court*, all about by *Tweeting Broadway*. I bet you can't call a name in *London* that I don't know where it is.

Moses   You're right, City, I can't.

Big City   Those boys know what they are doing.

Moses   They done this before?

Big City   Over and over.

Moses   Oh Lord, Jesus.

Big City   You want get out of this fucking country or not?

Moses   Who say I do?

Big City   I say you do. I am not as stupid as Lewis and Galahad. You're tired of been everyone's top fellar and you must tek care of dem.

Moses   I never asked for that.

Big City   I know that. They don't, but I do. You are done with this country, Moses, I can see it in your eye. You want money, well come after this job, you will have more money than you need. Get on that plane and go, don't look back. Or maybe you too afraid to go.

Moses   Why would I be too afraid to go home, City?

Big City   You tell me?

Moses   Well, I'm not.

Big City   This is your chance then, Moses. These English bwois, they just funny that is all.

Moses   As in *Bob Hope* funny?

Big City   It's their country, we just living in it.

Moses   Don't chat to me about their country, City, half of them can't even speak their own language.

Big City   I don't care about that! Nor should you. Let them talk how they want. Or maybe you more London than you think.

Moses   Listen, boy, I have had about as much as I can take of London!

Big City   That's better!

Moses   So what about you, City? Why you are doing this? You're a hustler man, you're trying your best. You don't do this. You don't carry a gun.

Big City   I do now.

Moses   So, what happened to you?

Big City   I am just tired of being spat on, yelled at and treated like shit, alright? I am as British as they. I fly planes during the war for these ungrateful sons of bitches. If they don't want give, fine, from now on, I take!

Moses   You did not fly planes in the war, City, you fixed them.

Big City   Not one of them would make it in the air if it weren't for us! Fly off back to Trinidad if that is what you want, Moses. But I am staying right here. I'm going to take this city, this country for everything I can get. They owe us. They owe me! When this done, we go be rich! You interested?

Moses   Would I be asking otherwise?

Big City   So the mighty Moses come off his high cross at last! I tell the boys you are interested. This calls for a celebration. You coming to the park? There will no girls left tonight.

Only **Moses** *can see that* **Christina** *is now standing in the room.*

Moses I'll catch up. You gwan.

Big City *goes.* **Moses** *is alone with* **Christina**. *His memory has taken him back to Trinidad, 1949.*

Christina Stop looking at me like that.

Moses Like what?

Christina Like some dirty man.

Moses Then how should I be looking at you?

Christina Like a gentleman.

Moses Do I have to do everything?

Christina Such as?

Christina *leans in again, they kiss.*

Moses So?

Christina It was only a kiss.

Moses Would you like me to do it again?

Christina You really do love yourself.

Christina *and* **Moses** *kiss again.*

Moses Do you ever think your father kissed your mother like that?

Christina Is that what this is about? To make my father angry?

Moses This has nothing to do with your father.

Christina I am not a prize, Moses.

Moses I never said you were.

Agnes Don't, don't ever.

Moses' *memory goes forward several weeks later.*

Moses Your father wants me gone, you know?

Christina   I know.

Moses   He wants me to get on that boat sail all the way to England and never come back. Good money he has offered me.

Christina   So what do you want to do?

Moses   I can't stay here, Christina, there is nothing for me here.

Christina   What am I, a mirage?

Moses   I know what you are going to say.

Christina   How can you know what I am about to say?

Moses (*beside himself*)   Please!

Christina   Moses?

Moses (*loses it*)   What are you? What are you! Some spirit that will not leave me, just keep running through my head day and night?

Christina   Moses?

Moses   No! No. No. No!

Christina *sings 'Be Thou My Vision' again.* **Moses** *grabs both sides of his head.*

Moses   What do you want? Do you want me to say it, is that it, do you want me to say out loud? I'm sorry. I'M SORRY, CHRISTINA!

Act Two

Portobello Market

Lights up on **Agnes**, *by a fruit and veg stall waiting patiently to be served.*

Agnes Excuse me? I said excuse me. But you said you would be right with me a minute ago, I believe it is my turn, now do you mind? (*Listens.*) I'm sorry? Yes, I do have manners, would you like to borrow some of mine? (*Listens.*) But I was here first, now are you going to serve me or not? I would like, six potatoes, four cauliflowers, five onions, a bunch of carrots, and three cabbages, now please! (*Sees something.*) Just a minute, please? One moment? What was that? That, I said, I saw that, I saw what you just did. You were quick, but not quick enough, sir, not for me. I saw you do it. That is not fresh fruit you are picking. That must be your old fruit from last week I would care to guess or even further back than that. But I saw you, you are trying to get rid of those first. You are selling your nasty rotten pieces first. How dare you? Don't you shout over me. Do not do that. Very well. (*Shouts over him.*) Everyone, may I have your attention, please?

What we have here is the nastier fruit on Portobello Market, please check your bag all of you. This man is trying to con you. He is trying to poison you and your family with rotten pieces of fruit and vegetables. (*To the trader.*) Do you have no shame at all? I'm sorry? What do I want? Well thank you for asking. As I said, six potato, four cauliflower, five onions, large, a bunch of carrots, and three cabbage? From the front please? Nice and fresh, please?

The trader does as **Agnes** *asks.* **Agnes** *readies her shopping bag, the trader puts them all in.*

Agnes Thank you. (*Listens.*) I'm sorry? Sling my what? My hook? Do I take it that you wish me to leave expediently?

Gladly, you will not see me again, until next week, that is, where I will expect to see you have the freshest fruit and vegetables waiting for us all, or would you like us to go through this all over again? (*Listens.*) And a very good day to you, sir.

Lights up on **Lewis** *and* **Agnes** *in their room.*

Agnes   If you were there, Lewis, if only you could have seen me? You you would have been proud of me.

Lewis   Proud of you? To buy potato?

Agnes   It was more than that. It's like what your mother says, if it doesn't fit, you make changes.

Lewis   We can't change nuttin, they won't let us.

Agnes   Maybe if you gave them a chance?

Lewis   What do you think I have been doing for the past three years. Never mind me, what about them, why they won't give us a chance?

Agnes   They not all bad, Lewis.

Lewis   A few weeks here and you and my mother think you know.

Agnes   The man on the stall was so horrible to me at first, but when he knew I wouldn't leave, that I was making a stand, I left, he respected me, Lewis, for standing up to him, the way he smiled at me as I left.

Lewis   Agnes, I don't business, yeah!

Agnes   Why are you like this?

Lewis   I lost my job, remember.

Agnes   And why was that?

Lewis   What you mean why? This is the white man; this is their country, they don't need no reason. Don't trouble yourself.

Agnes   I could still find work, at the hospital, perhaps?

Lewis   What do you mean that he smiled?

Agnes   What?

Lewis   The fruit and veg man, you say him smiled?

Agnes   Yes, he did.

Lewis   What reason you give him to smile?

Agnes   No reason.

Lewis   You sure about that?

Agnes   Lewis, this is foolishness you are talking.

Lewis (*snaps*)   You don't give no man any reason at all to smile at you, you understand?

Agnes (*suddenly scared*)   Lewis?

Lewis   You go behave yourself, not go running round, mek eyes at men.

Agnes   I was not.

Lewis   Carry on like you is at a party. You understand?

Agnes   Yes, I understand.

Lewis *takes his hat and coat.*

Lewis   Good. I go to the park, see if I can catch some pigeon to eat.

Lewis *goes.*

Bayswater

Moses *is on his room writing.*

Moses   When summer come to the city and all them girls throw away heavy winter coat and wearing light summer fricks so you could see the legs and shapes that was hiding away from the cold blasts, William, and you could coast a lime in the park and negotiate ten shillings or a pound with the sports . . . (*Stops writing.*) What the hell are you doing, Moses man, he's only a boy. He don't need to hear.

Moses *tears the letter up. He starts again.*

Moses   Oh, what a time it is, William, when summer come to the city . . .

Lewis *appears by the window, he taps on it, alerting* **Moses**.

Moses   What the hell?

Moses *lets him in.*

Lewis, why the hell you can't come through the front door?

Lewis   I didn't want to see Agnes.

Moses   She your wife, man.

Lewis   I want to ask you something.

Moses   Hurry up.

Lewis   You see any men come round here, lately?

Moses   What kind of men?

Lewis   Just men! You know, when you are here, during the day?

Moses   What's this all about?

Lewis   Yu nuh answer my question.

Moses   Speak, Lewis.

Lewis   Agnes carrying on with some man, or men.

Moses   What?

Lewis   True talk mi I tell you.

Moses   You must be mad.

Lewis   She have man.

Moses   Your wife?

Lewis   Yes, Moses, mi wife.

Moses   You don't know that.

Lewis   I know it.

Moses   She said that?

Lewis   Of course she nuh say.

Moses   Well then, how do you know?

Lewis   Moses, I know!

Moses   Not all women bring men home when their husbands are out.

Lewis   But some.

Moses   Lewis?

Lewis   Agnes could be one of the some. What?

Moses   You chatting shit is what.

Lewis   But you see her, you all see her, you telling me you wouldn't.

There, you see? She drive me mad.

Moses   Are you sure that is it?

Lewis   Well, what else?

Moses   Never mind.

Lewis   If you were in my position, any one of you would.

Moses   Do what, Lewis?

Lewis   Box she down, of course! Now I am not saying I would, but it's what she deserve.

Moses   No.

Lewis   What you mean, no?

Moses   . . . It's not like Jamaica, women in this country have rights. Them mouth Bible, here.

Lewis   I know that.

Moses   You can't stay here, Lewis?

Lewis   You go let me think, Moses, just for one minute? I really love that woman.

Moses   Agnes is not fooling around, you know that.

Lewis   I don't know anything.

Moses   Write a letter.

Lewis   What?

Moses   A letter, about how you feel. If you can't talk, write.

Lewis   Like you, you always writing. Who to, I don't know.

Moses   And you won't, my letters, my business.

Lewis   What will I say?

Moses   I can't write this for you, Lewis.

Lewis   I know that. Just help me out.

Moses   Just write, man. Write what's in there (*Points to his heart.*) Not what is in there. (*Points at his head.*)

Lewis   You have paper?

Moses *hands him paper and a pen.*

Moses   Now write.

Lewis   What I tell she?

Moses   Lewis?

Lewis   It's myself I ask. That I is all. Sorry. Yeah, I is sorry. (*Begins writing.*) From now on, everything will be alright.

Moses *gets his coat.*

Lewis   Where you go?

Moses   When I write, I like to be alone. The silence helps.

Lewis   Well, I am not you.

Moses   You'll be alright.

Lewis   Moses, it's cold.

Moses   It's always cold, it's *London*. I'm just go walk down the street. Mek sure you done by then. Mind how you go.

Moses *goes.* **Lewis** *continues to write but soon the words begin to dry up. He looks helpless and feels it as well. He eventually gives up and crumples the letter in his hands and throws it to the floor. He takes out his flask and drinks from it.*

Chiswick

Several days later. Lights on **Galahad** *at work, packing boxes. When he sees* **Daisy**, *he tries to steal her away for a quick kiss.*

Galahad   Come on, Daisy, just one quick kiss? (*Listens.*) Since when do you call me Henry? I keep telling you, it's Galahad. I don't care, let them, let the whole world see us. Now, come on. (*Objects.*) Why does everyone have to say that? Like I don't know what country I am living in? Or what the people are like by now Do I look like a child? You're the one who kissed me first, remember? Outside the Coronet. (*Laughs.*) A moment of weakness, my eye! You kissed me because you wanted to. I kissed you back because I wanted to. Why are you so afraid?

Two workmen show up and see what **Galahad** *and* **Daisy** *are getting up to.*

Galahad   Good afternoon. How may I help you, gentlemen? (*Listens.*) I'm sorry? (*Objects.*) Now, just a moment. I can assure you I do not need to force myself on anyone, especially a lady. (*Defensive.*) That is none of your business, now if you will excuse us, come Daisy.

The two workmen block their path.

Galahad   I said please excuse us? (*Listens.*) I was not forcing her, I believe I have made that clear. Well, I do not believe she belongs to you either. Does she look like a cow to you? I don't see no number on her side. Well, you see gentlemen, I would gladly get on that boat and leave, but I am afraid, I am not done fucking yer mudda yet.

Galahad *is beaten senseless.*

Pimlico

Later that day. **Big City** *is putting on a handkerchief that covers his nose and mouth, He inspects the handgun.*

Big City (*listens*)   Say what? Yes, man, I am fine. He said yes. He yes. Moses will do the job with us now, are you sure there is plenty of money in that post office? This little something is enough to cover our faces? They won't recognise us or nuttin? Hey, I am only asking. I'm fine, don't you worry, I just want to know. So, I ask. It is what people do. Good. Good. That is good. That is all good. (*Listens.*) Look, I just told you, he said yes, Moses will not let me down. He will not, alright? He will, alright! (*Paces up and down.*) Let's go over the plan for tomorrow. The three of us go in, Moses will be waiting for us in the car, outside the post office, *Notting Well Fence.* (*Listens.*) That is what I said, *Notting Hill Gate.* Stop fucking me up. Come on.

Bayswater

Same day. **Galahad** *has his wounds treated by* **Moses**.

Moses   Jesus, those boys turn you out good! Hold still, boy, don't wince.

Galahad   I had one of them.

Moses   But there three of them.

Galahad   I buss his head, good.

Moses   There is no need to show off, Galahad.

Galahad   I am not showing off, I am telling you what happened.

Moses   Calm yourself.

Galahad   I am calm.

Moses   We have all had a beating from the white man at some point.

Galahad   It was not a beating.

Moses   If you say.

Galahad   It was a fight.

Moses   Of course, man.

Galahad   And I gave as good as I got.

Moses   Are you going to keep your head still or not?

Galahad   Can I ask you something, Moses?

Moses   What do you want to know?

Galahad   This colour problem, what do you think of it?

Moses   I never heard it called that before.

Galahad   Well?

Moses   I don't have an answer for you, I still don't know if I can work it out. I know they hate us. They hate us cos we love their women in the way they can't.

Galahad   It have nothing to wid women.

Moses   It has everything to do women. All the problems in the world always have to do with two things, two things only. Sex and money!

Galahad   I know how to please a woman.

Moses   I am not taking about that.

Galahad   Then what else is there? I give them what they want, exactly what they want, I don't business about the rest.

Moses   Now you sound like City.

Galahad   I don't care about City. Or Lewis. I don't care about any of them.

Moses   Well, I want you to care.

Galahad   Why?

Moses   It's important you get to know them.

Galahad   Important? You are a funny one, Moses.

Moses   I take that as compliment.

Galahad   Why are they like this, Moses? White people, them? All I want to do is get on, we all do, why are they like this?

Moses   I wish I could help you.

Galahad   You know more than you let on, Moses, I see you, your brain is always thinking. Always writing them letters to send back home. So, tell me, just tell me, why are they like this?

Lewis *comes in.*

Lewis   Moses!

Moses   What you want now, Lewis?

Lewis *shows the hole in the trousers he is wearing.*

Moses   What, what do you want from me?

Lewis   You see it? My backside through the hole of this trouser, can you see it?

Moses   Well, of course I can see it. You can fly a plane through it.

Lewis   I have a job interview this afternoon.

Moses   What exactly is it that you want me to do?

Lewis   Well, you know.

Moses   I see.

Lewis   You will have them back.

Moses   Oh shut up, man. You'll find a pair of trousers in the closet. One day you nuh, one day all of you are going to have to look after yourselves instead come crying to me all the blasted time.

Lewis   Yes, Moses, one day, one day indeed, but not today.

Moses   You are riding your luck now, Lewis.

Lewis   I bring them back to you.

Moses   If that makes you feel better.

Lewis   I gone.

Lewis *goes.*

Galahad   You really think?

Moses   That I will never see them again, come on. If Lewis had any brains and decided to use them for once, he would see that the trousers him go borrow are his trousers. I borrowed them from him, a year ago.

Galahad   So Moses did go to someone, without everyone coming to him.

Moses   It has been known to happen. So, you were asking?

Galahad   Never mind.

Moses   No, come on.

Galahad   I don't want to burden you with trouble too.

Moses   Look, what I said, I meant them. Not you.

Galahad   And I don't want to end up like them. Eat pigeon for the rest of my days? No thank you. It's like you always say, it's time I knew my way around.

Moses   Do you?

Galahad   Starting to.

Moses   Good.

The two men sit together as they quietly eat their stew. Once they finish, **Moses** *clears the table, puts the dishes in the sink and joins* **Galahad** *by the window and they share a cigarette, letting the time pass.* (*For over an hour.*)

Lights on **Lewis**'s *room. A record player is on.* **Tanty** *and* **Agnes** *are dancing together.*

Tanty   Well, of course he must continue to wrap the bread in paper. Who in their right mind would want to eat a loaf of bread after somebody has had their dirty fingers on it?

Not me.

Agnes   That is exactly what I said. You should have seen the looks he gives me, Tanty.

Tanty   Looks?

Agnes   Good look, like you know, one of respect.

Tanty   He was fortunate that you were there to remind him. Who could not help but respect a fine lady such as yourself?

Agnes   The finest language in the world.

Tanty   Oh, we are learning child, the two of we. You know, it only tek me a minute to find a policeman when I get lost one day in the city, trying to find *Grape Paul Street*.

Agnes (*corrects*)   Great Portland Street.

Tanty   That's right. And the day after that, it tek me ten minutes to persuade that man who run the corner shop to let me do my shopping, pay him back on credit. For him to trust me, a coloured woman him nuh know from Adam. But every Friday since, like clockwork, him see me come to pay what I owe!

Agnes   Just like home.

Tanty   This is home.

Lewis *enters.*

Tanty   Oh, here he come. Mister sour puss.

Agnes   How did it go? Did you get the job?

Lewis   Are those my records you are playing?

Tanty   Whose else would they be, Lewis?

Lewis   You had better not scratch them.

Agnes   Lewis, did you get the job?

Lewis   No, I did not get the blasted job.

Agnes   I was only asking. I'm sorry my love.

Lewis   Don't call me that.

Tanty   There will be other jobs, son.

Lewis   Not here, Mama, not for me, not in this country.

Tanty   Oh I see, self-pity.

Lewis   Mama, it's the truth.

Tanty (*quotes*)   'Man nuh dead, nuh call him duppy!'

Lewis   What?

Tanty   Don't give up.

Lewis   Oh, leave me alone, please?

Agnes   You know what, forget about all of that.

Lewis   What are you talking about, woman?

Agnes   Just for tonight. Forget about all of it. Tonight, we dance. Dance with me, Lewis.

Lewis   Agnes, have you gone mad?

Agnes   Just dance with me.

Lewis   No.

Agnes   It's been so long since we last danced.

Lewis   I don't care.

Agnes   But I care.

Lewis   I can't help you with that.

Tanty   Come on, boy, dance with your wife.

Lewis   Mama?

Agnes   Come on, Lewis.

Lewis   I don't feel like it.

Agnes   Dance with me.

Lewis   No, I said, now move!

Agnes (*snaps*)   Fine then, fine! I will find someone else to *dance* with me then.

Lewis   Meaning what?

Moses and **Galahad** *can hear from upstairs.* **Moses** *gestures* **Galahad** *to follow him down.*

Agnes   Nothing.

Lewis   Who else you dance with?

Agnes   No one.

Lewis   I knew it.

Tanty   Knew what? What is it that you think you know?

Lewis   What are you doing, Agnes?

Agnes   Nothing.

Lewis   Making eyes at my friends?

Agnes   I am not!

Lewis   Woman, you're slack!

Tanty Lewis!

Agnes You want to discuss our business in front of your mother?

Lewis So, there is business to discuss. You admit it?

Agnes Admit what, you blasted idiot?

Lewis Is who you chat to?

Agnes I have no idea. From the minute I come to this country, I am looking for my husband. Where him deh?

Lewis *strikes her and continues to hit.* **Moses** *and* **Galahad** *run in to pull him off her.* **Tanty** *runs to console* **Agnes**.

Tanty Agnes, my darling!

Moses Miss Tanty, get her out of here, now

Tanty *takes* **Agnes** *out.*

Moses You is a damn fool, Lewis!

Lewis Me? Agnes fooling around with some man. Dancing! She says so herself.

Moses If you carry on giving her licks to the head, she'll admit to the starting the fire of London, but does not make it so, man. You know Agnes better than most, you know she's not carrying on, but you want to believe it.

Lewis Moses, man, I don't know. Ever since I come to this island I just don't know about anything. You know I was never like this back home, yu nuh, Moses. I never raised my hand to nobody. It's like I am a different person here.

Moses Get in line. Take a walk, Lewis.

Lewis *leaves.*

Galahad You act like you don't care, Moses, but you do, more than any of us.

Moses You think?

Galahad   I know.

Moses   Well look 'pon this! Like a duck back when rain fall. You still have a hell of a lot to learn about me.

Galahad   I've learned enough.

Moses   Boy, you haven't even started.

Galahad   I know about the job.

Moses   Job, what job?

Galahad   Post office, Big City, those white boys. Tomorrow, right?

Moses   City should learn to keep his mouth shut.

Galahad   Are you crazy or what?

Moses   Excuse me?

Galahad   Why the hell would you want to do this for?

Moses   If you have to ask, you really don't know me.

Galahad   I know you're fed up.

Moses   Boy, I am past fed up.

Galahad   But all angry and bitter like City, I would never have thought.

Moses   Galahad, there is no other way to put this other than to say, mind yer own fucking business!

Galahad   No.

Moses   Say again?

Galahad   No, I said no.

Moses   Oh, you really want to live up to your name. Why do you care so much?

Galahad   You're my friend.

Moses   Well, you're not mine.

Galahad   You're lying.

Moses   If I lie, I die.

Galahad   No, not this time, Moses. From the minute I arrive here, I hear you do nothing but complain about them, Lewis want this from you, Big City needs that from you, a whole heap of fellars, one after the other, coming to you, need a room to stay, place to find work, Moses the man you want speak to, him help you out! No peace for you!

Moses   That's right, not a single moment of blasted peace.

Galahad   When was the last time you ask any of them for help? When have you ever trusted them, as much as they trust you? When have you ever let them? Let me? Just for once, for the sheer hell of it. Let me help you, man.

Moses   You want to help? This is how you can help. Go and look after Lewis, make sure he has something to eat every single day. Protect him from himself. Stop him from beating up on his wife. Share your last cigarette with Big City, but never leave without putting a smile on his face. That is how you can help, they are your fellars now, go!

Galahad   Moses, I never beg a man for anyting in my life, but I am begging you, don't do this.

Moses   You don't understand.

Galahad   Then mek me!

Moses   I can't die here, not in this country, I just can't.

Piccadilly Circus

The next day. **Galahad** *and* **Daisy** *are together. Two Teddy Boys (not seen but heard by* **Galahad***) appear.*

Galahad   Look, I don't want any trouble, alright? Daisy! You let her go, you don't touch her. Take your dirty hands off her. Daisy! Go now. Go!

Daisy *runs off.*

Galahad   Let's get this over with.

The Teddy Boys circle **Galahad***, one of them throws a punch,* **Galahad** *side steps it, and connects with a punch to the assailant's face. He then throws a punch followed by a kick to the one behind him. The rest of the gang then set about* **Galahad** *with punches and kicks to his stomach and head. But* **Galahad** *is putting up a very good fight, even though he is now very bloody he's still not down as the kicks and punches continue. The sound of a police siren cause the fight to end as the Teddy Boys run off.*

Galahad *staggers to his feet*

Galahad (*screams*)   Daisy? Daisy!

Daisy *appears.*

Galahad   Where did you go? Are you alright? I just wanted to make sure. Alright, I will go. I said I will go, but kiss me first. I don't care. I don't care. I'm dead already, see me? You're right, maybe I still don't know where I am. I have no idea, but I know how I feel when I'm with you. Daisy? Daisy please?

Daisy *leaves.*

Galahad (*calls*)   Daisy! Renk! This whole fucking country, is renk!

Bayswater

Later that day. **Moses** *in his room, writing. His mind takes him back once more to Trinidad, 1949.* **Christina** *enters.*

Christina   So, is it true?

Moses   Oh God!

Christina   Is what Father saying to me true, Moses?

Moses (*pleads*)   Why can't you leave me alone?

Christina   Tell me if it's true?

Moses   Yes, yes, it's true.

Christina   Look at me. At least have the decency to look at me.

Moses *does not want to turn around.*

Moses   What good would that do?

Christina   Let me see you.

Moses *forces himself to turn around. This memory is unbearable for him.*

Moses   Alright, so what now?

Christina   You can't.

Moses   Christina?

Christina   You can't go, you know you can't.

Moses   Watch me.

Christina   You can't go.

Moses   Stop this!

Christina   I won't let you.

Moses   I have to.

Christina   All of the things you said to my father, that was a lie? You said you would do what is right protect my honour.

Moses   Stop it, why do you love to go on?

Christina   Don't you care about me?

Moses   I have to.

Christina   You don't have to.

Moses   The mother country is calling!

Christina   But you don't have to go.

Moses   I don't have to go? I did hear you right, Christina, I heard you say, I don't have to go? What the hell is here for me?

Christina   Me! Our boy, your son.

Moses   How do you even know it's a boy?

Christina   I just know.

Moses   What makes you so sure, what the hell do I have to offer him?

Christina   Your love.

Moses   It's not enough.

Christina   How can you say that?

Moses   Because I can't die here. I just can't.

Christina   No.

Moses   Go home, Christina.

Christina   You are not saying this to me because you believe it.

Moses   Then why then, tell me?

Christina   You want to believe it because you are going.

Moses   Don't think I won't walk away from you right now, don't think I wouldn't.

Christina   If you go.

Moses   What? What will you do? I'm not what you want, don't you see?

Christina   Don't tell me what I want.

Moses   Just find another man for your son.

Christina   You bastard!

Moses   It's best he don't know me.

Christina   But he will know you, Moses. Because I will tell him. I will tell him your name; I will tell him everything he needs to know about you. I will tell him how you left him behind. I will make sure he will grow up hating you, so much that if your face was on fire and he only had a glass of water he would drink it. Every day he will curse your name, Moses Aloetta! I make sure of this, Before God, I will.

Moses   I am getting on that boat, Christina. Do what you feel is best.

Christina *is beside herself. She runs off.*

Moses (*to himself*)   Enough, enough now.

Moses *is brought back to his present time when* **Galahad** *comes in, slamming the door behind him,*

Moses   Oh man. White boys again? They see you with your girl? Galahad? Talk ti me, boy.

Galahad   I want to go home.

Moses   I see.

Galahad   I want go home, Moses, right now.

Moses   Just like that?

Galahad   I don't want to be English any more.

Moses   Sit down before you fall down.

Galahad *slumps down on a chair. He stares hard at his hands.* **Moses** *tends to* **Galahad**'s *wound with a wet cloth.*

Galahad   You can forget what I said to you before, every word of it.

Moses   And why is that?

Galahad   Why you think?

Moses   You want keep still for me, Galahad?

Galahad   It's Henry now. You call me Henry. I don't want to be Galahad no more. Lawd knows what I was thinking.

Moses   OK, *Henry,* now what?

Galahad (*raises his hands*)   You know what this is, Moses?

Moses   Your hands?

Galahad   We are black.

Moses   Oh my! Does your mother know?

Galahad   I'm serious.

Moses   You're angry.

Galahad   It is this that is causing all the trouble, not us, but this, this black!

Moses   Talk sense.

Galahad   Why the hell couldn't we be blue, or red, or green, if we can't be white? Why did we have to be black? We have done nothing to upset these people, nothing! It is not us, Moses, it is this, this fucking black! Look at it, Moses, look. So black and innocent and yet all this time it's causing nothing but misery, this black! Why the hell it can't change colour? I don't love it, I hate it. I hate this black! I want to go home.

Moses   No you don't.

Galahad   I'll come with you on the job.

Moses   What?

Galahad   We do the post office together, let's go. Right now.

Moses   Galahad?

Galahad   Henry, now!

Moses   Alright, Henry, no.

Galahad   What you mean no? We do the post office, get our money. We can leave together. Tell this country what to go and do with itself. Yes? I say yes? Moses? You were right, I was wrong, let's do this.

Moses   And then what?

Galahad   What do you mean?

Moses   I mean, and then what? What do we tell them all when we go back?

Galahad   The truth, man.

Moses   The truth? Will we tell them the weather is so cold it turns the people against us? That our life is so hard that in big Britain we sleep in a tiny room with broken cupboards, and holes in the windows? That we only own one pair of shoes, that we are so lonely we sleep with prostitutes for company? How do you think they would feel about us then, the men who left that tiny island with all the big dreams and big talk. Are you going to tell them you've come back with your tail between your legs because England beat you? I just lay there on the bed thinking about my life, how after all these years I aint got no place at all, I am still the same way, neither forward nor backward. That is the reason I tell everyone as to why I came back? Galahad, I turned my back on the only woman who ever loved me, so I can come here. Now she's dead. How can I go back and show my face there, how? You think I haven't tried, but all she does is run around in my head.

Galahad   You aint tried shit, Moses!

Moses *reaches under his bed and pulls out a shoe box inside of which are lots and lots of letters and his personal journal.*

Galahad   What is this?

Moses *hands his letters over to* **Galahad**.

Moses   Read it, out loud. Just read it.

Galahad (*reads from* **Moses'** *letter*)   It was the grimmest of all the winter evenings William. The fog would be sleeping restlessly over the city and the lights showing the blur as if is not London at all but some strange place on another planet, but there was I, William, . . . William?

Moses   Go on

Galahad (*continues*)   . . . hoping to meet a fellar who was coming from Trinidad on the boat train. And his name was Henry Oliver. You wrote about me?

Moses   Another.

Galahad   Who is this William?

Moses   Another.

Galahad   . . . someone from work, a white man called Darren, you could say he was my first white friend, told me I should go to Marble Arch and ask for where Speaker's Corner is. I hear this white man, dressed all in black saying the most horrible things about West Indians. When I look over, I see Darren, applauding him. He looked right over at me, and smiled.

Moses   Read another.

Galahad   You made yer point, man.

Moses   No I haven't, read another!

Galahad *reads another letter.*

Galahad   Dearest William, I went to see Mandy again today. I wish you could see her gorgeous red hair. I always believe when she say . . . I don't want to read no more!

Moses *snatches the letter and reads it himself.*

Moses   I am her favourite client! Why would we tell anyone this? There are times when I lay down on my bed, and I ask the Lord, what is it we people do in this world that we have to suffer so? What it is we want that the white people and them find it so hard to give? A little work, a little food, a little place to sleep. We are not asking for the sun; we left the sun behind.

Galahad   It's not we that the people don't like. Is the colour, black. Big City is right, you should do the job, and I want to come.

Moses   I am not going, I am not doing the job with City?

Galahad   You're not? Why? Because you're afraid?

Moses   I have some pigeon stew left; you want some?

Galahad   Who is William, Moses?

Moses   My boy. My little seven-year-old son. His mother was Christina, Frankie's sister.

Galahad   The one who died in that storm?

Moses (*snaps*)   Yes, Galahad, the one who died in that storm!

Galahad   And you wrote letters to your son?

Moses   I must have over a hundred in this box, all in their own envelopes, all bound for home. For him. Every detail of my life since I come here. Yet I haven't posted a single one of them.

Galahad   Why not?

Moses   Because I can't.

Galahad   You haven't seen him, have you?

Moses   Frankie send a picture of him once, when he was a baby. The boy hates me. Christina said she would make sure he will grow up hating me.

Galahad   Christina is dead, Moses.

Moses *begins composing another letter.*

Galahad   What are you doing now?

Moses   I'm writing another letter. Tell him about today, about Lewis losing his mind.

Galahad But you are never going to post it.

Moses But I am still going to write it. You want to stay?

Galahad No, I know how you like to be on your own when you write . . .

Moses Stay man, stay.

Galahad What about City?

Moses You let me worry about City.

Galahad You want me to go and talk to him?

Moses For what?

Galahad In case he gets fresh. I know how wild he can be.

Moses *laughs.*

Galahad What? You don't think I can take him? Do I look that soft to you?

Moses No offence, Galahad, but City would tear off yer arse and hand it to you.

Galahad You have a lot of faith in me, Moses.

Moses I tell you, Galahad, this London, man! The way it gets inside of you.

Galahad How? How does it get inside of you?

Moses You won't get it, man.

Galahad Try me. Come on, Moses. Tell me? Tell me how London gets inside of you.

Moses The changing of the seasons. The cold slicing winds, the falling leaves. Sunlight on green grass, snow on the land. Oh, what it is and where it is and why it is, no one knows, but to have said: 'I walked on Waterloo Bridge', 'I rendezvous at Charing Cross', 'Piccadilly Circus is my play-ground', to say these things, to have lived these things, to have lived in the great city of London, centre of the world.

To one day lean against the wind walking up Bayswater
Road, to see the leaves swirl and dance and spin on the
pavement, to write a casual letter beginning: 'Last night, in
Trafalgar Square . . .' What it is that a city have, that any
place in the world have, that you get so much to like it you
wouldn't leave it for anywhere else? Why is it, that although
they grumble about it all the time, curse the people, curse
the government, say all kind of this and that, why is it, that
in the end, everybody cagey about saying outright that if the
chance come they will go back to them green islands in the
sun.

Moses *sees that* **Galahad** *is fast asleep.*

Moses *covers his friend with a blanket.*

Christina *appears, carrying her new born baby son in her arms.*
She rocks him gently from side to side, she ever so quietly and gently
sings him to sleep with a lullaby. **Moses** *watches and smiles as*
mother and son walk off.

Big City *then enters the room, looking dishevelled, gun in his hand.*

Moses   City?

Big City   That's my name.

Moses   Are you alright?

Big City   Do I look?

Moses   Not really.

Big City   I waited for you.

Moses   I know that, and I am sorry.

Big City   Half a hour, we waited.

Moses   I couldn't come, City.

Big City   Thirty blasted minutes.

Moses   Why don't you put the gun down for me?

Big City   Why?

Moses   Put it down.

Big City   You think I am going to shoot, Moses?

Moses   The thought had occurred.

Big City   The gun fire already, so don't worry.

Moses   Fire already, you do the job?

Big City   The job?

Moses   Police on your tail? You can't be here, City, don't bring the police to my door, man.

Big City   Let me tell you about the job. We waited half an hour for you.

Moses   I said I was sorry.

Big City   Until Timmy say we should go on without you.

Moses   Timmy? One of the white boys?

Big City   You know any self-respecting fellar that would call himself, *Timmy*?

Moses   Not really.

Big City   He ask if he could see my gun, he takes it in his hand, goes on about it being better than his. That it looks just like the gun John Wayne use in his cowboy films. The man is jealous, Moses, jealous, about a blasted gun! At one point, I thought he was going to kiss the damn thing, ask it to marry him. All of this was going on as we are driving to the post office you know. We pull up outside, Timmy still waving it about around in the air. Like a jack arse. I know he didn't mean for it to happen.

Moses   What did happen? Tell me, City.

Big City   Charlie, the other boy, tried to grab it off him.

Moses   Oh no.

Big City   They struggled. The gun went off.

Moses Oh Lord.

Big City The fucking idiot shoot off his own toe. His big toe, mind. Left foot. Crying like a new-born as Charlie take him to *Paddy Town* hospital.

Moses (*corrects*) Paddington hospital.

Big City That's what I said, stop fucking me up, Moses.

Moses Alright.

Big City As far as I know he is still there, bawling.

Moses I'm sorry, man.

Big City Sorry for what? You were right. Them white boys are funny, Bob Hope, funny! Jerry Lewis, funny. You are not going to laugh, are you, Moses?

Moses (*fighting hard not to laugh*) No.

Big City Good. Cos I don't feel like laughing.

Moses Of course. (*Offers him a cigarette.*) You want smoke?

Big City It's your last one.

Moses Take it, man.

Big City Are you laughing?

Moses No.

Big City You are laughing, man. You are laughing at me.

Moses I'm not, I swear.

Big City Timmy lose his entire big left toe, Moses. There is nothing left of it on his foot. He might never walk properly again for the rest of his life.

Moses My heart bleeds.

They finally burst out laughing.

Galahad (*still sleeepy*) Hey man, what's all the noise?

Moses   Nothing, go back to sleep, Galahad.

Big City   You know what I am, Moses?

Moses   What are you, Big City?

Big City   Not a hustler. That's what I am.

Moses   That is true.

Big City   I can't do anything right.

Moses   That is not true. Your life is not a race, City. You will get there. We will all get there.

The two men share the cigarette, way into the night.

The next morning. Lights on **Agnes**, *watched by* **Tanty**, *packing a suitcase.*

Tanty   Child, you sure about this?

Agnes   I grew up in a house where my father did nothing but raise his fists to my mother. She always forgave him, she always believed him when he said he would change. Every other day. I swore I would not be like her. Lewis knows this. I told him before we were married. I'll be fine. My cousin Mabel arrived last month to join her husband in Birmingham. She said I can stay with them. They have plenty of room. They also have hospitals there, and they are always looking for nurses. I will be fine.

Tanty   And what am I supposed to do?

Agnes   Do you want to make me cry, Tanty? (*Embraces her.*)

Tanty   Remember what I say to you. This is your country now. It can only be what you make of it, child. If it don't fit, you make changes.

Agnes   I'm the one who doesn't fit.

Tanty   Now stop that.

Agnes   He has not touched me, Tanty.

Tanty   What do you mean?

Agnes   Nobody give love like Lewis does. At least when he was back home.

Tanty   Not once? Even when I am not here.

Agnes   Tanty, please, this is not easy for me to say.

Tanty   That wurtless sonofabitch.

Agnes   That is your son you know.

Tanty   I don't care. He's my only child, I say what I like.

Agnes   Well. Time to go.

Tanty   I have a present for you.

Agnes   Where is it?

Tanty (*recites, it is pitch perfect*)   Two toads, totally tired, trying to trot to Tewkesbury!

Agnes *laughs with delight. She claps her hands to applaud.*

Tanty   Wait nuh! (*Recites again.*) Peter Piper picked a peck of pickled pepper. A peck of pickled pepper Peter Piper picked. If Peter Piper picked a peck of pickled pepper, where's the pickled pepper Peter Piper picked? Well?

Agnes (*delighted*)   Well done, well done, you are English now!

Tanty   As are you, my darling. My sweet baby girl.

The two friends embrace each other again.

Lewis *appears.*

Lewis   Are you sure that suitcase big enough?

Agnes   Don't try and stop me, Lewis.

Lewis   I'm not. I won't.

Agnes   When the children come, they are living with me.

Lewis   Fair enough.

Agnes   What has happened to you? There was never anyone.

Lewis   I know.

Agnes   Do you understand?

Lewis   Yes!

Agnes   Then why, why Lewis?

Agnes *thinks going over to console* **Lewis**. *She is divided.*

Agnes   You know how much I love you?

Lewis   Yes.

Agnes   But I cannot help you.

Agnes *gives* **Lewis** *a gentle peck on the cheek before leaving.*

Lewis   Alright, Mama, just say what you have to say.

Tanty   Whatever happen to that sweet little bwoi . . .

Lewis   Yeah, here it come.

Tanty   . . . who used to run around naked in the backstreet of Kingston?

Lewis   Oh Lawd, I am tired of hearing that! Every time, you have to remind me when I was a little boy running around arse naked. So you mind me, so what? I'm a man, Mama, stop calling me boy. Why did you have to leave that warm place to come here and freeze to death?

Tanty   You are the one who write to me, bragging that you getting paid five pound a week.

Lewis   I know what I said.

Tanty   So, of course, I was going to come.

Lewis   But I only send for Agnes, not you.

Tanty   So all of this is my fault? You are blaming me?

Lewis   You come to give me grey hair before my time. And if I didn't have enough worry.

Tanty   What about you and your *nonsense*, eh?

Lewis (*denial*)   What?

Tanty   White girls, Lewis, and you know the kind I mean.

Lewis   I don't.

Tanty   I am not talking about what you were doing when you were here by yourself, I'm talking about now.

Lewis   Mama, you have it wrong.

Tanty   You think I don't know what goes on in that park? Catch pigeon my eye! Mind you don't catch something else.

Lewis (*cringes*)   Alright!

Lewis *leaves.*

Tanty   Is that what sweeten up so many of you to come to *London*? Your own kind of gal not good enough? Your wife is a beautiful woman. But you don't even blink on she.

Lewis   Mama?

Tanty   You're no son of mine.

Lewis *leaves.*

Tanty   Yes, go. Run away to your friends. Go to yer white gal!

Moses *lets* **Lewis** *in.*

Tanty *turns the record player back on. She sings to herself quietly.* ('*London is the Place for Me?*')

Moses *offers* **Lewis** *his last cigarette and lights it for him.* **Lewis** *bursts into tears.* **Moses** *takes him in his arms and cradles him as* **Tanty** *continues to sing.*

Several more days have passed. (Three weeks perhaps.)

Galahad, *watched by* **Big City**, **Moses** *and* **Lewis** *as he attempts to snatch a pigeon from* **Moses'** *window sill.*

Galahad   Quee, quee? Quee, quee? Quee, quee? Quee?

Big City   I swear, him say that one more time. I go kill him.

Galahad   Quee?

Big City   Enough with the noise, boy, grab it nuh!

Lewis   Just like I taught you, Galahad, you are almost there.

Big City   We is hungry! He's not going to do it.

Moses   He almost has it.

Galahad *manages to grab one.*

Big City   Yes!

Lewis   Now kill it.

Galahad *pinches the pigeon's neck and snaps it.*

Lewis   Oh yes!

Big City   The boy broke his cherry at last!

Moses   He's one of the boys now. Congratulations.

Lewis   So, who's hungry?

Moses   Boys. (*Recites.*) Pigeon meat . . .

Big City/Lewis/Galahad   . . . is sweet!

Moses   Believe that!

Galahad   Save me a wing, please?

Big City   Move, I ask for a wing first.

Galahad   You look more like a breast man, City.

Big City   Never mind what I look like.

Moses   Hey, why don't we cook the damn thing first?

Big City   Listen to the big man. He would have been a hundred pounds happy if he had listened to me.

Galahad   Why didn't you do it?

Big City   Moses let me down.

Galahad   So?

Big City   I couldn't go without him.

Galahad   Why?

Big City   Him love his questions, about 'Why' and 'So'!

Galahad   But why?

Big City   Bwoi, shut up.

Moses   He would never have done it anyhow. Cos he knows, like me them white boys did not have a brain cell to share between them. Why else would one of them shoot off his own toe? Big City is tough, but he don't like jail.

Big City   Hear him, so! Moses by name, Moses by nature.

Moses   I can only be myself City, I just want to get on like the rest of you.

Big City   Get on with what though?

Lewis   Agnes gone!

Galahad   And we so hungry for food, we have to eat pigeon.

Moses   Yes. But we have each other, right? We go on, right? Like it or not, fellars, but this is our home, our place. Now, we are lonely, yes. But we are not alone!

Big City   We're not as strong as you, Moses!

Moses   How can you put up with all this shit if you're not, City? From winter to winter. Summer to summer. Work after work, we sleep, we eat, we hustle, we work. You understand? Enough chat. Today is Sunday, now what you say, we pluck this nice plump juicy pigeon and go season it with salt and pepper, cook it with some onion, potato?

Lewis   Sweet potato?

Moses   Whatever you want, man, but you had better high tail it to the greengrocer before it shut, if you want sweet. Then, we go yam its arse off, yes?

Big City   Sound like a plan.

Galahad *smiles over at* **Moses**.

Moses   I don't know what yer smiling at?

Galahad   I knew you wouldn't leave.

Moses   Change that to couldn't, and you might be onto something, *London* man!

Galahad   Why do we love it so much?

Moses   When I know, I will tell you. Landlord wants us all out. Him moving to Surrey!

Lewis   Mama and I find a place in *Kilburn*. Two of you want our floor?

Moses   Thank you, Lewis, it will only be for a couple of nights, I swear.

Lewis   We all hear that before . . .

Big City   Hey, Moses, I did hear about a couple of rooms going over in *Hammerstring*?

Moses   *Hammersmith*!

Big City   Or you could try over there by *Gloucestershire Street*

Moses   *Gloucester Road*, man!

Big City   That's what I say, stop fucking me up.

Galahad   Why do the you two love to go on so? And is it me or is it getting colder in here?

Big City Definitely not you.

Lewis But this is London.

Moses He shoulda been here in fifty-two!

Lewis Tell him, Moses!

Moses It get so bad here, when you try and speak,

Galahad . . . the words freeze and you have to melt it to hear the talk. Yeah, yeah, yeah . . .

Big City Bwoi, rude!

Moses The boy is renk!

The fellars continue to laugh and chat as the lights go down.

End.